Thank-you for creating such awesome recipes!! At the age of 37, I was diagnosed with diabetes, high cholesterol, and high blood pressure. I switched my diet to your recipes, and after 6 months was 50 pounds lighter and off all medications. To date, I have lost an amazing 110 pounds, and have gone from a size 22/24 to a 6/8! Your cookbooks are my bibles. They make it easy to make eating well a part of my daily life, and my husband and my daughter absolutely LOVE everything I make!

—MIRIAM GERACI OLSON, *New Britian, Connecticut*

Marlene, it has been exactly 3 months since I started my "health crusade" using your cookbook *Eat What You Love*. Since then, I have lost a total of 37 pounds and eagerly bought *Eat More of What You Love*. From it, I cooked each of my son's birthday dinners! Thank you for your great recipes!! —KATHY FOGELGREN, *Wilmington, Delaware*

I just had to tell you how wonderful your books are. I have a very picky husband and children, and couldn't be more pleased. All of the recipes are easy-to-follow, quick, and DELICIOUS. My husband now goes for seconds (a first for him), and my kids ask me to cook from your books. I had no idea it could be so easy to keep my family healthy AND happy.

—RHONDA WILLIAMS, *Scottsdale, Arizona*

I am over-the-top excited to share that with your cookbooks my husband has lost 55 pounds and I just reached 30 pounds today!!! Jim's blood sugar readings have gone from the 200's down to 95 to 100! We are so happy. You have taught us that you can eat healthy, and still have great tasting food for life! Thank you Marlene!

—HOLLY NELSON, *Ranchester, Wyoming*

I have lost 52 pounds and 4 dress sizes due to your wonderful recipes, and I am like a new person!! I can't thank you enough for the great tasting recipes you have created. The delicious food has helped me stay on the straight and narrow, and I never feel deprived. Thank you, thank you!! —ROSE MARIE YOUNG, *Trenton, New Jersey*

Books published by Running Press are available at special discounts for bulk purchases
in the United States by corporations, institutions, and other organizations. For more
information, please contact the Special Markets Department at the Perseus Books
Group, 2300 Chestnut Street, Suite 200, Philadelphia, PA 19103, or call (800) 810-4145,
ext. 5000, or e-mail special.markets@perseusbooks.com.

This book offers recipes and tips that should be included as part of an overall
healthy diet. Readers are advised to consult with a qualified health professional for
specific dietary needs or concerns.

ISBN 978-0-7624-5918-6
Library of Congress Control Number: 2013950314

E-book ISBN 978-0-7624-5190-6

9   8   7   6   5   4   3   2   1
Digit on the right indicates the number of this printing

Cover and Interior design by Susan Van Horn
Edited by Jennifer Kasius
Typography: Avenir, Mrs. Eaves, and Filosofia

Running Press Book Publishers
2300 Chestnut Street
Philadelphia, PA 19103-4371

Visit us on the web!
offthemenublog.com

EAT *what you* LOVE EVERYDAY

MARLENE KOCH

Photographs by
STEVE LEGATO

RUNNING PRESS
PHILADELPHIA · LONDON

For my mother who fed us with love everyday,
and to my husband Chuck for supporting me in all I do.

table of contents

introduction

Guilt-free goodness, times three! It's been said that the best things in life come in threes—and such is my promise as *Eat What You Love Every-day* joins *Eat What You Love* and *Eat More of What You Love*—the first two cookbooks in my (now, three-book) Eat What You Love cookbook series. The journey I have had with these books has been nothing short of incredible, and with over 500,000 books of the first two books sold, I am humbled and honored to have had so many people purchase them, cook from them, and recommend them to family and friends. From stories of tremendous weight loss and defeating diabetes, to having their "healthy hating" husbands and finicky teens run to the table for (unbeknownst to them) healthy meals, to the joy of discovering, or redrediscovering, cooking, countless readers have also been kindhearted enough to share the numerous ways the books have improved their lives—and for that I am most grateful.

I passionately believe that *everyone* deserves to eat the foods they love. As a cooking instructor and registered dietitian—who comes from a large family that loves to eat—I feel incredibly fortunate to be able to deliver both good health *and* great taste to my readers, and those they love. In that spirit I'm delighted to share that *Eat What You Love—Everyday!* offers 200 all-new, amazingly tasty, easy, healthy recipes that everyone can enjoy—every day of the week.

Like three notes in a chord, this book has been built to stand alone, as well as complement the other two Eat What You Love books in perfect harmony. "Firsts" for this book include my incredible Cook It Fast or Slow chapter, which features thirteen double-duty recipes; every delectable recipe in the chapter includes *both* pressure cooker and slow cooker instructions. (I'm pretty sure this is a first for any cookbook :) !) You'll also find new options for nondairy milk alternatives, gluten-free baking, and sweeteners. And for entertaining, you will find an expanded menu section with eight mouthwatering menus, along with even more tips and hints to make entertaining as easy and carefree as it is delicious.

As in the two previous much-loved titles, there are no repeated recipes (with the exception of my signature Unbelievable Chocolate Cake), and as always, all ingredients are easy-to-find and the recipes easy-to-make, with most recipes taking fewer than 30 minutes active time. Portion sizes are real, not skimpy, and nutrition information is comprehensive and accurate.

Most of all, while I've slashed the sugar, trimmed the fat, and cut the calories, taste *always* comes first! New Southern-style specialties like Savory Southern-Style Biscuits, Eggs, and Gravy will have your family popping out of bed, while Weeknight Chicken and Dumplings will have them running for the supper table. Fresh, fabulous restaurant makeovers (one of my specialties) include 14-Karat Carrot Cake Pancakes, Panda-Style Chicken Chow Mein, and Quicker-Than-Takeout Sweet and Sour Chicken. You'll find these recipes (and others), as seen in my revealing "Dare to Compare" notes, clocking in with up to 75% calorie savings, or more! Updated classics come by way of dreamy Deviled Eggs, savory Skillet Shepherd's Pie, and a much-requested holiday favorite, luscious Classic Green Bean "Casserole." If you are looking for recipes that offer a fun new twist with familiar, beloved flavors, you'll find plenty: my Pizza Frittata, Any Day Stuffin' Muffins, and 15-Minute Meat Loaf Dinner quickly come to mind. And of course, as usual, if you are a sweet lover

(like me!), I haven't forgotten you. Nothing says you care like baking for the ones you love. For every day, and any occasion, you'll discover plenty of guilt-free goodies, including creamy Red Velvet Cheesecake Cupcakes, 5-Ingredient Strawberry Blossom Pudding Cups, and Tiramisu, to name a few (each averaging fewer than 150 calories per serving!).

With so much to offer, perhaps the saying "the third time's a charm" says it best. I genuinely love this book and its wonderful range and variety of recipes. That said, mixing and matching recipes among all three Eat What You Love books (and the more than 700 recipes!), is not only allowed, but fondly encouraged. May you always eat what you love, and love what you eat!

My best to you and yours,

Marlene

EVERYDAY HEALTHY EATING TIPS

IF YOU HAVE EVER TRIED TO EAT "HEALTHY," YOU KNOW IT ISN'T ALWAYS EASY, because the hardest foods to give up are those we love best, and the foods we love best are often not the best for us! The fact is, foods that are high in sugar, fat, and salt taste great. And not only do they taste great, they make us feel great—at least while we're eating them. According to Pulitzer Prize–winning investigative reporter Michael Moss, sugar and fat send powerful signals to the pleasure centers of our brain, which makes eating such foods very, very, enjoyable. It's no wonder that giving up our favorite foods for the sake of health simply doesn't stick. And to think that anyone would expect us to do so, every day! Well, I'm here to tell you that it is possible to eat healthy, yep, every day (including holidays!). And not only can it be done, it can be fun! In this book you will find over 200 easy, delectable recipes guaranteed to help you effortlessly reduce the sugar, fat, and excess calories on your plate (and in your cup and bowl!).

I've made it my mission to create the types of wonderfully delicious foods we all love in a way we can all enjoy—no matter what our diet or health goals. In my world, when it comes to eating healthfully, there are no "rarely" or "never" foods. It's also my mission (and honor) to share my nutritional knowledge with you so that you, and those you love, can look and feel your very best. Throughout this book you will find loads of healthy eating and cooking tips. In addition to the recipes, be sure to read the chapter introductions and full-sized "For the Love of" pages. There you will find everything from why breakfast is the most important meal of the day, to how bacon can fit into a healthy diet! To start you off, here's a bit more information to help you eat what you love everyday—in the healthiest way:

KEEP CALORIES IN CHECK

While many health and diet books lure readers by offering "secrets" to good health, or the "fastest" way to lose weight, the fact is for optimal health, nothing trumps a healthy weight—and nothing affects your weight more than the number of calories you eat. Calories are simply a measure of the amount of energy a food provides. When you are at a healthy weight, keeping your calories in check means consuming an equal number of calories to those you burn each day. Alternately, when you are overweight, eating fewer calories than you expend each day will help you get to a healthier weight. (The USDA estimates the average person needs 2,000 calories a day to maintain their weight. To calculate *your* personal calorie needs go to www.marlenekoch.com and click on the Personal Calorie Calculator. For more information on calories, see Balancing Calories on page 27).

It may not sound like much, but even eating a mere extra 100 calories daily can add up to a weight gain of 10 pounds a year! Moreover, given the average restaurant meal has over 1,100 calories (not counting beverage, appetizer, or dessert!) or that beloved home-cooked dishes can be equally weighty, it's easy to see why keeping calories in check can be a challenge. Challenge aside, I also have good news: Every recipe in this book has been carefully crafted to deliver less calories and better health, and

oh-so-deliciously so. With restaurant-worthy pasta dishes averaging a meager 300 calories, enticing and flavorful chicken entrées at 250 calories, and unbelievably irresistible desserts at a slim 150, it's now oh-so-easy to keep your calories in check! And with my "Dare to Compare" feature accompanying many of the recipes, you'll

Eating a mere extra 100 calories daily can add up to a weight gain of 10 pounds a year!

see how enormous the calorie savings are when you "eat what you love everyday." (P.S.—For my Weight Watcher friends, the same significant savings can be found for keeping precious points in check!)

FINE-TUNE FATS

Fat, once heralded as a dietary villain, has become the darling of healthy headlines; including those that tout we should eat *more* fat! But before you grab that stick of butter, or good-for-you-oil, here's some sound information about fats to help you fine-tune the type, and amount, of fat you should actually eat. To start, a "no-fat" or nonfat diet is not only unhealthy (especially when fat is replaced with sugar and other highly refined starches as is often the case), it's also not very tasty. Fat adds flavor and aroma; it also imparts creamy or crispy textures to food. Even a small amount of fat can make a big difference in creating a truly delectable dish. Fat is also

It just makes sense that eating less fat can help keep your weight in check (keeping total fat at under 30% of your total calories is wise).

necessary for good health. Fatty acids help the body absorb essential vitamins and antioxidants, give structure to cells, and are important for optimal nerve, brain, and heart function.

But here's the caveat; all fats are not created equal. "Good fats," like those found in nuts, seeds, avocados, liquid oils, and fish are richly satisfying, can lower disease risk, and protect your heart. The so called "bad fats," such as saturated fats found in animal products like butter, meat, and full-fat cheeses, and especially trans-fats, found most often as hydrogenated oils used in crackers, baked goods, and some margarines, increase the risk for heart disease, diabetes, and more. This is why most health organizations recommend that most of the fats we eat (or drink) be of the "good" variety. Ten percent or less of our total daily calories should come from saturated fats and trans-fats minimized.

When it comes to weight, it's important to understand that all fats, whether "good" or "bad," are very dense in calories (fat has 9 calories per gram compared to 4 calories per gram for either protein or carbohydrates). To put it simply, foods high in fat are high in calories. Did you know that olive oil actually has more calories than butter at almost 500 calories per *quarter* cup? So, if eating excess calories translates to extra weight, and fat is dense in calories, it just makes sense that eating less fat can help keep your weight in check (keeping total fat at under 30% of your total calories is wise). Finally, while reducing the fat in recipes—especially in the luscious, creamy, crispy, gooey foods we all love—can be challenging, I'm proud to tell you that I've done it. Healthy fats like those found in creamy avocados, olive oil, salmon, and nuts (see page 308) are featured throughout this book, while all fats, and especially saturated fats, have been "stealthfully" reduced to healthy levels. Any now that *my* fine tuning is over, it's your turn to simply enjoy!

BE CARB CONSCIOUS

Carbohydrates are the most misunderstood of all the major nutrients, here's why. First and foremost, and you are going to love this if you are a "carb" lover: *We all need carbs.* Second, similar to fats, all carbohydrates are not created equal. Third, carbohydrates are found not only in bread, pasta, and rice, but also in milk, legumes, and beans. Even fruits and vegetables, including the non-starchy varieties, are almost exclusively carbohydrates. No matter what the source, all carbohydrates turn into glucose to provide fuel for bodies, including our muscles and our brain. The difference is that refined carbohydrates that are low in fiber—like sugar, unenriched white bread, and white rice—break down rapidly, and although they are a quick source of energy, they offer little beyond calories. Moreover, when eaten in excess, refined carbs contribute to weight gain and the risk for heart disease and type 2 diabetes. On the other hand, complex carbs found in food like whole grains, brown rice, fruit, beans, and vegetables are packed with essential vitamins, minerals, antioxidants, phytochemicals, and plenty of fiber which slows down the breakdown

Complex carbs should be eaten daily at each meal and simple carbs more sparingly.

of carbohydrates—thus minimizing their impact on insulin and blood sugar (see Fill Up with Fiber (page 13) for more information on this fabulous no-calorie carb).

Similar to fats, the key to being able to healthfully and happily indulge in carbs in any diet is to properly balance both the amount and type you eat. Complex carbs should be eaten daily at each meal and simple carbs more sparingly. (For more information on carbohydrate-controlled diets, see page 28.) With this in mind, every recipe is this book is what I call "carb-conscious." Wherever possible I use more nutritious, slow-burning complex carbs such as white whole-wheat flour, wholesome oats, fiber-rich beans, and fresh and frozen fruits, along with a varied assortment of nonstarchy veggies. I also use fewer refined carbs like sugar, white rice, and dense breads that offer no fiber. Most of all, the total amount of carbohydrates are kept in check for every recipe so that even those who are on carbohydrate-controlled diets—such as those for diabetes or weight loss—can eat the foods they love, in real portions, every day.

PENCIL IN PROTEIN

Whether you are trying to bulk up, or slim down, protein plays a vital part in every healthy diet, so when planning your menus, be sure to pencil in lean, satisfying protein at every meal. From helping to maintain your immune system to strengthening your bones to maintaining your muscles, especially as you diet or age, there are over 10,000 proteins at work in your body that need to be fueled. The recent surge in the popularity in protein is thanks to new studies on satiety (the feeling of being satisfied) and fullness. These studies reveal that protein reduces appetite, helps you feel full sooner, and stay full longer. You get the greatest appetite-curbing effect when you eat protein-rich foods at every meal, especially at breakfast. A protein-rich breakfast curbs the appetite not only until lunch, but as amazing as it seems, can even reduce your cravings for that late night snack!

I'm happy to report that I've included plenty of lean protein in my delicious everyday recipes. From smoothies and parfaits made with Greek yogurt, plus plenty

You get the greatest appetite-curbing effect when you eat protein-rich foods at every meal, especially at breakfast.

of egg-straordinary egg dishes for breakfast; to hearty and satisfying soups, salads, and sandwiches made with the leanest cuts of chicken, beef, and beans for lunch; to the most satisfying protein-packed entrées for dinner, including a dozen fast-fix, slim chicken dishes. I've got you covered. (P.S.— Be sure to check out my Marvelous Strawberry Mousse; I've even managed to bump up the protein in dessert.)

SIDELINE EXCESSIVE ADDED SUGARS

I love sugar, I really do, and my guess is that you do too. As I have said before, it's only natural because we are all born with an affinity for sweet-tasting things. And enjoying sweet treats, well, I think it's one of the *sweetest* things in life. Unfortunately, in the case against excess *added* sugars in our diet and their effect on our health, the evidence continues to mount.

It's important to know that there are actually two main sources of sugars in our diets: sugars that occur naturally in foods and those that are "added" during preparation or processing. Naturally occurring sugars are found in fruits, vegetables, and milk. They come bundled with a host of healthy nutrients such as vitamins, minerals, and anti-aging antioxidants, as well as protein and fiber, two nutrients that help slow the digestion and absorption of sugars into the bloodstream. Alternately, added sugars, which in part include syrups, honey, molasses, and white and brown sugars, enter the bloodstream much more rapidly and offer little more than calories (which very few of us need more of!). While small amounts of added sugar are *not* harmful, when eaten in excess they contribute to numerous health concerns including weight gain, type 2 diabetes, and heart disease. For this reason, health experts recommend that women consume no more than 6 teaspoons of added sugars a day and men 9. In contrast, on average we eat a whopping 22 teaspoons of added sugar a day! Where does all of this sugar come from, you may ask? Sugar is a

Health experts recommend that women consume no more than 6 teaspoons of added sugars a day and men 9.

prominent ingredient in many of the foods we love to eat, even those we don't think of as sugary, like Asian food and barbecue sauce, or sweet salad dressings and condiments. A quick glance at a traditional baking book reveals the average recipe to contain two to four cups of sugar (with a single cookie containing *two days'* worth of added sugar). And that medium-size coffee drink at the big "bucks" coffee shop, alas, it's pumped up with 24 teaspoons of added sugar!

As a sweet lover, a baker, and someone who has family members with diabetes, I am delighted to tell you that, with this book, you and yours *can* enjoy all of the sweet foods you love—and be healthy, too. I am also excited to share that on page 81, you will find more sweetener options than ever (including great baking options) for use in my recipes. From sweet and sour chicken and Luscious Coconut Cupcakes (with just one teaspoon of sugar instead of

the usual twelve!) to smoothies, muffins, beverages, sides, and of course lots more desserts, the sweet recipes in this book slash the sugar, but not its great taste. And that's very sweet, indeed!

FILL UP WITH FIBER

If you haven't yet done so, it's time to make friends with fiber. Fiber is categorized as a type of carbohydrate, but unlike other carbohydrates, it cannot be digested, hence fiber has no calories and does not raise blood sugar. (On a food label, the grams of fiber are included in the total grams of carbohydrates. Subtracting the fiber gives you what is known as "net carbs.") Fiber comes in two forms—nonsoluble and soluble—and many foods contain both. Nonsoluble, or insoluble, fiber is also referred to as roughage and best known for promoting

Fiber helps you feel full faster, and stay full longer!

regularity. Whole-wheat products, seeds, whole fruit, and vegetable skins are some common sources of insoluble fiber. Soluble fiber offers a wide range of health benefits. Once ingested, soluble fiber absorbs water and turns into a gel-like substance which in turn traps sugars, fats, and cholesterol. Adding soluble fiber to your diet can reduce the risk of heart disease, diabetes, high blood pressure, and obesity. Examples of foods that contribute more soluble fiber are oats, beans, barley, and peas. Soluble fiber helps you feel full faster, and stay full longer! Fiber can also speed up weight loss and help

Aim to eat both types of fiber for a total of 20 to 35 grams a day.

keep blood sugar in check. Aim to eat both types of fiber for a total of 20 to 35 grams a day to reap the most health benefits.

I'm always looking for tasty ways to increase fabulous fiber in my recipes, so you'll find old-fashioned oats, peas, beans, and of course plenty of whole fruits and vegetables (which also add texture and flavor). To further increase the amount of fiber in any of my recipes, feel free to add even more of these terrific ingredients. Other products I love that are excellent sources of fiber, but that you may be less familiar with, are high-fiber tortillas, light wheat bread, and higher fiber pastas. See the ingredients section to learn more about these high fiber, family-friendly ingredients.

SHAKEDOWN SODIUM!

Scientists may debate the extent to which we love salt is by nature or nurture, but we all know that there is no debate about the fact that salt (aka sodium chloride) makes just about everything taste better. In addition to adding its own flavor, one that many of us love, salt has the ability to enhance sweet flavors and suppress those that are bitter. One need look no further than the sodium content of a restaurant menu—where a single dish can deliver over 5,000 milligrams of sodium—to see how chefs rely on salt to create crave-worthy foods (check out my Dare to Compare on page 188). Sodium does have a downside, however, when it comes to health. High intakes of sodium are linked to high blood pressure, heart attacks, and stroke. Health experts recommend that we consume no more than 2,300 milligrams of sodium; that's the equivalent of one teaspoon of added salt a day (with less for some

The simplest way to give sodium a shakedown is to prepare your own meals.

people, including those who already have high blood pressure). Our current consumption is closer to 4,000 milligrams per day per person.

The best way to reduce or maintain healthy blood pressure is achieve a healthy weight and to eat a diet high in fruits and vegetables, whole grains, low-fat dairy products, and lean meats, moderate in sodium (as above), and low in added sugar and fats (sound familiar?). The simplest way to give sodium a shakedown is to prepare your own meals. While like any chef, taste is my first priority, I also work hard to limit the sodium in my recipes (and am glad that many of my readers report their blood pressure dropped after adding more of my recipes into their diets). Throughout this book you will use reduced-sodium products, such as reduced-sodium broth, and healthier preparation techniques, like draining and rinsing canned goods before adding them to the recipes. In baking, beyond the use of baking soda or powder, salt is rarely added, and the minimum amount is added to soups, stews, and entrées. If you want to reduce the sodium even more in any of the recipes, choose no-salt tomato products where applicable, reduce the amount of added salt, and look to my lower-sodium recipes for chicken stock and marinara. For recipes that appear slightly higher in sodium, rest assured that each and every recipe is lower in sodium than its traditional sky-high salty counterpart (with many of the restaurant makeovers boasting as much as a 75% sodium reduction or more!).

EVEN MORE EVERYDAY
HEALTHY EATING TIPS

1. Always eat breakfast.

2. Eat more nonstarchy vegetables and whole fruit.

3. Drink more water.

4. Eat regular meals with your family most days of the week.

5. Cook everyday!

EVERYDAY INGREDIENTS

I AM OFTEN ASKED HOW I AM ABLE TO CREATE RECIPES THAT ARE LOW in sugar, fat, and calories—yet taste so decadent. Much of the secret—as you've probably guessed—lies in the choice of ingredients. Moreover, the magic comes not from a perfect ingredient, but the perfect mix. To that end, I spend hours at the market and online doing research, always on the lookout for ingredients that help me live up to my promise of delivering the ideal blend of good health and great taste!

In this section, you will find additional information on some of the everyday ingredients used in this book, and most importantly, why I used them. I place a high value on common ingredients that are economical and easy-to-find, but also realize there are times you may need to make substitutions, so you will find tips for doing that here too. The information I offer is meant as a guide to help you get the same results in your kitchen as I do in mine, but do feel free to adjust ingredients, especially the spices, to create the everyday flavors you and *your* family love.

Additional information on selecting and substituting ingredients can be found throughout the book, including on the full-size "For the Love of" pages (see Index, page 340). One final note: When it comes to baked goods, with the exception of spices and add-ins, such as nuts, it's important to use the ingredients listed (unless otherwise noted in the recipe itself or in this section), for the best results.

AGAVE NECTAR

I am often asked about agave nectar, or syrup. Agave nectar is a mild-tasting sweet syrup made from the agave plant. While agave has been praised for its lower glycemic index (the rate at which it raises blood sugar), agave is still a sugar, and a concentrated one at that (with more calories and ~ 1.3 times the sweetening power of sugar). As it is very high in fructose, I recommend using agave, like all sugars, in moderation. For substituting agave in my recipes, see page 81.

BACON

Bacon, you ask? Yep, bacon! This book has a bit more of the smoky meat in it than my others—and deliciously so! No worries, I've found lots of creative ways to temper the customary fat, sodium, and calories; lean center-cut bacon, precooked bacon bits, and liquid smoke are just three ingredients in my "bacon" flavor arsenal. See page 264 for more bacon information.

BREADS

I am happy to say there are more "light" choices on the bread aisle than ever for those calorie- and/or carb-conscious. "Light" breads not only have less calories and carbs (about 45 and 9 per piece respectively), but they often also contain more fiber and protein per ounce. Pepperidge Farm brand offers a nice selection. Their soft 100% Whole Wheat Hamburger Buns with 110 calories, 3 grams of fiber, 6 grams of protein—and the carbs of just one slice of regular bread—hit the good health, great taste mark, as do many of the new "100-calorie" products available.

BUTTERMILK

Buttermilk adds great flavor to recipes and lightens and tenderizes baked goods. To make your own, place 1 tablespoon of vinegar or lemon juice in a measuring cup; pour in enough low-fat milk (or soy or almond "milk") to make 1 cup, let it sit for 5 to 10 minutes, and then stir before using. Alternately, mix ½ cup nonfat or low-fat plain yogurt with ½ cup of milk.

COCOA POWDERS

I prefer Dutch-processed cocoa powder. The Dutch process reduces cocoa's natural acidity and bitterness, mellowing the cocoa and imparting a richer, darker color (which is especially helpful when cooking with less sugar). I use Hershey's brand Special Dark cocoa powder (found next to the regular cocoa powder in most markets), but any unsweetened cocoa powder may be used.

COOKING AND BAKING SPRAYS

The difference between cooking and baking sprays are that baking sprays also contain flour, making them a convenient way to grease *and* flour a pan (especially the hard-to-coat spots), which helps baked products release with ease. Be sure to select a flavorless vegetable or canola oil-based spray, and remember to keep the "trigger finger" light—two to three seconds is all it should take. (Use a dusting of flour with a cooking spray if you don't have baking spray.)

COTTAGE CHEESE

Cottage cheese is one of my favorite sneaky ingredients for cutting calories and fat and adding hunger-curbing protein to recipes—especially when it's creamed. To cream it, whether alone or with other ingredients, blend it (with an immersion blender or in a food processor) until no curds are left (think thick sour cream). Trust me, many a cottage cheese hater (like my boys) will never notice it when cooked, luscious and creamy, into a dish. Low-fat or 2% cottage cheese is my choice for the best outcome.

CREAM CHEESE

While there are some good store brands, Philadelphia brand cream cheeses are my reliable go-to's, especially for reduced-fat and nonfat cream cheeses (which can vary in taste greatly). Neufchâtel cheese can also be used in place of light tub-style cream cheese in any of the recipes. Nonfat cream cheese has fewer calories, but does not have the taste or texture to stand

on its own. Using a higher ratio of it in my recipes will negatively affect the taste and texture and is not recommended. (Regular cream cheese works well, but of course, has more calories.)

DAIRY AND NONDAIRY MILK ALTERNATIVES

Because for me taste comes first, I prefer reduced- or low-fat dairy products over nonfat products. One percent milk is richer and has better body than skim, light sour cream is much creamier than nonfat, and reduced-fat cheeses have more flavor and meltability than the nonfat kind. If you have nonfat brands you prefer, you may use them, but the taste and texture may change. If you prefer to use any of the nondairy beverages or milk alternatives, such as soy or almond "milk," please see page 38. They can be used in most recipes with little adjustment. (Note: Nondairy "milks" cannot thicken instant pudding mix.)

EGGS AND EGG SUBSTITUTES

To keep the total fat, cholesterol, and calories in check, and still maintain the taste and texture of whole eggs, I use a higher ratio of egg whites to yolk (or only egg whites when appropriate). I find this best particularly in baking (and because eggs are so much cheaper than egg substitutes, it's also cost effective). There are some recipes, though, such as smoothies and egg casseroles, where liquid egg substitute is the perfect fit. If you choose to make additional substitutions, it is helpful to keep in mind: 1 large egg = 2 large egg whites = 1/4 cup liquid egg substitute.

FLAVORINGS

Good-quality spices and flavorings make a big flavor difference in all recipes, and even more so in reduced-sugar and/or reduced-fat recipes. I always bake with real vanilla for example. Alternate flavorings like coconut extract can be found next to the vanilla, and dried spices should still be fragrant when you open the jars. One teaspoon of a dried spice = 3 teaspoons when fresh.

FLOURS

When it comes to flours, all-purpose flour is considered the gold standard. It has the perfect amount of protein for structure, offers a mild taste, and creates a light texture. Cake flour has less protein than all-purpose and as such creates an even lighter, more tender crumb. To make your own cake flour, place 2 tablespoons of cornstarch in a one-cup measure, and fill it with all-purpose flour for each cup of cake flour. For whole grain goodness, white whole wheat flour is my pick. It has a lighter taste than traditional whole wheat flour, yet the same fabulous fiber. The most common brand is King Arthur. You can replace white whole wheat flour with all-purpose flour if

you choose, or to maintain wholesomeness, a 50/50 blend of white and wheat flours. When it comes to gluten-free baking, there is no other single flour that can replace all of the properties of wheat, but there are many good alternatives. See page 124 for more information.

LEAN GROUND BEEF, TURKEY, AND PORK

Lean ground beef, turkey, and pork make it possible to keep a lot of everyday family favorites on a healthy table. For the recipes in this book, I used 93% lean ground beef and turkey, and 95% lean ground pork. (Tip: The fat content ranges from 30% to 39% of the calories; the "% lean" on the label is the percent of fat per weight, not calories.) I find meat that is any leaner to be too dry and mealy. I occasionally mix ground meats for flavor, but all of one type or the other can be used in any of the recipes.

LIGHT WHIPPED TOPPING

Light whipped topping has only a fraction of the fat of real whipped cream and works great as a whipped replacement. Lite Cool Whip sold in a tub in the freezer section of most markets is my light topping of choice. Be sure to thaw it before using, noting that this can take up to a couple of hours. (Tip: Place it in the fridge, not the freezer, when you bring it home.) My preference is light, *not* nonfat, whipped topping. The additional calorie savings are not worth the difference in taste and texture. For garnishing, at just 15 calories per 2 tablespoons, light real whipped cream sold in aerosol cans is a calorie bargain (just don't overdo it!). It does not work, however, as a substitute for light whipped topping for mixing into recipes.

MARGARINE OR BUTTER

In the margarine versus butter battle, I specify margarine first as it has 65% less saturated fat. One of my favorites is Smart Balance Original Buttery Spread (in the tub, 67% fat). You may substitute any brand of stick margarine you prefer, but I recommend you choose one with little trans-fat. Soft and tub margarines with less than 65% fat by weight do not work as well in cooking and baking, as their water content is too high. For flavor, well, butter can't be beat. With 8 grams of saturated fat in each tablespoon, however, I choose to use it in small quantities when it makes a big taste difference. Use it where and when it suits you best.

MAYONNAISE

With 90 calories per tablespoon (and 1,440 per cup), regular mayonnaise packs a weighty punch. Fortunately, after testing mixtures of mayonnaise (at every fat level), with yogurt and every other common mayonnaise replacement, I've found that a 50/50 blend of light mayonnaise and low-fat (or nonfat) plain yogurt is a great tasting replacement. You may also simply use light mayo if you prefer. I do not recommend low-fat mayonnaise, as it will not give the same delicious results.

NONFAT HALF-AND-HALF

Nonfat or fat-free half-and-half has the creamy richness of regular half-and-half but without the fat. The only quality substitute for nonfat half-and-half is real half-and-half (which adds some extra fat and calories). Nonfat milk is not an in-kind substitute.

OATS

Old-fashioned oats, rolled oats, and the quick-cooking variety may be interchanged (I personally prefer the larger-cut, old-fashioned or rolled variety, especially for toppings). Instant oatmeal is not a suitable replacement for either.

OILS

All liquid oils contain the same amount of fat, so it's the flavor (or lack of), primarily, that determines the type I select. For flavorless oil, I use canola, which is high in monounsaturated fat—but any flavorless vegetable oil can be substituted. For flavor, I like olive oil. Here's a buying tip: For most applications, regular olive oil is fine. As heat breaks down olive oil's flavor, reserve pricy extra-virgin olive oil for dressings and drizzling versus cooking. Distinct flavored sesame oil (made from sesame seeds) can be found in the Asian section of most markets, and has no equal substitute.

ORANGE JUICE (LIGHT)

Light orange juice offers the taste of regular orange juice with one-half as much sugar, carbs, and calories. Trop50 (found in the refrigerated juice case), is a popular brand. If you see simply "orange juice" listed as the ingredient instead, it means that the difference in carbs and calories between using regular and light orange juice was not significant. Either juice will work fine.

PASTA

The pasta aisles of today are a far cry from the past with a huge array of different types of pastas to choose from. From traditional semolina pasta and whole grain "blend" pastas, to those higher in fiber or protein, and even those that are gluten-free, there are plenty of delicious, nutritious pastas available. Traditional pasta has 210 calories and 2 grams of fiber per 2 ounces (dry). For fewer calories and more nutrients, check labels (unless gluten-free, I suggest using one of the many types of pasta that offer at least 5 grams of fiber). Whole wheat pasta is one choice, but so are blended and specialty pastas that offer the benefits of whole wheat without the heavy

wheaty taste. As for gluten-free pastas, there are many options. Those that are blended with corn are my favorites. Last, while I have specified the shape of pasta for all of the pasta dishes based on the sauce and other ingredients, feel free to vary the shape based on your taste and what you have on hand (as I often do!).

PRUNE PUREE

Pureed prunes are great for low-fat baking. I find it convenient to keep a couple of containers of baby food "prunes" (including prunes and apples sold in a 2-pack), on hand. To make your own prune puree, combine 11/4 cups pitted prunes and 6 tablespoons very hot water in a food processor, and blend until smooth. You can store it in a covered container in the refrigerator for one to two months.

NO-CALORIE GRANULATED SWEETENER

Bulk no-calorie sucralose-based granulated sweetener, which is derived from sugar, was used for testing and analyzing the recipes in this book, as was stevia and sugar. (*For more sweetener options, see agave, stevia, and page 81.*) You will find several types of sucralose sweeteners (like Splenda) next to the sugar in most markets. For cooking and baking, the granulated product sold in large bags—which measures 1:1 for sugar—works best. One cup has 96 calories and 24 grams of carbohydrate, compared with 770 calories and 192 grams respectively for granulated sugar. Wherever I list "(or X packets)," you many use sucralose or stevia-based packets (see below) with good results. (For cold recipes, if you have another favorite no-calorie sweetener, you may use that as well.) Each no-calorie packet, while it does not measure as such, equals the sweetness of 2 teaspoons of sugar or no-calorie granulated sweetener. Please note: Splenda Sugar Blend for Baking is a 50/50 combination of sucralose and granulated sugar. If you substitute it for the no-calorie sweetener, or sugar, *use one-half as much—as it has twice the sweetening effect.* Expect slightly longer baking times.

STEVIA-BASED NO- AND LOW-CALORIE SWEETENERS

Stevia is a sweet-tasting natural sugar substitute derived from the stevia plant. When it comes to most sugar substitutes, all brands that are packaged the same way are equal, but this is not the case with stevia products, which vary widely in sweetness, taste, and quality. Three brands whose products passed my easy-to-find, economical, and most of all, great taste requirements for use in my recipes, are Truvia, Domino, and C&H. Truvia no-calorie packets and no-calorie

"spoonable," can be used anywhere you see "(or X packets)." Each packet equals the sweetness of 2 teaspoons of sugar or no-calorie granulated sweetener. For baking, Truvia for Baking (made with 25% real sugar), or Domino Light or C&H Light (both made with 50% real sugar), work well in ALL recipes. If you substitute any of them for the no-calorie sweetener, or sugar, *use one-half as much—as they have twice the sweetening effect.* Expect slightly longer baking times.

All of the products are shelved on the baking aisle with other sugars.

YOGURT

For the first time in my Eat What You Love books, you might note that I now specifically list Greek yogurt in my recipes. The difference between it and regular yogurt is that they strain off more of the whey (the watery part of the milk), when making traditional Greek yogurt. The result is a creamier, thicker texture, and nutritional superiority. Plain Greek yogurt averages half the carbs and sugar, and double the protein of traditional American-style yogurts. Either nonfat or low-fat (2%) Greek yogurt can be used. Two tips: To ensure the yogurt is truly "Greek," check the label. The only ingredients should be milk and active cultures, and it should have over 20 grams of protein per cup. To make your own Greek-style yogurt, place a fine mesh or yogurt strainer—or line a regular strainer with cheesecloth—and place it over a bowl. Add "American-style" yogurt, and let it drain for several hours or until very thick. Discard the liquid whey.

TORTILLAS

Reduced-carbohydrate, high-fiber tortillas are widely available and found next to the regular tortillas. In addition to the traditional flour variety you will also find many flavors to choose from. Mission Carb Balance and La Tortilla Factory Smart and Delicious wraps are two brands to look for. (Mission Carb Balance wraps are the perfect swap for regular white tortillas and thin pizza crusts.) When shopping for high-fiber tortillas, look for wraps that offer over 10 grams of fiber each. 100% corn tortillas are a great gluten-free substitute.

ZEST

Orange, lemon, and lime zest add great fresh flavor in cooking and baking (and work beautifully when reducing sugar). To zest a piece of fresh fruit, wash it and grate off the brightly colored outer layer (rind) of the whole fruit (avoiding going deeper into the bitter white pith). Zest is best when finely grated. If you do not have zester, use a box grater and then mince finely with a knife before adding it to the recipe.

EVERYDAY MEAL PLANNING

IF YOU ARE LIKE MOST AMERICANS, YOU DON'T THINK ABOUT WHAT YOU are going to eat until it's time to eat! With increasingly hectic on-the-go lifestyles, a recent survey revealed that 88% of us did not know what we would be eating for dinner an hour before we expected to do so. In my previous *Eat What You Love* cookbooks I shared that meal planning was not required to enjoy my incredible recipes, or perhaps more importantly, to reap the health benefits, and this book is no different. Please feel free to simply cook from this book knowing that every recipe has been crafted to deliver great taste and better health, so that you, like many of my readers, will find yourself feeling "better than ever."

That said, taking a little bit of time to plan what you and your family will eat can yield big benefits. Meal planning saves time and money, and eases the "chore" of cooking every day. Meal planning, whether it is for a single meal or a week's worth, is also key to making the switch to healthier eating habits or to maintain a diet that can help achieve health goals, such as weight loss or keeping blood sugar in check. In this section, you will find a wide array of information regarding meal planning, from how to plan and shop to calm the chaos at dinnertime and enjoy a variety of delicious healthy meals every day, to how to use the calorie, carbohydrate, or food exchanges in this book to help you achieve or maintain your healthiest best. At the end of this section you will find detailed information about how the nutritional information for each recipe was calculated, including portioning, sauces, and optional ingredients. (For a week's worth of weight loss/carb-controlled menus featuring the recipes in this book, go to www.marlenekoch/sample-menus/.)

Seven Super Tips for
EVERYDAY MEAL PLANNING AND SHOPPING

1. Make a weekly meal calendar.

Set aside a few minutes on the weekend to map out meals for the coming week. It needn't take long or be fancy; I use a free calendar I received in the mail, and it takes me about 15 minutes to jot down my ideas. Mix your go-to recipes with the new ones you want to try. Have fun with theme nights like Meatless Monday or Taco Tuesday. Serve pasta every Wednesday or fish every Friday; narrowing menu choices streamlines planning. And be sure to plan for leftovers. (When you have an a few nights of leftover entrée pickings, make one side dish that compliments them all and have a leftover Smörgåsbord!)

2. Set time aside each week to look for new recipes.

Grab your cookbooks and/or check out your favorite websites, and get inspired (there are over 700 recipes in my Eat What You Love cookbook series!). Look for one or two new recipes to try each week, and have fun. If you love a recipe and plan to bring it into your go-to rotation, consider writing the ingredients on an index card for easy shopping.

3. Engage the family.

Have family members help pick out a new recipe or suggest an old favorite that can be added to your weekly meal calendar. Have them contribute to preparing "their" special meal (if only setting the table).

4. Shop wisely.

Use grocery market circulars or online ads to see what's on sale, and factor these items into your meal plans. With menus set, make a shopping list. Going food shopping *after* you have eaten keeps temptation and impulse buying at bay. Take advantage of coupons and sales to save money on your favorite brands and to stock up on canned goods or other less perishable goods you routinely use.

5. Keep pantry staples well stocked.

Keep your cupboard, fridge, and freezer stocked with healthy staples, especially for recipes you make often. I keep skinless boneless chicken breasts, tilapia, shrimp, and lean ground beef in my freezer at all times. With pantry staples like whole grain pasta, instant brown rice, reduced-sodium broth, canned tomato products, spices, and beans—along with any fresh (or canned or frozen) veggies I have on hand—I can always throw together a delicious and healthy meal.

6. Prep ahead.

When you get home from the market, wash vegetables so they will be ready to use. On Sunday prepare a big batch of marinara (page 188), chicken stock (page 215), or Moist and Flavorful Chicken for Days (page 260), and use these for meals throughout the week.

7. Fix it and freeze it.

Soups, stews, and chilis not only freeze well, but also taste just as good, or sometimes even better, when reheated. Other great-for-freezing items are meatballs, meat loaf (cooked or ready to cook), and muffins. Slice quick breads or on-the-go bars, and wrap individual servings. A quick reheat in the microwave on high power for 30 seconds brings back fresh-baked goodness.

EVERYDAY MEAL PLANNING
with Your Plate

In June of 2011, First Lady Michelle Obama introduced "MyPlate," a new tool developed to help Americans eat healthier. The color-coded plate was in, and the old food pyramid was out. I have used the color-coded plate method for many years, and what I love about it is its simplicity. To use it, all you need to do is follow the instructions on how to fill it, and you're on your way to better health. My plate (aka "Marlene's Plate") differs slightly from the government's version in that I recommend a slightly higher portion of protein, less starch, and even more vegetables to encourage better satiety, weight control, and blood sugar management.

To create a healthy meal that is moderate in both carbs and calories, use a 9-inch

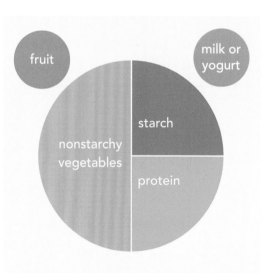

MEAL PLANNING BY THE PLATE

dinner plate (no larger). Fill half the plate with nonstarchy vegetables and salad, and then fill one-quarter of the plate with one of my starchy sides (about one serving of any recipe from the Sensational Sides chapter) or bread. The remaining quarter should be comprised of any lean meat or seafood entrées in my book. If you're dining on pasta, dish up one serving and fill the rest of the plate with salad and nonstarchy veggies.

To complete your meal, add one 8-ounce glass of skim or low-fat milk or yogurt, and a single serving of whole fruit. (If you need to keep tighter control of your carbs, you can save either your dairy or fruit servings for snacks.)

BALANCING CALORIES

A sure-fire way to keep weight in check is to balance the number of calories you eat each day with what you expend. While the idea of counting calories is tedious or burdensome for some people, for others it is a way of life. According to a recent survey by the International Food Information Council Foundation, 27% of Americans routinely monitor the calories they eat—but only 9% are able to accurately estimate the number of calories they should consume each day!

The number of calories you require depends on many factors, including your sex, age, height, current weight, and activity level. Setting a daily calorie "budget" also takes into account your goals (whether you are trying to lose, maintain, or gain weight, and how quickly). *I believe that everyone, whether or not they choose to diligently track their daily caloric intake, should know the number of calories they require.* Without knowing how many calories you require, the amount of calories in a particular food or dish has no context. For example, when you know that your daily

calorie budget is 1,800 calories, the fact that a restaurant entrée has 2,000 calories, or a single piece of cake has 900, has far more meaning. To assist you in determining your personal calorie budget, you will find a Personal Calorie Calculator that can help you determine it at www.marlenekoch.com (look for the tools tab).

Every recipe in this book has been designed to deliver more taste with fewer calories. Even better, the calorie reduction comes in large part not from reducing the

A moderately active woman usually requires between 1,800 and 2,200 calories per day, and a man, 2,200 to 2,700 calories for weight maintenance. Subtract 500 calories per day to lose one pound of fat per week.

portion size (a sneaky trick too often used), but from trimming excess fat and sugar, two unhealthy ingredients none of us need more of. To give you a general estimate (and to put my recipes' calorie counts and "Dare to Compares" in perspective): A moderately active woman usually requires between 1,800 and 2,200 calories per day, and a man, 2,200 to 2,700 calories for weight maintenance. Subtract 500 calories per day to lose one pound of fat per week.

USING FOOD EXCHANGES

The exchange system, a traditional meal planning tool for weight loss and diabetes, groups similar foods together, such as starches, meat, and dairy foods, to form "exchange lists." The foods within each list contain a similar amount of calories and major nutrients, and affect blood sugar similarly. This allows one food in the group to be "exchanged" or traded for another. For example, the value of a starch exchange is 80 calories, 15 grams of carbohydrate, and 1 to 2 grams of fat. In the starch group this equates to a single slice of bread, one-half cup of cooked oatmeal, or one-third cup of pasta (yes, just one-third cup for traditional pasta). So when you follow a meal plan based on the exchange system, you can "exchange" a slice of toast for one-half cup of cooked oatmeal or one-third of a cup of pasta. By varying the number of servings among the various groups, the exchange system ensures that all your nutrient needs are met and that carbs, fat,

and calories are kept in check. The number of servings you are allowed to choose from each group at each meal or snack is based on your individual needs and is best determined by a qualified health provider, such as a registered dietitian or certified diabetes educator. Food exchanges can be found on every recipe. The individual food groups include:

- **STARCH** (breads, pasta, rice, beans, potatoes, and corn)

- **VEGETABLE** (all nonstarchy vegetables)

- **FRUIT** (all fruits and fruit juices)

- **MILK** (nonfat and low-fat yogurt)

- **MEAT** (lean and medium-fat meats, cheese, and eggs)

- **FAT** (oil, butter, margarine, nuts, and other added fats)

- **CARBOHYDRATE** (sugar and desserts)

COUNTING CARBOHYDRATES
Carbohydrate Counting

A healthy diet for anyone—and that includes people with diabetes—is one that includes wholesome, good-for-you foods such as fruits and vegetables, whole grains, and low-fat dairy. That said, of all the nutrients you eat, carbohydrates have the greatest impact on blood glucose. Controlling the amount of carbohydrates you eat at every meal can help control blood sugar, insulin levels, and energy. Thus, for those with elevated blood sugar or diabetes, moderating carbs is vital.

Carbohydrate counting, or carb counting, is a meal-planning tracking system that helps you monitor the carbohydrates

A carb-counting budget for diabetes or weight loss averages 45 grams of carbohydrates per meal for most women and 60 grams for most men. In addition, 2 to 3 snacks are allowed each day ranging between 15 and 22 grams of carbohydrate.

you eat. When carb counting, whether you're eating a snack or a meal, you simply add up all of the carbohydrates you eat at the same time (subtracting fiber), and strive to keep the total within a designated budget. Like calories, the amount of carbohydrates every individual needs varies based on several factors, including gender, weight, activity, and any medications you may take. (For a personalized carbohydrate budget, go to www.marlenekoch.com, click on the tools tab, and use the Carbohydrate Budget Calculator.) A carb-counting budget for diabetes or weight loss averages 45 grams of carbohydrate per meal for most women and 60 grams for most men. In addition, 2 to 3

snacks are allowed each day and ranging between 15 and 22 grams of carbohydrate. Tip: To keep blood sugar in check and on an even keel (and your energy level optimum), it's best to spread the carbohydrates you are budgeted evenly throughout the day.

Carbohydrate Choices

At the end of each recipe you will find "Carbohydrate Choices." Because some diabetes educators use "carbohydrate choices" as a method for budgeting carbohydrates, I have also included this tool. Carbohydrate choices, or carb choices, are simply a calculation of the total number of carbs in a food divided by 15 (see *Carbohydrate Choices Chart* on page 30). As such, each carb choice = 15 grams of carbohydrate. Many common

Carbohydrate choices, or carb choices, are simply a calculation of the total number of carbs in a food divided by 15.

foods average 15 grams of carbohydrate, including a single slice of bread, a single serving of fruit, or a cup of milk. Most women with diabetes average 3 carb choices per meal and men, 4. Snacks average 1 to 1½ carb choices.

Grams of Carbohydrate	Carbohydrate Choices
0–5	0
6–10	½
11–20	1
21–25	1½
26–35	2
36–40	2½
41–50	3
51–55	3½
56–65	4

A last note on carbohydrate counting: Counting carbs (with the right information in hand) is easy, but keeping within a carbohydrate budget can be very challenging, especially when you want to eat the traditional carbohydrate-rich foods you love. The recipes in this book are fantastic for s-t-r-e-t-c-h-i-n-g a carbohydrate budget. If you need more information on carbohydrate counting or a personalized menu plan, a registered dietitian or certified diabetes educator can help you.

More Information on
THE NUTRITION INFORMATION IN THIS BOOK

A complete nutritional analysis complements every recipe so you are able to make healthy choices every day based on your personal needs. The information was calculated using ESHA Nutrition Food Processor software in conjunction with manufacturers' food labels.

FOOD EXCHANGES follow the guidelines set forth by the American Diabetes and American Dietetic Associations. Values have been rounded to the nearest one-half for ease of use. For more information see Food Exchanges, page 28.

CARBOHYDRATE CHOICES have been calculated in accordance with the American Diabetes Association. See Counting Carbohydrates on page 28 and the Choices Conversion Chart on this page for more information.

WEIGHT WATCHERS AND POINTSPLUS are registered trademarks of Weight Watchers International, Inc. I have made a comparison using the most current information available for the points plus system. Calculations include all ingredients, (including otherwise "free" fruits and vegetables).

PORTION SIZE

I am a stickler about offering realistic *and* satisfying portion sizes. There is nothing more annoying than getting excited about the nutrition numbers only to find they relate to nothing more than a mere bite or tiny sliver (and I find this all too common!). I also use common sense when it comes to how recipes are measured and/or

---

Use the nutrition numbers as a guide, but when eating, simply sit back and enjoy. Numbers don't taste nearly as good as great food!

---

normally served. For example, for a recipe that includes four chicken breasts and a pan sauce (that serves four), each person gets one chicken breast and an equal portion of sauce. I do not give the exact amount of sauce, as the exact amount of a pan sauce is not always consistent (measuring it is also messy and tedious). Just divide such items evenly, and you're good to go. Measurements by the cup

or spoonful are provided where it is realistic that a food will be measured in this way. Casseroles and other one-dish meals are actually easier to divide by simply portioning the pan, so I list serving sizes as "one-fourth or one-sixth of the dish." As a nutritionist from a large family, I am also well aware that appetites and caloric needs vary. Feel free to adjust the portions to your own or your family's needs and desires. Here are a few more things you need to know:

- Garnishes that are normally eaten (e.g., sprinkled green onions or powdered sugar) are always included in the nutritional analysis.

- Optional ingredients are not included in the nutritional analysis.

- Items that are added to taste are not included. If a choice is given, the first item listed was used for the nutritional analysis.

(Psst . . . I have created the recipes in this book so you and yours can eat what you love—and have the food you eat love you back! Use the nutrition numbers as a guide, but when eating, simply sit back and enjoy. Numbers don't taste nearly as good as great food!)

EVERYDAY WITH DIABETES

OF ALL THE REWARDS THAT HAVE COME FROM WRITING MY BOOKS, none are more gratifying than the thank-you letters from those readers with diabetes who are kind enough to share how my work has improved their lives. I cannot tell you how incredible it is to read that blood sugar that was once out of control is now "in check," that eating is finally a "pleasure" again, or that a child, for the first time in years, feels "normal" now at birthday parties (thanks to my 90-calorie cupcakes with just 13 grams of carbs!). And then there is the story of Miriam, whose "before and after" you may have seen on television or read when it was featured in *Prevention* magazine. Not only did Miriam lose over 100 pounds by using my recipes; she defeated diabetes!

When I am asked if my recipes are good for those with diabetes, I answer with a resounding, "YES!" I have two family members with diabetes, and I am proud to say there isn't a single recipe in any of my book that they can't enjoy. From pizza and pasta to burgers and dessert, nothing is off limits. All the nutrition information is listed, and the carbs, fat, and sodium have been curbed in every delectable recipe so that they fit easily into diabetes-friendly meal plans. Moreover, for those who need to lose weight (and doing so is the single most important thing that can be done to help control blood sugar), these recipes can help do that too. Diabetes is a condition that must be lived with and managed every day, so I am delighted to help each and every one of those days be more delicious.

WHAT IS DIABETES?

Diabetes is a condition in which the body is unable to handle glucose properly, allowing an excessive amount to build up in the bloodstream. To understand diabetes, it is important to know about two of the things that normally circulate in your blood—glucose and insulin. Glucose is a simple sugar, and it fuels every cell in your body, and insulin is a hormone that is required to move the glucose into your cells. Upon digestion, the carbohydrates you get from eating foods such as bread, fruit, vegetables and milk, break down into glucose and it enters your bloodstream. Insulin (produced in your pancreas) acts as a key to allow the movement of the glucose from your blood into your cells. Because of this, insulin is a critical component in main-

Diabetes is a condition in which the body is unable to handle glucose properly, allowing an excessive amount to build up in the bloodstream.

taining the proper amount of sugar in your blood. In type 1 diabetes, the body, for reasons not fully known, is unable to produce insulin. In type 2 diabetes, the body does not produce enough insulin and/or is not able to use what is produced properly.

(The most common condition that affects the effectiveness of insulin is called "insulin resistance." An excessive number of fat cells can cause insulin resistance.) No matter what the cause, high blood sugar, unfortunately, can result in both short-term and long-term negative health consequences.

PREVALENCE OF DIABETES

If you or someone you love has diabetes, you are not alone. An estimated 26 million people in the United States have diabetes, and that number is rising rapidly. Another 79 million, or *one in three Americans*, have what is called prediabetes. Prediabetes is a condition in which your blood sugar is higher than normal, but not quite high enough to be classified as diabetes—yet. If left unchecked, the majority of people with prediabetes will go on to develop type 2 diabetes within 10 years. It's estimated that one out of every two Americans over 65 years of age have either diabetes or prediabetes.*

PREVENTING DIABETES

Although there are many factors that contribute to type 2 diabetes, including genetics, ethnicity, and age, the single factor that contributes the greatest risk is not whether diabetes is in your genes, but the size of the jeans you are in! When it comes to decreasing your risk for type 2 diabetes, there is nothing more important than maintaining a healthy weight. Ninety-five percent of those diagnosed with diabetes have type 2, and 8 out of 10 of these cases can be prevented or delayed with weight loss, regular physical activity, and a diet high in fiber and low in saturated fat and trans-fats (see Everyday Healthy Eating Tips, page 8). If diagnosed with diabetes, you will need to eat healthier every day, so why not start now? If you already have prediabetes, it has been clinically proven that the combination of modest weight loss (losing as little as 5 to 7 percent of your body weight) and moderate exercise (30 minutes of walking five days a week) can

When it comes to decreasing your risk for type 2 diabetes, there is nothing more important than maintaining a healthy weight.

delay or even prevent the onset of type 2 diabetes! And last, if you have diabetes, taking control of it will keep it from controlling you. (See Everyday Meal Planning on page 24.)

EAT WHAT YOU LOVE WITH DIABETES

This is the fun part! Whether you want to reduce your risk for diabetes, push back prediabetes, or keep diabetes in check, you *can* still enjoy the foods you love, including all the scrumptious recipes in this book

I've made it my mission to make eating with diabetes easy (and tasty!).

(and all of my books) and achieve your health goals, too! Let's face it, diabetes can be tough, but I've made it my mission to make eating with diabetes easy (and tasty!). Beyond the recipes, you'll find plenty of healthy eating and shopping tips, a section to help you with menu planning, along with a diabetes-focused nutritional analysis for every recipe. Most of all, these recipes for every meal, every day, and every occasion make eating well with diabetes, well, a piece of cake! (P.S.—Go to www.marlenekoch. com for a week's worth of calorie/carb-controlled menus.)

* The American Diabetes Association recommends that all persons who are 45 years of age or older and overweight, or younger than 45 and overweight with additional risk factors such as family history of diabetes, high blood pressure, or heart disease, plus those who are African American, Hispanic, or Native American, or have had gestational diabetes be screened for high blood sugar.

EAT *what you* LOVE

RECIPES

for Every Day & Every Occasion

Sippers, Smoothies, Shakes, and Cocktails

Iced Green Tea Refresher

Raspberry Lemonade

Citrus Cucumber Spa Water

Strawberry Kiwi Smoothie

Luscious Lemon Slim Smoothie

Banana Berry Super Smoothie

PB&J Smoothie

Mocha Fudge "Mudslide" Milk Shake

Soda Fountain Float Freezes

Starbucks-Style Blended Strawberries & Cream Frappe

Blended Strawberry Daiquiri

65-Calorie Peppermint Mocha

BBQ Bloody Marys

Skinny Margaritas

SOME OF MY FAVORITE "FOOD" MEMORIES ARE NOT OF FOOD at all—but of beverages. From making fresh homemade lemonade with my boys, to drinking root beer floats with my best friend, to sipping margaritas with my husband, I can't imagine *not drinking* any of life's sensational sippers. Unfortunately, studies show that calories from such drinks are usually of the "extra" kind, and most of us consume far too many. It's estimated that one in four Americans gulps down at least 200 sugar-laden calories a day (or enough to gain 20 pounds in a year!) Considering that one large drink can pack up to 1,000 calories, it's easy to see how quickly the calories—and the pounds—can add up.

But if you think you need to drink plain water only in order to look and feel your best, I have wonderful news for you! Whether you are in the mood for an icy cold drink, a soda fountain freeze, or an end-of-the-day cocktail, the only consequences you'll get from drinking these beverages are the fond memories you can make.

Looking for the perfect drink to share on a hot summer's day? Go fruity and refreshing with real fruit Raspberry Lemonade. Need a smoothie that will fill you up but not out? Try the bright Luscious Lemon Slim Smoothie (only 100 calories!) or the vitamin-packed Banana Berry Super Smoothie to power you through your day. Love the coffeehouse, but not the cost? Have a coffee klatch at home for a fraction of the sugar, calories, and fat with my Starbucks-Style Blended Strawberries & Cream Frappe or 65-Calorie Peppermint Mocha. And when it comes to entertaining, I'm thrilled to introduce lower-calorie cocktail offerings for all your needs, whether it's Sunday brunch with a BBQ Bloody Mary or Friday night with an authentic Skinny Margarita. At fewer than 150 calories, they're both worth raising your glass for!

MILK

Moo-ve over milk! It's hard not to notice the vast variety of nondairy beverages and milk alternatives that now line the supermarket aisles and inhabit the dairy case. For me, when it comes to across-the-board use for cooking and baking—including nutrient content, texture, taste, and cost—good old cow's milk is still the gold standard (low-fat of course), but that's not saying that there's not a lot to love about nondairy milk replacements.

For those who are allergic or lactose intolerant, these beverages are lifesavers, for those seeking less carbs or calories, they're great alternatives, and for those adventurous in the kitchen, nondairy milks can be a delicious swap. Here's a guide to selecting and substituting nondairy beverages that will ensure both good recipe results and good health:

Marlene's Tips for Nondairy Beverages:

- Choose carefully. Milk alternatives vary greatly in taste, texture, and nutritional content.

- For the lactose intolerant, lactose-free cow's milk (like Lactaid) is a good choice.

- Read labels. While some beverages are low in calories, others have more sugar and fat, and far less protein than cow's milk. Look for beverages fortified with calcium and vitamin D. Almond milk, for example, is low in protein while rice milk is high in carbs.

- Pick the right "milk," for the dish. Nondairy beverages, such as soy and almond milk, come in many flavors. Use *plain* varieties for savory recipes, such as soups, sauces, or pasta dishes. Light vanilla varieties can be used for sweet foods, such as cookies, cakes, and quick breads.

- Soymilk is the most similar to milk in cooking and baking applications. Light, unsweetened soymilk is close in protein and similar in fat content to 1% milk.

- Unsweetened almond milk is lowest in calories and carbs. At just 40 calories and 3 grams of carb per cup (instead 110 and 12 respectively), it's great for breakfast cereals and skinny smoothies and shakes.

- Use nondairy alternatives, cup for cup, in place of cow's milk. To make up for less body in soups and sauces, add up ¼ to ½ teaspoon of cornstarch per cup of "milk."

- Make your own nondairy buttermilk. Just add 2 teaspoons of vinegar or lemon juice to 1 cup of light soymilk. (It will not curdle but will work the same.)

Note: Nondairy beverages cannot thicken instant pudding.

Iced Green Tea Refresher

WHEN I WAS GROWING UP, the only time we drank green tea was when we ate Chinese food. How times have changed! With studies touting the incredible health benefits of green tea, it's no wonder that it is now so commonplace. Inspired by the popular cocktail, the Mojito, this refreshing, lightly sweetened, all natural iced tea combines good-for-you green tea with fresh lime and mint. To create a green tea "mo-tea-to" cocktail, add additional sweetener to taste and an ounce or two of your favorite rum.

MAKES 2 SERVINGS

1½ cups water

2 green tea bags

8 fresh mint leaves

2 teaspoons granulated sugar

2 teaspoons fresh lime juice

½ teaspoon lime zest

Crushed ice

1. Pour the water into a small saucepan and bring to a low boil. Let cool 1 minute, add tea bags and steep for 5 minutes. Remove tea bags and discard. Let the tea cool to room temperature.

2. Place the mint leaves into a pitcher and sprinkle with sugar. Using a wooden spoon or muddler, gently mash the mint leaves to release their flavor. Pour the tea into a pitcher. Add the lime juice and zest, and stir.

3. To serve, fill each glass with crushed ice, and add the tea (distributing mint leaves evenly). Garnish with additional mint leaves, if desired.

Marlene Says: *This is a lightly sweetened drink. For a sweeter tea, add two more teaspoons of sugar (adds 15 calories per serving). Or to keep carbs in check, opt for a packet of a sugar substitute. As a rule, all sugar substitute packets are calibrated to equal the sweetness of 2 teaspoons of sugar.*

NUTRITION INFORMATION PER SERVING: (1 cup with ice) Calories 20 | Carbohydrate 5g (Sugars 4g) | Total Fat 0g (Sat Fat 0g) | Protein 0g | Fiber 0g | Cholesterol 0mg | Sodium 0mg | Food Exchanges: Free Food | Carbohydrate Choices: 0 | Weight Watcher Plus Point Comparison: 0

Raspberry Lemonade

WHILE MOST RASPBERRY LEMONADES TEMPT YOU WITH THE PRETTY RED HUE of raspberries—but offer little raspberry taste—in this lemonade, the sweet taste of raspberries shine. The only thing you'll find lacking here is the customary 10 teaspoons, or more, of added sugars per serving. For a twist, use sparkling water instead of plain. Fresh raspberries and a twist of lemon on each glass are perfect garnishes.

MAKES 4 SERVINGS

1 (10-ounce) package unsweetened frozen raspberries

3 cups water, divided

½ cup granulated no-calorie sweetener (or 12 packets)*

1 tablespoon granulated sugar

½ cup fresh lemon juice (about 3 lemons)

2 teaspoons lemon zest

Crushed ice

1. Place the raspberries in a medium, microwave-safe bowl and microwave on high for 1 minute. Stir in 1 cup of the water while lightly crushing the berries. Strain the juice through a sieve or strainer (pressing on the berries to force all the juice out). Discard the pulp and seeds.

2. Add the remaining water, sweetener, sugar, lemon juice and zest to the raspberry juice and stir well.

3. Serve over crushed ice.

DARE TO COMPARE: The frozen lemonade mixers at Auntie Anne's are almost as popular as their pretzels. Their smallest raspberry lemonade drink contains 15 teaspoons of added sugar and 240 calories.

*See page 81 for sweetener options.

NUTRITION INFORMATION PER SERVING: (1 cup) Calories 35 | Carbohydrate 9g (Sugars 6g) | Total Fat 0g (Sat Fat 0g) | Protein 0g | Fiber 0g | Cholesterol 0mg | Sodium 0mg | Food Exchanges: ½ Fruit | Carbohydrate Choices: ½ | Weight Watcher Plus Point Comparison: 1

Citrus Cucumber Spa Water

WHO WOULD THINK YOU WOULD NEED A RECIPE FOR WATER? Well, as it turns out, I did! After enjoying the perfect blend of citrus and cucumber in a refreshing beverage at the Culinary Institute of America in Napa, I set out to make it at home. I quickly learned that the ratio of fruit and cucumber to water, and the length of time the mixture sits, makes a big difference. Here's to the perfect water recipe!

MAKES 8 SERVINGS

½ medium orange

½ medium lemon

½ cup thinly sliced cucumber

4 cups water

1. Slice the orange and lemon halves into thin, round slices and place in the bottom of a 2-quart pitcher. Add the cucumber and water, stir, and refrigerate for 1 to 2 hours.

2. Fill the pitcher with ice and stir before serving.

Marlene Says: *Have a "spa day" at home with this delicious refresher. When you finish drinking the pitcher of water, top the fruit off with another 4 cups of water. Let it sit 8 hours, or overnight, in the refrigerator, add ice, and enjoy another batch.*

NUTRITION INFORMATION PER SERVING (1 CUP): Calories 5 | Carbohydrate 2g (Sugars 1g) | Total Fat 0g (Sat Fat 0g) | Protein 0g | Fiber 0g | Cholesterol 0mg | Sodium 0mg | Food Exchanges: Free Food | Carbohydrate Choices: 0 | Weight Watcher Plus Point Comparison: 0

Strawberry Kiwi Smoothie

FRUIT SMOOTHIES MAY SOUND HEALTHY, but the all-fruit smoothies at most smoothie shops contain more concentrated fruit juice than they do whole fruit, rendering them sky high in simple sugars and low in healthy fiber. The carb content in the smallest size often equals that of 6 pieces of fruit, without the fiber! A better bet is this truly healthy dairy-free smoothie—packed with real fruit, it has 4 grams of fiber and delivers over two days' worth of vitamin C.

MAKES 1 SERVING

½ cup light cranberry juice

½ cup frozen strawberries, halved

1 medium kiwi, peeled and quartered

1 tablespoon or 2 packets granulated no-calorie sweetener*

¾ to 1 cup crushed ice

1. Place all the ingredients, except the ice, in a blender. Blend to mix.

2. Add crushed ice and blend on high until the ice is completely incorporated and drink is frothy.

DARE TO COMPARE: The average strawberry kiwi smoothie from a smoothie shop, made with strawberries and concentrated juice blends, clocks in with 375 calories and 90 grams of carbohydrate (84 of them from sugar). Plus Point value for the "healthy" drink is 10.

*See page 81 for sweetener options.

NUTRITION INFORMATION PER SERVING: Calories 105 | Carbohydrate 25g (Sugars 18g) | Total Fat 0g (Sat Fat 0g) | Protein 1g | Fiber 4g | Cholesterol 0mg | Sodium 5mg | Food Exchanges: 1½ Fruit | Carbohydrate Choices: 1½ | Weight Watcher Plus Point Comparison: 2

Luscious Lemon Slim Smoothie

ADD A RAY OF SUNSHINE TO YOUR MORNING with this luscious lemon smoothie—for only 100 calories! Lemon sugar-free pudding mix adds body, while milk and Greek yogurt pump up the protein for a waist-whittling drink that's sure to satisfy. In a rush? Add a slice of whole grain toast and you're out the door.

MAKES 1 SERVING

⅓ cup low-fat milk

1 tablespoon lemon sugar-free instant pudding mix

⅓ cup cold water

⅓ cup plain nonfat Greek yogurt

2 teaspoons fresh lemon juice (optional)

1 cup crushed ice

1. Place the milk and pudding mix in a blender. Blend briefly. Let pudding set up for one minute.

2. Add the water, yogurt, and lemon juice, if using. Blend to mix, add crushed ice, and blend on high until the ice is completely incorporated. Serve immediately.

Marlene Says: *Studies show that thicker beverages satisfy hunger better than thin ones. To make a sensational PEANUT BUTTER BUTTERSCOTCH SLIM SMOOTHIE, replace the lemon pudding mix with butterscotch sugar-free instant pudding mix and add 2 teaspoons peanut butter in step 2. (Adds 60 calories, 5 grams fat, 3 grams protein, and 2 grams carbohydrate, and 1 "point.")*

NUTRITION INFORMATION PER SERVING: Calories 100 | Carbohydrate 14g (Sugars 7g) | Total Fat 1.5g (Sat Fat 0.5g) | Protein 10g | Fiber 0g | Cholesterol 5mg | Sodium 350mg | Food Exchanges: ½ Low-fat Milk, 1 Lean Meat | Carbohydrate Choices: 1 | Weight Watcher Plus Point Comparison: 3

Banana Berry Super Smoothie

DESPITE MY NUTRITION KNOWLEDGE, I must admit that I never found the idea of putting "greens" in a smoothie very appealing—but this drink changes that. With some help from a blended fruit and veggie mix found readily at the store, and three "superfood" all-stars, blueberries, spinach, and Greek yogurt, this big belly-filling 110-calorie smoothie serves up two fruit and vegetable servings, and it tastes great! No spinach? No problem. Feel free to leave it out.

MAKES 1 SERVING

½ cup frozen blueberries

¾ cup V8 V-Fusion Light Strawberry Banana juice drink

1 cup fresh spinach, lightly packed

2 tablespoons plain nonfat Greek yogurt

⅓ cup crushed ice

1. Place all the ingredients except the ice in a blender. Blend to mix.

2. Add crushed ice and blend on high until the ice is completely incorporated. Serve immediately.

Marlene Says: *This smoothie contains 70% of your daily requirement of Vitamin A and over 100% of Vitamins C and K. At breakfast I pair it with a boiled egg or handful of nuts for additional protein. In the afternoon it does a great job at blasting away my hunger cravings!*

NUTRITION INFORMATION PER SERVING: Calories 110 | Carbohydrate 24g (Sugars 18g) | Total Fat 1g (Sat Fat 0g) | Protein 4g | Fiber 3g | Cholesterol 0mg | Sodium 85mg | Food Exchanges: 1 Fruit, 1 Vegetable | Carbohydrate Choices: 1½ | Weight Watcher Plus Point Comparison: 3

PB&J Smoothie

SMOOTHIES MADE WITH PEANUT BUTTER ARE NOTORIOUS for being sky high in fat and calories. They're also incredibly delicious. Inspired by one of the most popular versions at a national chain smoothie shop, this newly fit, yet still delectable smoothie, blends peanut putter, bananas, and jam together beautifully in what may soon be called your daily favorite. To turn this into a "power" smoothie add 1 tablespoon of your favorite protein power or ¼ cup liquid egg substitute.

MAKES 1 SERVING

½ cup low-fat milk

½ medium banana, frozen

1 rounded tablespoon peanut butter

2 tablespoons sugar-free or low-sugar strawberry jam

1 cup crushed ice

1. Place all the ingredients except the ice in a blender. Blend to mix.

2. Add crushed ice and blend on high until the ice is completely incorporated. Serve immediately

DARE TO COMPARE: A small Peanut Power Plus Strawberry at Smoothie King has 680 calories and packs the equivalent of 24 teaspoons of sugar. Jump up to the medium size, and you're looking at a staggering 1,020 calories and 42 teaspoons of sugar.

NUTRITION INFORMATION PER SERVING: Calories 220 | Carbohydrate 32g (Sugars 18g) | Total Fat 10g (Sat Fat 2.5g) | Protein 9g | Fiber 2g | Cholesterol 5mg | Sodium 135mg | Food Exchanges: 1 Fruit, ½ Low-fat Milk, 1 Fat | Carbohydrate Choices: 2 | Weight Watcher Plus Point Comparison: 6

Mocha Fudge "Mudslide" Milkshake

THIS MILKSHAKE IS SOOO GOOD! Thick, creamy, and rich with the taste of coffee and chocolate fudge, it reminds me of the famous mudslide pie made with coffee, chocolate fudge, and sliced almonds. I find this shake super satisfying just as it is, but feel free to kick it up another notch by adding the whipped cream and almonds options.

2 teaspoons sugar-free fudge ice cream topping

⅔ cup low-fat milk

1 tablespoon vanilla sugar-free instant pudding mix

2 teaspoons instant coffee powder (regular or decaffeinated)

2 teaspoons granulated no-calorie sweetener (or 1 packet)*

½ cup light, no-sugar-added vanilla ice cream

⅔ cup crushed ice

light whipped cream (optional)

sliced almonds (optional)

1. Using a teaspoon, smear the fudge sauce along the inside walls of a tall glass. Place in the fridge while making the shake.

2. Combine the milk and pudding mix in a blender. Blend to mix. Let set for 1 minute. Add remaining ingredients and blend until the ice is completely incorporated and the shake is thick and creamy. Carefully pour milkshake into the prepared glass. Top with light whipped cream and sliced almonds, if desired.

DARE TO COMPARE: A restaurant-style sundae made with coffee ice cream, fudge, whipped cream, and nuts will set you back 1,350 calories and 75 grams of fat! Two tablespoons of light whipped cream and a teaspoon of sliced almonds adds just 25 calories to this sensational shake.

*See page 81 for sweetener options.

NUTRITION INFORMATION PER SERVING: Calories 205 | Carbohydrate 35g (Sugars 12g) | Total Fat 4.5g (Sat Fat 3g) | Protein 8g | Fiber 4g | Cholesterol 5mg | Sodium 480mg | Food Exchanges: 1½ Carbohydrate, ½ Low-fat Milk | Carbohydrate Choices: 2 | Weight Watcher Plus Point Comparison: 5

Soda Fountain Float Freezes

IF YOU'VE NEVER HAD A SODA "FREEZE," now is a good time. Cool, creamy, and delightfully sweet, drinking one will make you feel like a kid again. The trick to making them is soda ice cubes. Keep an ice cube tray in the freezer filled with soda pop, and you will always be ready for a freeze. I'm partial to root beer float freezes, but my boys also love to make cherry cola, orange soda, and Dr Pepper freezes. Have a favorite soda flavor? Give it a whirl! With only 55 calories a freeze, you can try them all!

MAKES 1 SERVING

1¼ cups sugar-free soda, divided

⅓ cup light, no-sugar-added vanilla ice cream

1. Pour ½ cup of the soda into an ice cube tray and freeze for several hours until frozen.

2. Place the remaining ¾ cup of soda, ice cream, and frozen soda cubes in a blender and blend on high until the cubes are completely incorporated. Serve immediately.

DARE TO COMPARE: The dubious honor of worst "freeze" in America with 820 calories and 34 teaspoons of sugar goes to the large Root Beer Freeze served at A&W restaurants. Downsize to a small and you are still looking at nearly 15 teaspoons of added sugars (close to two days' worth).

NUTRITION INFORMATION PER SERVING: Calories 55 | Carbohydrate 8g (Sugars 3g) | Total Fat 2g (Sat Fat 1.5g) | Protein 2g | Fiber 3g | Cholesterol 0mg | Sodium 90mg | Food Exchanges: ½ Carbohydrate | Carbohydrate Choices: ½ | Weight Watcher Plus Point Comparison: 1

Starbucks-Style Blended Strawberries & Cream Frappe

HERE'S ANOTHER WELL-KNOWN COFFEEHOUSE FAVORITE, only this one is coffee-free! After testing this makeover recipe several times (and enjoying the process immensely), my kitchen assistants and I did a back-to-back tasting with the big 'bucks original. Our luscious drink was just as creamy; but even better, it offered a much fresher strawberry flavor than the original. We immediately declared this marvelous makeover a winner!

MAKES 1 SERVING

½ cup low-fat milk

¼ cup nonfat half-and-half

⅔ cup frozen strawberries (about 6 large)

3 tablespoons granulated no-calorie sweetener (or 4 packets)*

½ cup crushed ice

1. Place all the ingredients except the ice in a blender. Blend to mix.

2. Add crushed ice and blend on high until the ice is completely incorporated. Top with light whipped cream, if desired.

DARE TO COMPARE: Want to send your blood sugar soaring? While only 10% fat, a grande Strawberries and Crème Frappuccino Blended Crème at Starbucks (without whipped cream) clocks in with two meals' worth of carbohydrates—including the equivalent of 20 teaspoons of sugar.

*See page 81 for sweetener options.

NUTRITION INFORMATION PER SERVING: Calories 150 | Carbohydrate 25g (Sugars 16g) | Total Fat 1.5g (Sat Fat 1g) | Protein 7g | Fiber 2g | Cholesterol 5mg | Sodium 65mg | Food Exchanges: ½ Low-fat Milk, ½ Fruit, ½ Starch | Carbohydrate Choices: 1½ | Weight Watcher Plus Point Comparison: 4

Blended Strawberry Daiquiri

WHEN WE ENTERTAIN, I may be known for working my magic in the kitchen, but it's my husband, Chuck, who is known for working magic at the bar. You'd never guess this luscious, fruity drink isn't high in sugar, especially since it tastes just like the traditional blended bar version that can easily contain 40 grams of sugar or more. The addition of an umbrella is optional, but sure is fun. To make a Strawberry Margarita, Chuck says to use tequila instead of rum.

MAKES 1 SERVING

2 ounces light rum (¼ cup)

1 tablespoon fresh lime juice

3 large, whole, frozen strawberries

2 tablespoons granulated no-calorie sweetener (or 3 packets)*

½ cup crushed ice

Twist of lime (optional garnish)

1. Pour the rum and lime juice into a blender. Add the strawberries and sweetener and blend on medium until smooth. Add the crushed ice and blend on high until ice is incorporated and drink is thick.

2. To serve, pour into a cocktail glass and garnish with twist of lime, if desired.

*See page 81 for sweetener options.

NUTRITION INFORMATION PER SERVING: Calories 150 | Carbohydrate 6g (Sugars 3g) | Total Fat 0g (Sat Fat 0g) | Protein 0g | Fiber 1g | Cholesterol 0mg | Sodium 0mg | Food Exchanges: 3 Fat, ½ Fruit | Carbohydrate Choices: 0 | Weight Watcher Plus Point Comparison: 5

65-Calorie Peppermint Mocha

ONE OF THE MOST POPULAR DRINKS EVERY HOLIDAY SEASON at Starbucks is the Peppermint Mocha, a festive blend of coffee, milk, peppermint, and chocolate. When topped off with whipped cream, it's deliciousness defined. The downside is that this "deliciousness" comes with a hefty price tag—both to your wallet and your waistline. You can drink four of these for the calories in one of theirs—and also savor the significant savings in your wallet.

| MAKES 1 SERVING

1 tablespoon cocoa powder (preferably Dutch-processed)

2 tablespoons no-calorie sweetener (or 3 packets)*

¼ rounded teaspoon cornstarch

⅔ cup warm water

½ teaspoon instant coffee

⅛ teaspoon peppermint extract

¼ cup low-fat milk

2 tablespoons light whipped cream

1. Place the cocoa powder, sweetener, and cornstarch in a microwave-safe mug. Whisk in water and instant coffee and peppermint extract. Microwave on high for 1 minute (keep an eye on it to be sure it does not boil over). Whisk in the milk and heat for 30 seconds more.

2. To serve, top with whipped cream.

Marlene Says: *Feel free to omit the coffee for dark, delicious Peppermint Hot Chocolate. For a dairy-free option, try it with light vanilla soymilk and drop 10 more calories! A small (also known as a "tall") Peppermint Mocha with whipped cream at the 'bucks serves up 350 calories and 10 teaspoons of sugar.*

*See page 81 for sweetener options.

NUTRITION INFORMATION PER SERVING: Calories 65 | Carbohydrate 9g (Sugars 3g) | Total Fat 2g (Sat Fat 2g) | Protein 3g | Fiber 2g | Cholesterol 10mg | Sodium 20mg | Food Exchanges: ¼ Low-fat Milk, ½ Fat | Carbohydrate Choices: ½ | Weight Watcher Plus Point Comparison: 1

BBQ Bloody Marys

HERE'S A FUN TWIST ON AN OLD FAVORITE. I was pretty skeptical when I spotted a Blood Mary seasoned with barbecue sauce at a fancy food show, but was ready to re-create the drink after just one sip! The barbecue sauce lends a bit of smoky sweetness, complementing, rather than overpowering, the traditional drink. Pair this with my Savory Southern-Style Biscuits, Eggs, and Gravy (page 68) for a "down South" brunch that will completely wow your guests. (P.S.—Low-sodium V8 not only tastes great in this drink, but it also helps cut the usual sodium in half!)

MAKES 2 SERVINGS

3 ounces vodka
(6 tablespoons)

1 cup low-sodium V8

2 tablespoons fresh
lemon juice

1 teaspoon horseradish

1 teaspoon
Worcestershire sauce

2 teaspoons barbecue
sauce

½ teaspoon celery salt

¼ teaspoon black pepper

2 to 3 dashes Tabasco
sauce, or to taste

Crushed ice

2 trimmed celery stalks,
for garnish

1. In a large bar glass or 2-cup container, mix everything together except the ice and celery stalks.

2. To serve, fill each glass with ice and half the Bloody Mary mix, and garnish with a celery stalk.

Marlene Says: *For a fun twist, replace the celery garnish with a few Sweet 'n Spicy Pickled Green Beans (page 115).*

NUTRITION INFORMATION PER SERVING: Calories 140 | Carbohydrate 8g (Sugars 6g) | Total Fat 0g (Sat Fat 0g) | Protein 1g | Fiber 1g | Cholesterol 0mg | Sodium 395mg | Food Exchanges: 3 Fat, 1 Vegetable | Carbohydrate Choices: ½ | Weight Watcher Plus Point Comparison: 3

Skinny Margaritas

MADE WITH TEQUILA, ORANGE LIQUEUR, AND FRESH LIME JUICE, these margaritas are the real deal. Most "skinny" mixes use the essence of lime, but in my book, skinny doesn't mean skimping on taste, so you'll not find that here. Two-Minute Fire-Roasted Salsa (page 112) and chips, and Chicken Fajita Nachos (page 106), are two of my favorite accompaniments. Whether shaken (see step 2), or served over ice, these are top shelf.

MAKES 4 SERVINGS

¾ cup tequila

½ cup fresh lime juice

½ cup water

¼ cup orange liqueur (like Triple sec or Grand Marnier)

3 tablespoons granulated no-calorie sweetener (or 4 packets)*

Lime wedge (optional)

Coarse salt (optional)

1. Pour tequila, lime juice, water, orange liqueur, and sweetener into a pitcher. Stir well.

2. For each drink, pour ½ cup of the mixture into a shaker filled with ice and shake well. Wet the rim of an ice-filled rocks glass with the lime wedge, and dip in salt, if desired.

3. Alternatively, pour ½ cup margarita mixture over ice in a tall glass and stir.

Marlene Says: *Alcohol, in moderation, may actually have health benefits. If you choose to imbibe, opt for drinks without sugary mixers, and don't forget to count the calories! If you have diabetes, you may be pleased to know that alcohol itself does not raise blood sugar. Check with your doctor or a registered dietitian for personalized guidelines on alcohol consumption.*

*See page 81 for sweetener options.

NUTRITION INFORMATION PER SERVING: Calories 140 | Carbohydrate 7g (Sugars 5g) | Total Fat 0g (Sat Fat 0g) | Protein 0g | Fiber 0g | Cholesterol 0mg | Sodium 0mg | Food Exchanges: 3 Fat, ½ Starch | Carbohydrate Choices: ½ | Weight Watcher Plus Point Comparison: 3

Breakfast and Brunch

Apple Pie Oatmeal

Everyday Granola

Breakfast-Style Egg Salad Sandwich

Anyday Egg "Muffins"

Pizza Frittata

Perfect Puffy 150-Calorie Cheese Omelet

Hearty Breakfast Bake

Savory Southern-Style Biscuits, Eggs, and Gravy

Joe's Special Spinach and Egg Scramble

Mexican-Style Steak & Eggs

14-Karat Carrot Cake Pancakes

Sweet and Savory French Toast Sandwiches

Whole Grain Apple Popover Pancakes

Apple Dapple Yogurt Parfait

Maple Bacon Waffles

REAKFAST IS MY FAVORITE MEAL OF THE DAY, and it's a good thing, because studies show just how important the first meal is. For example, it may appear that skipping breakfast would save calories, but recent research reveals that what is eaten at breakfast influences the appetite far beyond the morning hours. Not only do people who skip breakfast tend to make up the calories later in the day with richer, less healthy foods, but eating a protein-rich breakfast can keep even those late-night cookie cravings in check!

It's fun to get excited about a breakfast that hits the culinary trifecta of easy, nutritious, and delicious, and my Everyday Granola does just that. Made with wholesome oats, nuts, and coconut, it has the decadent taste of commercially packaged granola with less than half the carbs, calories, and fat. Another is a warm bowl of homemade Apple Pie Oatmeal with its apple-icious taste and wholegrain goodness. It takes just minutes to make and is sure to make the old "packets" a thing of the past.

If a higher protein breakfast is what you are looking for, you'll find plenty of quick weekday protein-packed entrées to keep you full and fit—from the easy Breakfast-Style Egg Salad Sandwich (at just 170 calories), to Anyday Egg "Muffins" (perfect for toting), or Apple Dapple Yogurt Parfait (that boasts the protein of two eggs). And last, for leisurely mornings and entertaining, you'll find amazing restaurant-inspired dishes. Your family is sure to smile when you serve Maple Bacon Waffles or 14-Karat Carrot Cake Pancakes topped with maple cream cheese, walnuts, and whipped cream (no need to tell them they are just 300 calories instead of the usual 1,120!), and your guests will never want to leave after eating Savory Southern-Style Biscuits, Eggs, and Gravy. You're going to love breakfast!

Apple Pie Oatmeal

ONE OF MY FAVORITE BREAKFAST FOODS GROWING UP was a bowl of apples and cinnamon oatmeal prepared from an instant packet. Funny how our palates change; I recently tried it again and found the consistency pasty, the taste a bit salty, and the bits of dried apples in need of an upgrade. My fast-fix version infuses pieces of fresh apple with sweet cinnamon-y goodness before adding the oats to give it the homey taste of apple pie. The instant packets are now packed away for good.

MAKES 1 SERVING

½ medium apple, peeled, cored, and chopped

½ teaspoon cinnamon

2 tablespoons granulated no-calorie sweetener (or 3 packets)*

⅓ cup old-fashioned oats

½ teaspoon vanilla extract

1. In a medium, microwave-safe bowl (at least 2-cup capacity), combine the apple, ¼ cup water, cinnamon, and sweetener, and stir. Microwave on high for 2 minutes.

2. Remove from microwave and add oats, ¾ cup water, and vanilla, and stir. Microwave on high for 3 more minutes. Remove, stir again, and let cool for 1 minute.

Marlene Says: *Oats contain more protein than any other grain, are high in cholesterol-lowering soluble fiber, and have been shown to keep you full longer than other, more refined cereals. The beta-glucan in oats also helps to slow the rise of blood sugar, making oats a superb choice for those with diabetes.*

*See page 81 for sweetener options.

NUTRITION INFORMATION PER SERVING: Calories 160 | Carbohydrate 30g (Sugars 8g) | Total Fat 2g (Sat Fat 0g) | Protein 4g | Fiber 4g | Cholesterol 0mg | Sodium 0mg | Food Exchanges: 1½ Starch, ½ Fruit | Carbohydrate Choices: 2 | Weight Watcher Plus Point Comparison: 4

Everyday Granola

SWEET, NUTTY, AND PACKED WITH PLENTY OF OAT CLUSTERS, this granola is easy to make, economical, and healthy enough to eat every day. Feel free to switch up the nuts and dried fruit, but do keep the wheat flakes. They lend an extrasatisfying crunch and a boost of fiber. Stored in an airtight container, this will keep fresh in the cupboard for up to two weeks and in the freezer for a month or more.

MAKES 18 SERVINGS

3 cups old-fashioned oats

1½ cups wheat flakes (like Wheaties)

½ cup unsweetened coconut

½ cup sliced almonds

1 teaspoon cinnamon

⅛ teaspoon salt

½ cup sugar-free maple syrup

½ cup granulated no-calorie sweetener*

1½ tablespoons canola oil

2 large egg whites

1 teaspoon vanilla extract

½ teaspoon coconut extract

⅓ cup raisins (I like golden)

1. Preheat the oven to 350°F. In a large bowl, combine oats, cereal, coconut, nuts, cinnamon, and salt.

2. In a small bowl, whisk together remaining ingredients, except the raisins. Pour the syrup mixture over oats and toss.

3. Spread the granola onto a baking sheet or jelly roll pan and bake for 15 minutes. Turn granola with a spatula, add raisins, and bake an additional 10 minutes. Let cool on baking sheet before placing in an airtight container.

DARE TO COMPARE: Seemingly "healthy" granolas are not healthy everyday fare when packed with sugar, fat, and calories. One-half cup of commercially prepared Vanilla Almond Granola clocks in with 250 calories and 12 grams of fat.

*See page 81 for sweetener options.

NUTRITION INFORMATION PER SERVING: (⅓ cup) Calories 125 | Carbohydrate 16g (Sugars 3g) | Total Fat 5g (Sat Fat 1.5g) | Protein 4g | Fiber 3g | Cholesterol 0mg | Sodium 55mg | Food Exchanges: 1 Starch, 1 Fat | Carbohydrate Choices: 1 | Weight Watcher Plus Point Comparison: 3

Breakfast-Style Egg Salad Sandwich

I NEVER THOUGHT OF EGG SALAD AS A BREAKFAST FOOD until inspiration struck, and I created this open-faced sandwich. As it happens, creamy egg salad is actually perfect for breakfast, especially when spread over warm toast, topped with bacon, and garnished with green onions! I really recommend you try this great on-the-go breakfast option. High in protein and flavor and low in fat and calories, I find it egg-ceptional.

MAKES 1 SERVING

2 large hard-boiled eggs*

1 green onion, chopped, white separated from green

1½ teaspoons light mayonnaise

1½ teaspoons plain nonfat Greek yogurt

Salt and black pepper to taste

1 slice light white or wheat bread

1½ teaspoons real bacon bits (like Hormel)

1. Peel the eggs, cut them in half, remove the yolk from one of the eggs, and discard it. Using the coarse shred on a box grater, grate the egg and egg white into a small bowl (you can also mash the eggs with a fork, but the grater makes for a much creamier egg salad). Add the white part of the onion, mayonnaise, yogurt, and salt and pepper. Stir well to combine.

2. Toast bread, and spread the egg salad on the warm toast, sprinkle the bacon bits on top, and garnish with the green part of the onion.

*See page 103 for my hard boiled egg tips.

NUTRITION INFORMATION PER SERVING: (1 sandwich) Calories 170 | Carbohydrate 12g (Sugars 1g) | Total Fat 8g (Sat Fat 2g) | Protein 14g | Fiber 3g | Cholesterol 190mg | Sodium 420mg | Food Exchanges: 2 Lean Meat, 1 Starch, 1 Fat | Carbohydrate Choices: 1 | Weight Watcher Plus Point Comparison: 4

Anyday Egg "Muffins"

WHEN YOU ARE FACED WITH A HECTIC MORNING, having these protein-packed "muffins" made and ready-to-eat could save the day. So, when time permits, make a batch, enjoy some for breakfast, and pop the leftovers in the fridge or freezer for those crazy times when you're running late but still want a breakfast that can get you through the morning.

MAKES 12 SERVINGS

3 to 4 teaspoons dry breadcrumbs

¾ cup shredded reduced-fat Cheddar cheese

½ cup chopped green onions

¼ cup diced red pepper

½ cup Canadian bacon, diced

¼ cup low-fat milk

3 tablespoons light mayonnaise

6 large eggs

1 cup liquid egg substitute

¼ teaspoon black pepper

1. Preheat the oven to 350°F. Lightly spray 12 muffin cups with non-stick cooking spray. Sprinkle a generous ¼ teaspoon of bread-crumbs in the bottom of each cup and gently tap the pan to evenly distribute the crumbs. Add 1 tablespoon of cheese to each cup.

2. Place the green onions and red pepper in a small, microwave-safe bowl, cover with plastic wrap, and cook on high for 2 minutes. Uncover and stir in the Canadian bacon. Set aside.

3. In a medium bowl or large measuring cup, whisk together the milk and mayonnaise. Add the eggs, egg substitute, and black pepper, and whisk until smooth.

4. Distribute the vegetable mixture evenly in the muffin cups (about 1 tablespoon in each), and pour the egg mixture over the vegetables, filling each cup ¾ full. Bake for 22 to 24 minutes, or until the center of the muffins are set and firm to the touch.

NUTRITION INFORMATION PER SERVING: (1 muffin) Calories 95 | Carbohydrate 2g (Sugars 0g) | Total Fat 6g (Sat Fat 2g) | Protein 9g | Fiber 0g | Cholesterol 100mg | Sodium 195mg | Food Exchanges: 1 Lean Meat, 1 Fat | Carbohydrate Choices: 0 | Weight Watcher Plus Point Comparison: 3

Pizza Frittata

THIS RECIPE OFFERS ALL THE DELICIOUS ELEMENTS OF A PIZZA—in a frittata! The first time I tasted eggs with pizza sauce, I fell in love with the combination, and I think you will too. Loaded with veggies and pepperoni, you get a generous portion (half of the frittata) for only 210 calories. As an added bonus, you don't have to think twice about excess carbs. This may just become your new favorite pizza for dinner, too.

MAKES 2 SERVINGS

2 large eggs

2 large egg whites

¼ teaspoon garlic salt

¼ teaspoon dried oregano

1 teaspoon olive oil

½ small red onion, thinly sliced

½ medium green pepper, cut into half rings

1 cup sliced mushrooms

¼ cup jarred pizza sauce

¼ cup part-skim mozzarella cheese

9 slices turkey pepperoni

1 tablespoon grated Parmesan cheese (optional)

1. Preheat the broiler. In a medium bowl, whisk together the eggs, egg whites, garlic salt, oregano, and 2 teaspoons water. Set aside.

2. Heat oil in a large, ovenproof, nonstick skillet over medium heat. Add the onion, and cook for 4 minutes, or until softened. Add green pepper and cook for 1 minute. Add mushrooms and 1 tablespoon of water, and cook for an additional 2 to 3 minutes, just until the mushrooms slightly soften.

3. Add the eggs to the skillet. Using a heat-resistant rubber spatula, gently lift and push cooked edges toward the center, allowing uncooked egg liquid to flow to the edge of the pan. Repeat until eggs are even across the bottom of the pan and set, but still moist.

4. Spread the pizza sauce over the eggs. Sprinkle the mozzarella over the sauce and top with pepperoni. Sprinkle with Parmesan, if desired, and place under the broiler for 3 minutes, or until cheese is melted. Use a spatula to loosen the frittata around edges and slide onto a plate. Cut into wedges and serve.

NUTRITION INFORMATION PER SERVING: (½ frittata) Calories 210 | Carbohydrate 9g (Sugars 5g) | Total Fat 11g (Sat Fat 3.5g) | Protein 17g | Fiber 2g | Cholesterol 230mg | Sodium 650mg | Food Exchanges: 2 Lean Meat, 1 Fat, ½ Vegetable | Carbohydrate Choices: ½ | Weight Watcher Plus Point Comparison: 5

Perfect Puffy 150-Calorie Cheese Omelet

THE SECRET TO CREATING a puffy diner-style omelet is to incorporate lots of air into the eggs. I have seen techniques ranging from separating the eggs and whipping the whites, to even folding fat-laden whipped cream into the egg mix to do so, but you won't find an easier way to create a puffy-style omelet than what you'll find here. I have purposely kept this omelet simple (as I do when I make it most days), but feel free to add your favorite omelet stuffers—at a starting point of 150 calories, there's room to spare!

MAKES 1 SERVING

1 large egg

¼ cup liquid egg substitute (or 2 large egg whites)

Black pepper to taste

¼ cup chopped spinach (optional)

2 tablespoons reduced-fat cheese

1 tablespoon salsa

1. Crack the egg into a small mixing bowl, add egg substitute and 1 tablespoon water, and blend with an immersion blender or mixer until eggs are thick and frothy and have doubled in volume (about 30 seconds).

2. Spray a small, nonstick skillet with cooking spray and warm over medium heat. Add the eggs to the hot pan. Roll the pan gently to allow the eggs to evenly cover the bottom, and cook the eggs until they start to set. Using a heat-resistant rubber spatula, gently lift and push the cooked edges toward the center, while tilting the pan to allow the uncooked egg liquid to flow to the edge of the pan. Repeat until no more liquid flows and eggs are set, but still moist.

3. Sprinkle the eggs with black pepper to taste. Place spinach, if desired, and cheese on half the eggs, and fold the plain half over the cheese. Spoon 2 teaspoons water into the pan (on the side away from the omelet), and immediately cover the pan with a lid. Reduce heat slightly and let omelet steam for 1 minute. Uncover, transfer omelet to a plate, top with salsa, and serve.

DARE TO COMPARE: A basic two-egg cheese omelet at IHOP has 510 calories and 34 grams of fat. Want ham with that? A Hearty Ham and Cheese Omelet—without any sides—clocks in at 910 calories, including an entire day's worth of fat. Instead, add 2 ounces of lean ham to this omelet for only 75 additional calories.

NUTRITION INFORMATION PER SERVING: Calories 150 | Carbohydrate 1g (Sugars 0g) | Total Fat 8g (Sat Fat 2g) | Protein 17g | Fiber 0g | Cholesterol 195mg | Sodium 195mg | Food Exchanges: 2½ Lean Meat, 1 Fat | Carbohydrate Choices: 0 | Weight Watcher Plus Point Comparison: 4

Hearty Breakfast Bake

THIS SAUSAGE, EGG, AND POTATO BAKE is one of my favorite no-brainer brunch dishes. You can whip it up the night before, refrigerate, and pop in the oven about an hour before guests arrive. In our house, extra portions never go to waste—my teenaged boys have been known to eat them for dinner. Be sure to use packaged shredded potatoes (either refrigerated or thawed frozen), fresh potatoes will discolor.

| MAKES 8 SERVINGS

1 medium onion, chopped

8 ounces lean turkey breakfast sausage

4 large eggs

1½ cups liquid egg substitute

1½ cups low-fat cottage cheese

¾ cup low-fat milk

1 cup reduced-fat shredded Cheddar cheese

3 cups shredded potatoes, refrigerated or thawed frozen

½ teaspoon dried thyme

1 teaspoon black pepper, or more to taste

1 small green pepper, diced (optional)

2 tablespoons grated Parmesan cheese

2 tablespoons chopped fresh parsley

1. Spray a large, nonstick skillet with cooking spray, and place over medium heat. Add the onion and sauté until soft, about 5 minutes, stirring occasionally. Crumble in sausage and cook, breaking up the meat, for 5 to 6 minutes, or until browned. Remove from the pan and set aside.

2. In a large bowl, combine the next 9 ingredients (eggs through optional green pepper). Add the sausage mixture, and stir well to combine. Cover and refrigerate for 1 hour or up to overnight.

3. Preheat the oven to 350°F. Coat a 13 x 9-inch baking pan with cooking spray. Pour the egg mixture into the prepared pan and bake for 45 minutes. Top with Parmesan cheese and bake another 10 to 15 minutes, or until the top is set and edges are lightly browned. Sprinkle with parsley and serve.

Marlene Says: *This bake has one-half the calories and one-third of the fat of the original recipe, thanks in part to cottage cheese. While my boys would* never *knowingly eat cottage cheese, they gobble up this incredibly nutritious dish.*

NUTRITION INFORMATION PER SERVING: (⅛ of casserole) Calories 220 | Carbohydrate 17g (Sugars 5g) | Total Fat 10g (Sat Fat 3g) | Protein 21g | Fiber 1g | Cholesterol 115mg | Sodium 470mg | Food Exchanges: 2½ Lean Meat, 1 Starch, ½ Fat | Carbohydrate Choices: 1 | Weight Watcher Plus Point Comparison: 7

Savory Southern-Style Biscuits, Eggs, and Gravy

THIS IS THE PERFECT DISH FOR A SUNDAY MORNING when you have the time to savor every bite. My husband calls these Southern-Style Eggs Benedict, and while I wholeheartedly agree with the "benedict" comparison, I find this dish even more comforting than the original. Soft, savory biscuits cradle fluffy scrambled eggs that are topped with bacon-tinged cream gravy. It's like a hug on a plate.

MAKES 4 SERVINGS

4 Savory Southern Biscuits (page 92)

1 slice center-cut bacon, cut in half

2 tablespoons all-purpose flour

1 cup reduced-sodium chicken broth, divided

⅛ teaspoon black pepper

Pinch of thyme

3 tablespoons nonfat half-and-half

Salt to taste

4 large eggs

4 large egg whites

Pepper to taste

¼ cup fresh chopped parsley, for garnish

1. Prepare biscuits, set aside.

2. In a small saucepan, over medium heat, cook bacon until crisp. Remove from pan, crumble, and set aside. Add the flour to the pan and slowly whisk in ½ cup of broth. When smooth, whisk in remaining broth and black pepper, and crush in thyme with your fingers. Bring gravy to a boil, reduce heat, and simmer for 3 to 4 minutes, whisking occasionally until gravy thickens. Whisk in half-and-half, add the bacon, and simmer for 1 minute. Adjust salt to taste and remove from heat.

3. Spray a medium, nonstick skillet with cooking spray, and place over medium heat. In a medium bowl, whisk together eggs, egg whites, 2 tablespoons water, and a pinch of salt and pepper to taste. Pour the egg mixture into the heated skillet and cook eggs, stirring occasionally until eggs are set.

4. Warm biscuits if necessary, and cut in half horizontally. Place a cut biscuit on each plate. Divide eggs among biscuits and top each with 2 tablespoons of gravy. Garnish with fresh parsley.

DARE TO COMPARE: The Biscuits & Gravy Combo at IHOP is served with 2 biscuits and a side of sausage gravy (without eggs) at a whopping 1,380 calories. The average person would have to walk for close to 4 hours to burn that many calories!

NUTRITION INFORMATION PER SERVING: (2 topped biscuit halves) Calories 220 | Carbohydrate 20g (Sugars 6g) | Total Fat 9g (Sat Fat 3g) | Protein 14g | Fiber less than 1g | Cholesterol 215mg | Sodium 510mg | Food Exchanges: 1½ Starch, 2 Lean Meat, ½ Fat | Carbohydrate Choices: 1½ | Weight Watcher Plus Point Comparison: 6

Joe's Special Spinach and Egg Scramble

THE ORIGINAL VERSION OF THIS DISH dates back to the 1920s when it was served at New Joe's Italian restaurant in San Francisco. Today you'll find it as the signature dish at the San Francisco restaurant institution known as Original Joe's. I first tasted it as a child when my mother made it from a recipe she found in the local paper. Here I've given the classic recipe a fresh update by replacing the beef with ground turkey and the frozen spinach with fresh. If you like to eat breakfast for dinner, this dish is perfect.

MAKES 4 SERVINGS

9 to 10 ounces fresh baby spinach

4 large eggs

4 large egg whites

1 medium onion, chopped

½ pound lean ground turkey

1 (8-ounce) package mushrooms, chopped

1 teaspoon dried oregano

¾ teaspoon garlic salt

1 teaspoon Worcestershire sauce

¼ teaspoon black pepper (or more to taste)

Grated Parmesan cheese (optional)

1. Place the spinach and 2 tablespoons water in a large, microwave-safe bowl. Cook on high for 1 to 2 minutes or until wilted. Set aside. Whisk together eggs and eggs whites. Set aside.

2. Spray a large, nonstick skillet with cooking spray, and place over medium heat. Add the onion and sauté, stirring occasionally, until lightly softened. Crumble in the ground turkey and cook, breaking up the meat, for 3 minutes, or until it starts to brown. Add the mushrooms, oregano, garlic salt, and Worcestershire sauce, and cook for another 3 to 4 minutes, or until the mushrooms begin to soften.

3. Reduce the heat to low, stir in the spinach, and pour the eggs over the vegetable mixture, stirring gently to distribute the eggs. Cook for 2 to 3 minutes, while gently stirring, until eggs are set. Sprinkle with pepper and optional Parmesan cheese, and serve.

NUTRITION INFORMATION PER SERVING: (1¼ cups) Calories 220 | Carbohydrate 9g (Sugars 3g) | Total Fat 10g (Sat Fat 2.5g) | Protein 24g | Fiber 2g | Cholesterol 255mg | Sodium 450mg | Food Exchanges: 3½ Lean Meat, 1 Vegetable, ½ Fat | Carbohydrate Choices: ½ | Weight Watcher Plus Point Comparison: 5

Mexican-Style Steak & Eggs

ONE OF MY FONDEST MEMORIES of living in San Diego was Sunday morning breakfast at a local Mexican restaurant. I loved the scrambled eggs served with warm tortillas—eaten taco-style. Now you can eat your eggs the same way, but with the addition of tasty strips of lean steak, peppers, and onions. When I serve this dish, I place the skillet in the middle of the table along with warmed tortillas, and let the family help themselves. Shredded cheese and sliced avocado make great garnishes.

MAKES 4 TO 8 SERVINGS

4 large eggs

4 large egg whites

6 ounces boneless sirloin, cut into thin strips

¾ teaspoon garlic salt

⅛ teaspoon black pepper

1 medium green pepper, thinly sliced

1 small onion, thinly sliced

8 (6-inch) corn tortillas

½ cup salsa (like Two-Minute Fire-Roasted Salsa, page 106)

1. In a medium bowl, whisk together the eggs and egg whites; set aside. Season the steak with garlic salt and black pepper, and set aside.

2. Spray a medium, nonstick skillet with cooking spray, and place it over medium-high heat. Add the peppers and onions, and cook, stirring often, about 5 to 6 minutes, until they begin to soften. Add 2 tablespoons water to the pan, stir, and continue to cook 1 to 2 more minutes, or until tender. Transfer to a plate and cover. Spray the skillet with cooking spray, add the steak, and cook for about 1 minute, or until barely cooked through. Place the meat on top of the peppers.

3. Wipe out the skillet, spray with cooking spray, and add the eggs. Cook, stirring gently for 3 to 4 minutes, or until curds form and eggs are set. Add the vegetables and stir gently to combine all ingredients.

4. Wet the tortillas with a small amount of water, stack them, wrap them in a paper towel, and microwave on high for 1 minute. Place a heaping ⅓ cup of egg mixture on each tortilla, fold in half, and top with a tablespoon of salsa.

NUTRITION INFORMATION PER SERVING: (per taco) Calories 140 | Carbohydrate 15g (Sugars 2g) | Total Fat 4g (Sat Fat 1g) | Protein 12g | Fiber 2g | Cholesterol 95mg | Sodium 260mg | Food Exchanges: 1½ Lean Meat, 1 Starch, ½ Vegetable | Carbohydrate Choices: 1 | Weight Watcher Plus Point Comparison: 3

14-Karat Carrot Cake Pancakes

INSPIRED BY THE CARROT CAKE PANCAKES AT IHOP, my husband says these are as good as gold. Perfectly spiced and topped with a drizzle of cream cheese, they are wholly worthy of their "cake" title, yet healthy enough for breakfast. My husband tops his with a couple teaspoons of chopped walnuts, but a drizzle of sugar-free pancake syrup is more than enough for me.

MAKES 4 SERVINGS

¼ cup light tub-style cream cheese

3 tablespoons sugar-free maple syrup, divided

1¼ cups all-purpose flour

¼ cup granulated no-calorie sweetener (or 6 packets)*

2 teaspoons ground cinnamon

1½ teaspoons baking powder

½ teaspoon baking soda

½ teaspoon ground nutmeg

2 large eggs

1½ cups low-fat buttermilk

¾ teaspoon vanilla

¼ teaspoon coconut extract

¾ cup finely grated carrot

1. In a small bowl, whisk together the cream cheese and 1 table-spoon of syrup. Add remaining syrup and 1 tablespoon water, and whisk until smooth. Set aside.

2. In a medium bowl, combine the next 6 ingredients (flour through nutmeg). In another medium bowl, whisk together eggs, butter-milk, and extracts. Stir in the carrot and mix until thoroughly combined. Pour the liquid ingredients into the dry ingredients, and stir until mixed. (Batter will be slightly thick.) Let batter rest 5 minutes.

3. Spray a nonstick skillet or griddle with cooking spray, and place over medium heat. Pour ⅓ cup of batter per pancake into the skillet and spread into a 4-inch circle. Cook the pancake for 3 to 4 minutes, or until underside is golden. Flip the pancakes and cook until done, about 2 to 3 more minutes. Stack on a plate and cover to keep warm. To serve, place two pancakes on a plate and drizzle with 2 tablespoons maple cream cheese topping (and additional toppings if desired).

DARE TO COMPARE: An order of Carrot Cake Pancakes at IHOP has 1,120 calories, the better part of a day's worth of carbs (including 76 grams of sugar), and 47 grams of fat. To make these lighter pancakes over-the-top dessert-worthy, top with 2 tea-spoons chopped walnuts and 2 tablespoons light whipped cream (adds 45 calories).

*See page 81 for sweetener options.

NUTRITION INFORMATION PER SERVING: (2 pancakes with maple topping) Calories 255 | Carbohydrate 37g (Sugars 8g) | Total Fat 5g (Sat Fat 3g) | Protein 12g | Fiber 3g | Cholesterol 65mg | Sodium 500mg | Food Exchanges: 2½ Starch, 1 Lean Meat | Carbohydrate Choices: 2½ | Weight Watcher Plus Point Comparison: 6

Sweet and Savory French Toast Sandwiches

MY INSPIRATION FOR THIS RECIPE came by way of the show The Best Thing I Ever Ate. *The combination of creamy peanut butter, bananas, and sweet maple syrup—stuffed into a French toast sandwich—looked divine, but the 800 calories and over 50 grams of fat that came with it didn't dazzle me. If peanut butter and banana doesn't tickle your taste buds, check out the savory recipe below. These also freeze well and are easily reheated in the toaster for a breakfast-to-go.*

MAKES 3 SERVINGS

1 large egg

2 large egg whites

⅓ cup nonfat half-and-half

2 teaspoons all-purpose flour

½ teaspoon baking powder

¼ teaspoon cinnamon

½ teaspoon vanilla extract

3 teaspoons creamy peanut butter

6 slices light whole wheat bread

1 tablespoon sugar-free maple syrup

1 large banana, thinly sliced (about ³⁄₈-inch thick)

1. In a shallow bowl, whisk together the first 7 ingredients (egg through vanilla) until smooth. Set aside. Coat griddle or large skillet with nonstick cooking spray, and place over medium heat.

2. Spread 1 tablespoon of peanut butter on 3 of the bread slices, drizzle each with 1 teaspoon of syrup, top with banana slices, and cover with another slice of bread.

3. Quickly dip each side of the sandwiches into the egg mixture, taking care not to soak it all the way through. Place the sandwiches in the hot skillet and cook until the underside is golden brown. Turn and cook until the second side is golden brown and peanut butter is melted. Serve with additional syrup if desired.

Marlene Says: *For HAM AND CHEESE FRENCH TOAST SANDWICHES, prepare the egg mixture as directed, omitting the cinnamon and vanilla. Spread slices of French bread with 2 teaspoons Dijon mustard, and top each with 2 thin slices reduced-sodium deli-style ham and 1 slice reduced-fat Swiss cheese. Cover, dip, and cook as directed. (Each sandwich has 255 calories, 30g of carbohydrate (3g of sugar), 6g of fat, and 18g of protein.*

NUTRITION INFORMATION PER SERVING: (1 sandwich) Calories 300 | Carbohydrate 37g (Sugars 16g) | Total Fat 11g (Sat Fat 2.5g) | Protein 14g | Fiber 6g | Cholesterol 70mg | Sodium 410mg | Food Exchanges: 2 Starch, 2 Lean Meat, 1 Fat | Carbohydrate Choices: 2 | Weight Watcher Plus Point Comparison: 8

Whole Grain Apple Popover Pancakes

PUFFED APPLE GOODNESS FOR TWO is as easy as it can be! With this simple recipe, you can quickly whisk your way to sweet popover-style pancake perfection. What's more, a single serving delivers as much protein as 2 eggs and 4 grams of fabulous fiber. A dusting of powdered sugar adds only 10 calories and makes for a beautiful presentation. Sugar-free syrup can be drizzled on top or served on the side.

MAKES 2 SERVINGS

1 large egg

1 large egg white

½ cup plain nonfat Greek yogurt

2 tablespoons sugar-free maple-flavored syrup

½ teaspoon cinnamon

½ cup white whole wheat flour

½ cup finely chopped apple

1½ teaspoons powdered sugar (optional)

additional sugar-free syrup for drizzling (optional)

1. Preheat the oven to 425°F. Lightly spray 6 muffin cups with non-stick cooking spray.

2. In a medium bowl, whisk together the first 5 ingredients (egg through cinnamon). Whisk in flour until mixture is smooth. Stir in the apple.

3. Evenly divide the mixture among 6 muffin tins. Bake for 15 minutes, reduce the oven temperature to 375°F, and bake an additional 15 minutes, or until well browned. Remove popovers from pan, dust with powdered sugar, if desired, and serve immediately.

NUTRITION INFORMATION PER SERVING: Calories 200 | Carbohydrate 28g (Sugars 7g) | Total Fat 3.5g (Sat Fat 1g) | Protein 15g | Fiber 4g | Cholesterol 105mg | Sodium 90mg | Food Exchanges: 2 Lean Meat, 1½ Starch, ¼ Fruit | Carbohydrate Choices: 1½ | Weight Watcher Plus Point Comparison: 5

Apple Dapple Yogurt Parfait

THIS YUMMY GREEK YOGURT PARFAIT has more protein than two eggs, in addition to five grams of healthy fiber. Even better than its belly-satisfying quality, however, is the wonderful taste and texture combination of creamy peanut butter–flavored yogurt, topped with sweet maple-drizzled apples and crunchy oats. Eating one of these could easily become a daily habit!

MAKES 1 SERVING

2 tablespoons old-fashioned oats

½ cup plain nonfat Greek yogurt

1 scant tablespoon peanut butter

4 teaspoons granulated no-calorie sweetener (or 2 packets)*

⅛ teaspoon cinnamon

½ small apple, chopped

1½ teaspoons sugar-free maple syrup

1. Place a small, nonstick skillet over medium heat. Add the oats and cook for 1 to 2 minutes, or until the oats are lightly toasted, stirring occasionally. Remove from heat and set aside.

2. In a small bowl, combine next 4 ingredients (yogurt through cinnamon), stirring well to combine.

3. Top the yogurt with the apple, drizzle with syrup, and sprinkle with the toasted oats.

Marlene Says: *Greek yogurt is made by straining the whey (or watery portion) out of regular yogurt. The result is thicker, creamier yogurt that boasts twice as much protein with half the carbs of traditional yogurt. To ensure you are reaping the benefits of Greek yogurt, check the label. A cup of real Greek yogurt has over 20 grams of protein and less than 10 grams of carbohydrate. Some "Greek-style" yogurts simply add thickeners to regular yogurt to mimic Greek yogurt's texture.*

*See page 81 for sweetener options.

NUTRITION INFORMATION PER SERVING: (1 parfait) Calories 210 | Carbohydrate 26g (Sugars 12g) | Total Fat 7g (Sat Fat 1g) | Protein 16g | Fiber 5g | Cholesterol 0mg | Sodium 65mg | Food Exchanges: 2 Lean Meat, ½ Low-fat Milk, 1 Starch, ½ Fruit | Carbohydrate Choices: 1½ | Weight Watcher Plus Point Comparison: 6

Maple Bacon Waffles

IF YOU ARE A BACON LOVER, I probably had you at the title. Now, imagine a Belgian-style waffle studded with bits of smoky bacon and sweet maple flavor, hot off the griddle, for only 210 calories. I needed a follow-up recipe to equal my Crispy Waffles from Eat More of What You Love, *and I believe I've done so with this one. Feel free to top with an over easy egg or scrambled eggs, drizzle with maple syrup—or just do as I do, and eat one out of hand straight off the waffle iron. They also freeze beautifully.*

MAKES 4 SERVINGS

¾ cup white whole wheat flour

3 tablespoons cornstarch

½ teaspoon baking powder

¼ teaspoon baking soda

4 teaspoons granulated no-calorie sweetener (or 2 packets)*

1 tablespoon brown sugar

1 large egg

1 cup low-fat buttermilk

1 tablespoon canola oil

¼ teaspoon liquid smoke

1 teaspoon maple extract

¼ cup real bacon bits

1. In a medium bowl, combine the first 6 ingredients (flour through brown sugar). In a small bowl, whisk together remaining ingredients. Pour over the flour mix and stir until well combined, but do not overmix. Let batter rest for 15 minutes.

2. Spray waffle iron with nonstick cooking spray and preheat. Ladle about ½ cup of batter, or amount recommended for your waffle maker, onto the iron. Close the waffle iron and cook until the steam subsides and the waffle is golden on both sides. Serve immediately with topping of your choice.

*See page 81 for sweetener options.

NUTRITION INFORMATION PER SERVING: (1 waffle) Calories 210 | Carbohydrate 26g (Sugars 7g) | Total Fat 7g (Sat Fat 1.5g) | Protein 9g | Fiber 2g | Cholesterol 60mg | Sodium 450mg | Food Exchanges: 1½ Starch, 1 Fat | Carbohydrate Choices: 1½ | Weight Watcher Plus Point Comparison: 5

Muffins, Bars, Breads, and Coffee Cakes

Cinnamon Sugar "Donut" Muffins

Chocolate Breakfast Muffins

Raspberry Cream Cheese Muffins

Chocolate Chip Cookie Muffins

Blueberry Bran Muffin Tops

Bananarama Breakfast Bars

Gluten-Free Oatmeal Spice Bars

Blueberry Biscones

Savory Southern Biscuits

Quick Sour Cream and Onion Biscuits

Jalapeño Cheddar Muffins

Pumpkin Banana Miniloaves

Classic Zucchini Bread

Apples and Cinnamon Quick Cake

Cinnamon Sour Cream Coffee Cake

MY GOAL IN WRITING A CHAPTER INTRODUCTION is to highlight not only what I find special about a few scrumptious recipes (although I do love to single out my favorites), but also to sum up what I find unique about the collection of recipes as a whole. In this chapter what stands out, besides the warmth and delicious comfort that homemade quick breads are known for, is the range of delectable recipes to choose from. From sweet and savory muffins and on-the-go bars to luscious loaves for eating or gifting, to fluffy biscuits and amazing coffee cakes—there's something for every taste—and every diet!

Muffins start the chapter and come with plenty of new twists. There are Cinnamon Sugar "Donut" Muffins—that taste like donuts, but with a fraction of the calories—and Chocolate Chip Cookie Muffins that will remind you of the famous cookies. Jalapeño Cheddar Muffins will bombard your taste buds with both cheesy and spicy flavors, and Blueberry Bran Muffin Tops, well, they come with just the crave-worthy top. Beyond the muffins you will find two whole grain, calorie-conscious snack bars, including one that's gluten-free. Perfect for breakfast on-the-run or a mid-afternoon snack, these oat-y nutty bars, with just 120 calories, are easy-to-make delights that are low in sugar and high in flavor and nutrients.

Pumpkin, banana, and zucchini are the stars of the quick-loaves. Not sure whether to make pumpkin or banana bread? My Pumpkin Banana Miniloaves combine the classic flavors of both! At the end of the chapter, you'll find two fabulous coffee cakes. I highly recommend the Apples and Cinnamon Quick Cake with its top layer of thinly sliced sweet cinnamon apples, served warm from the oven (yes, it's a favorite).

SUGAR
sweetener options

Cooking, and especially baking, sweet foods with less sugar can be challenging as sugar not only adds sweetness to recipes, but also has the unique ability to add texture, structure, volume, and color. The great news is that while sugar substitutes do not have these unique qualities, they are super at sweetening. Moreover, I'm delighted to be able to offer you a greater range of sweetening options than ever. Choose what's best for you and yours, and enjoy!

SUCRALOSE: All of the recipes in this book were tested with granulated and/or packets of no-calorie sucralose-based sweeteners. Sucralose is safe, easy to find, economical, and delivers great tasting results, with the least calories, for both cooking and baking. All brands of sucralose products are the same. If you prefer to use **splenda sugar for baking, use ½ as much** as the recipe specifies for no-calorie granulated sweetener (it's twice as sweet).

STEVIA: There are many types and brands of all natural stevia-based sweeteners, and they differ in sweetness, taste, and safety. The easiest to find, best tasting, no-calorie choice is Truvia® brand packets and its equivalents. Use it, or other packets of your choice, wherever I list (or X packets). Truvia Baking Blend, made with 25% real sugar, or C&H or Domino Light, made with 50% real sugar, can be used in *all* recipes in this book. **When using sugar blends, use only ½ as much** as the recipe specifies for no-calorie granulated sweetener. Baking time may need to be extended.

SUGAR: Even with real sugar, my reduced-fat sweet recipes are healthier than traditional recipes. When using real sugar in baked goods, omit ¼ teaspoon of baking soda per cup of flour and expect to increase baking time by as much as 7 to 10 minutes for cakes, 5 minutes for muffins, and 3 to 5 minutes for cookies. Check all baked goods according to the recipe's test for doneness. (Tip: **The normal substitution for sugar is 1:1 for measured granulated no-calorie sweetener,** however you can cut one-fourth of the sugar called for with the only effect being slightly reduced sweetness.)

AGAVE NECTAR OR HONEY. Both agave nectar or syrup, and honey, are approximately 1.3 times sweeter than sugar—and have more carbs and calories (15 carbs and 60 calories per tablespoon versus 12 carbs and 48 calories for sugar). Agave syrup may raise blood sugar less than sugar, but is high in fructose and as a sugar, should be limited. In baking, agave and honey require recipes designed specifically for liquid sweeteners. For use in beverages, dressings, and sauces, use one-third less of either than the specified amount of sweetener.

*NOTE: When using packets, use the number specified (each packet equals the sweetness of 2 teaspoons of granulated no-calorie sweetener).

Cinnamon Sugar "Donut" Muffins

SOME MORNINGS, NOTHING TEMPTS MORE than a good ol' donut. Of course, when it comes to eating healthy, it's not new news that donuts are on the "do-not" list. If you're a donut lover, I've got great news—at just 70 calories, these sweet (almost) nothings clock in with 75% less carbs and 90% less fat than their gut-busting donut counterparts, yet deliver the sugar and spice that will answer your craving. I find eating two satisfies just right.

MAKES 24 SERVINGS

⅔ cup low-fat buttermilk

¼ cup unsweetened applesauce

1 large egg

2 large egg whites

1½ teaspoons vanilla extract

1½ cups all-purpose flour

2 teaspoons baking powder

¼ teaspoon baking soda

½ cup granulated no-calorie sweetener*

4 tablespoons granulated sugar, divided

2½ teaspoons cinnamon, divided

¼ teaspoon nutmeg

¼ cup shortening

1. Preheat the oven to 375°F. Lightly coat a 24 minimuffin baking pan with nonstick baking spray. In a medium bowl, whisk together the first 5 ingredients (buttermilk through vanilla). Set aside.

2. In a large bowl, combine the flour, baking powder, baking soda, sweetener, 2 tablespoons sugar, ½ teaspoon cinnamon, and nutmeg. Using your fingertips or a pastry blender, cut the shortening into the flour mixture until thoroughly incorporated. Make a well in the center, pour in the buttermilk mixture, and using a large spoon or spatula, stir just until the dry ingredients are moistened.

3. Spoon the batter evenly into the prepared muffin tins, filling each cup two-thirds full. In a small bowl, combine the remaining sugar and cinnamon. Place 1 tablespoon of the mixture on a small plate. Sprinkle the remaining mixture evenly over muffins, and bake for 10 minutes, or until the center springs back when lightly touched. Cool for 3 minutes in the pan. While still hot, remove the muffins, and dip the bottoms in the plated cinnamon sugar mixture. (Best served warm.)

Marlene Says: *If all-natural Truvia Baking Blend is your sweetener of choice, remember to use ½ as much as directed for the granulated no-calorie sweetener.*

*See page 81 for sweetener options.

NUTRITION INFORMATION PER SERVING: (1 muffin) Calories 70 | Carbohydrate 10g (Sugars 3g) | Total Fat 2.5g (Sat Fat 0.5g) | Protein 2g | Fiber 0g | Cholesterol 10mg | Sodium 70mg | Food Exchanges: 1 Starch (1½ for 2 muffins) | Carbohydrate Choices: 1 | Weight Watcher Plus Point Comparison: 2 (3 for 2 muffins)

Chocolate Breakfast Muffins

HIGH IN SUGAR, FAT, AND CALORIES, most muffins do not qualify as healthy to eat anytime, let alone as a good way to start the day (see my Dare to Compare). These muffins are a tasty exception. Low-fat ricotta sneakily adds richness and protein; cocoa powder offers antioxidant-rich chocolaty goodness, and a touch of old-fashioned oats is the perfect topping, making them as breakfast-worthy as they are delicious.

MAKES 12 SERVINGS

3 tablespoons old-fashioned oats

3 tablespoons brown sugar, divided

1½ cups all-purpose flour

1½ teaspoons baking powder

¾ teaspoon baking soda

1 cup granulated no-calorie sweetener*

⅓ cup mini semisweet chocolate chips

⅓ cup cocoa powder

½ teaspoon instant coffee

¾ cup low-fat ricotta cheese

2 tablespoons canola oil

1 large egg

2 large egg whites

1. Preheat the oven to 350°F. Line 12 muffin cups with foil or paper liners, and spray insides lightly with nonstick cooking spray. In a small bowl, combine oats and 1 tablespoon brown sugar. Set aside.

2. In a large bowl, combine flour, baking powder, baking soda, sweetener, and remaining 2 tablespoons of brown sugar. Stir in the chocolate chips.

3. Measure cocoa powder and instant coffee into a medium bowl. Whisk in ¾ cup warm water until smooth. Stir in the ricotta, oil, egg and egg whites, stirring well after each addition. Create a well in the center of the dry ingredients, and pour in the wet mixture. Using a large spoon or spatula, stir just until the dry ingredients are moistened.

4. Spoon the batter evenly into prepared muffin tins, filling each cup ⅔ full. Sprinkle each muffin with 1 teaspoon of the oat mixture. Bake for 15 to 17 minutes, or until the center springs back when lightly touched. Cool for 5 minutes before removing to a wire rack.

DARE TO COMPARE: With a hefty 530 calories, the Double Chocolate Chunk Muffin at Au Bon Pain delivers as much fat, more calories, and twice the sugar of a chocolate-filled croissant.

*See page 81 for sweetener options.

NUTRITION INFORMATION PER SERVING: (1 muffin) Calories 150 | Carbohydrate 21g (Sugars 5g) | Total Fat 5g (Sat Fat 1g) | Protein 5g | Fiber 1g | Cholesterol 5mg | Sodium 170mg | Food Exchanges: 1 Starch, 1 Fat | Carbohydrate Choices: 1½ | Weight Watcher Plus Point Comparison: 4

Raspberry Cream Cheese Muffins

THESE ARE BEAUTIFUL, CAKEY MUFFINS. The addition of cream cheese blended into the batter keeps them incredibly moist, while bright red raspberries add a burst of color. I find they have the best texture and appearance when made with fresh raspberries, but frozen can also be used. If using frozen raspberries, do not thaw them first, but mix them into the batter gently to keep them from breaking apart.

MAKES 12 SERVINGS

3 tablespoons margarine or butter, softened

½ cup tub-style reduced-fat cream cheese

3 tablespoons granulated sugar

1 cup granulated no-calorie sweetener*

2 large egg whites

1 large egg

1½ teaspoons vanilla extract

¾ teaspoon almond extract

¾ cup low-fat buttermilk

1¾ cups all-purpose flour

2 teaspoons baking powder

½ teaspoon baking soda

1¼ cups raspberries (fresh or frozen, unthawed)

1. Preheat the oven to 375°F. Lightly spray 12 muffin cups with nonstick cooking spray (paper or foil liners can be added before spraying).

2. In a large bowl, with an electric mixer, beat the margarine and cream cheese until light and creamy (about 3 minutes). Add the sugar and sweetener and beat to incorporate. Add egg whites, and then the whole egg, beating after each addition until creamy. Beat in the vanilla, almond extract, and buttermilk.

3. In a medium bowl, combine the flour, baking powder, and baking soda. Remove 1 tablespoon of the flour mixture and toss it with the berries to lightly coat. Create a well in the center of the flour mixture and pour in the creamed mixture. Using a large spoon or spatula, stir just until the dry ingredients are moistened. Gently fold in the raspberries.

4. Spoon the batter evenly into the prepared muffin tins, filling each cup ¾ full. Bake for 17 to 19 minutes, or until the center springs back when lightly touched. Cool for 5 minutes before removing to a wire rack.

Marlene Says: *For LEMON-BLUEBERRY CREAM CHEESE MUFFINS, substitute fresh or frozen blueberries for the raspberries and add 1 teaspoon lemon zest to the flour mix.*

*See page 81 for sweetener options.

NUTRITION INFORMATION PER SERVING: (1 muffin) Calories 150 | Carbohydrate 22g (Sugars 6g) | Total Fat 5g (Sat Fat 2g) | Protein 5g | Fiber 2g | Cholesterol 25mg | Sodium 240mg | Food Exchanges: 1½ Starch | Carbohydrate Choices: 1½ | Weight Watcher Plus Point Comparison: 4

Chocolate Chip Cookie Muffins

COOKIES FOR BREAKFAST! Your family is guaranteed to bounce out of bed the minute you pull these out of the oven. A touch of brown sugar and a good dose of vanilla are the secret to the chocolate chip cookie smell and taste, while white whole wheat flour adds wholesome goodness. My boys went crazy for these. I think they are the perfect guilt-free cookie fix.

MAKES 12 SERVINGS

¼ cup margarine or butter, softened

¼ cup brown sugar

½ cup granulated no-calorie sweetener*

1 large egg

1 large egg white

¾ cup plus 2 tablespoons low-fat milk

1½ teaspoons vanilla extract

1 cup all-purpose flour

1 cup white whole wheat flour

2 teaspoons baking powder

½ teaspoon baking soda

6 tablespoons mini semisweet chocolate chips

1. Preheat the oven to 375°F. Line 12 muffin cups with foil or paper liners and spray insides lightly with nonstick cooking spray.

2. In a medium bowl, with an electric mixer, beat margarine and sugar until light and creamy (about 3 to 4 minutes). Add sweetener and beat to incorporate. Add egg and egg white and beat until creamy. Beat in the milk and vanilla. Set aside.

3. In a large bowl, combine the flours, baking powder, and baking soda. Create a well in the center, and pour in the creamed mixture. Using a large spoon or spatula, stir just until the dry ingredients are moistened. Gently stir in the chocolate chips.

4. Spoon the batter evenly into the prepared muffin tins, filling each cup two-thirds full. Bake for 15 to 17 minutes, or until the center springs back when lightly touched. Cool for 5 minutes before removing to a wire rack.

Marlene Says: *Breakfast foods high in sugar and simple carbohydrates quickly elevate blood sugar, then leave you in a slump by mid-morning. A chocolate chip muffin at Dunkin' Donuts has 550 calories; most of which are refined carbs.*

*See page 81 for sweetener options.

NUTRITION INFORMATION PER SERVING: Calories 150 | Carbohydrate 22g (Sugars 7g) | Total Fat 5g (Sat Fat 2g) | Protein 4g | Fiber 2g | Cholesterol 20mg | Sodium 50mg | Food Exchanges: 1½ Starch, ½ Fat | Carbohydrate Choices: 1½ | Weight Watcher Plus Point Comparison: 4

Blueberry Bran Muffin Tops

YEARS AGO, I WORKED IN A HOSPITAL that got fresh blueberry bran muffins delivered daily to the cafeteria. The muffins were delicious, but fragile. There was always at least one that arrived unable to sell, and my fellow coworkers and I would descend upon that broken muffin all vying for the same thing— the precious top! The closest thing I have tasted since are these fresh-from-the-pantry muffin tops. When we tested these, my current kitchen crew also descended upon them, but this time everyone got a top!

MAKES 8 SERVINGS

¾ cup bran flakes cereal

½ cup low-fat buttermilk

1 large egg white

1 tablespoon canola oil

1 teaspoon vanilla extract

½ cup all-purpose flour

2 tablespoons brown sugar

½ teaspoon cinnamon

½ teaspoon baking powder

¼ teaspoon baking soda

½ cup fresh blueberries

1. Preheat the oven to 400°F. Spray a baking sheet with cooking spray (or use a silicone liner).

2. Place the bran flakes in a medium bowl, and roughly crush the bran flakes using your fingers. Stir in the buttermilk, egg white, oil, and vanilla, and let sit for 5 minutes. Stir again.

3. In another medium bowl, combine the next 5 ingredients (flour through baking soda). Add the wet cereal mixture and mix just until the dry ingredients are moistened. Gently stir in the blueberries.

4. Scoop 3 tablespoons of batter onto the prepared sheet for each muffin top, rounding off edges and slightly flattening the tops. Bake for 10 to 12 minutes, or until the center springs back when lightly touched. Cool for 5 minutes before removing to a wire rack.

Marlene Says: *A touch of added brown sugar is all it takes here for the perfect sweetness. With less than 1 teaspoon of added sugar in each "top," I do not recommend omitting, or switching it.*

NUTRITION INFORMATION PER SERVING: (1 muffin top) Calories 75 | Carbohydrate 13g (Sugars 4g) | Total Fat 2g (Sat Fat 0g) | Protein 2g | Fiber 1g | Cholesterol 0mg | Sodium 125mg | Food Exchanges: 1 Starch | Carbohydrate Choices: 1 | Weight Watcher Plus Point Comparison: 2

Bananarama Breakfast Bars

BANANAS AND CHOCOLATE ARE ALWAYS A WINNING COMBINATION, and here I combine them with chewy old-fashioned oats for a nutritious grab-and-go bar that's simple to make and fun to eat. I also like to switch this recipe up by using a multigrain oat mix instead of the usual oats. Quaker Oats offers a nicely textured multigrain mix of rye, barley, oats, and wheat that can be found with the rest of the oats.

MAKES 12 SERVINGS

½ cup mashed banana (about 1 medium)

1 tablespoon canola oil

1 tablespoon molasses

1 teaspoon vanilla extract

¼ teaspoon almond extract

3 large egg whites

2 cups old-fashioned oats

½ cup white whole wheat flour

⅔ cup granulated no-calorie sweetener*

¼ teaspoon ground nutmeg

¾ teaspoon baking soda

¼ cup mini semisweet chocolate chips

1. Preheat the oven to 350°F. Lightly coat a 9-inch square baking pan with nonstick cooking spray.

2. In a medium bowl, combine the first 6 ingredients (banana through egg whites). In a large bowl, combine the next 5 ingredients (oats through baking soda). Stir in the banana mixture until just combined. Stir in chocolate chips. Scrap the batter into prepared baking pan and smooth the top.

3. Bake for 16 to 18 minutes, or until the center springs back when touched or an inserted toothpick comes out clean. Let cool on a wire rack for 5 minutes, cut into 12 bars, and remove from the pan (bottoms will become slightly wet if left in pan). Store in air-tight container.

Marlene Says: *These bars also freeze well. Cool, cut, and wrap separately. Defrost to room temperature or, for a warm "fresh-baked" treat, pop them in the microwave for 15 to 20 seconds before eating.*

*See page 81 for sweetener options.

NUTRITION INFORMATION PER SERVING: (1 bar) Calories 120 | Carbohydrate 19g (Sugars 5g) | Total Fat 3g (Sat Fat 1g) | Protein 4g | Fiber 2g | Cholesterol 0mg | Sodium 95mg | Food Exchanges: 1 Starch, ½ Fat | Carbohydrate Choices: 1 | Weight Watcher Plus Point Comparison: 3

Gluten-Free Oatmeal Spice Bars

GLUTEN-FREE BAKING CAN BE A CHALLENGE with its uncommon flour alternatives and all-too-often undesirable results. That's why I am really excited to share this recipe. Using my Bananarama Breakfast Bars (page 89) for inspiration, I swapped out the wheat flour with ground almonds, and then for good measure, added an extra dose of spice. These bars give off such a fragrant aroma when baking that you'll be hard pressed to wait the five minutes to let them cool.

MAKES 12 SERVINGS

1 medium ripe banana, mashed (about ½ cup)

1 tablespoon canola oil

1 tablespoon molasses

1 teaspoon vanilla extract

3 large egg whites

2 cups old-fashioned oats

½ cup almonds, finely ground

⅔ cup granulated no-calorie sweetener*

½ teaspoon ground nutmeg

1 teaspoon cinnamon

¾ teaspoon baking soda

½ teaspoon baking powder

¼ cup raisins, chopped

1 cup crisped rice cereal

1. Set the cooking rack in the lower third of the oven and preheat the oven to 350°F. Lightly coat a 9-inch square baking pan with nonstick cooking spray.

2. In a medium bowl, combine the first 5 ingredients (banana through egg whites). In a large bowl, combine the next 7 ingredients (oats through baking powder) and stir. Add the banana mixture and stir together until combined. Stir in raisins and rice cereal. Pour into prepared baking pan and smooth the top.

3. Bake for 16 to 18 minutes, or until the center springs back when touched or an inserted toothpick comes out clean. Let cool on a wire rack for 5 minutes, cut into bars and remove from pan (bottoms will become slightly wet if left in pan).

Marlene Says: *To grind almonds, place them in a food processor, and process until they are the texture of coarse sand.*

*For sweetener options see page 81.

NUTRITION INFORMATION PER SERVING: (1 bar) Calories 130 | Carbohydrate 19g (Sugars 6g) | Total Fat 5g (Sat Fat 0g) | Protein 4g | Fiber 3g | Cholesterol 0mg | Sodium 120mg | Food Exchanges: 1 Starch, 1 Fat | Carbohydrate Choices: 1 | Weight Watcher Plus Point Comparison: 3

Blueberry Biscones

WHAT'S THE DIFFERENCE BETWEEN SCONES AND BISCUITS? Not much. While scones are traditionally sweeter, made with egg, and often a triangular shape, a biscuit-shaped scone and a dense, sweet biscuit are essentially one in the same. Fresh blueberries give these light-biscuit-style scones their best appearance. If you use frozen berries, roll them first in one tablespoon of flour and stir them lightly into the batter to avoid very blue blueberry biscones.

MAKES 12 SERVINGS

2 cups all-purpose flour

⅓ cup granulated no-calorie sweetener*

2 teaspoons baking powder

½ teaspoon baking soda

¼ teaspoon salt

1 cup fresh blueberries

1 cup low-fat buttermilk

3 tablespoons margarine, melted

1 large egg

½ teaspoon almond extract

2 teaspoons granulated sugar

1. Preheat the oven to 425°F. Lightly spray a cookie sheet with non-stick cooking spray.

2. In a large bowl, mix together the flour, sweetener, baking powder, baking soda, and salt. Stir in blueberries; set aside. In a small bowl, whisk together the buttermilk, margarine, egg, and almond extract. Pour this wet mixture into the dry ingredients, and stir just until moistened.

3. Drop by heaping spoonfuls (about ¼ cup) onto prepared baking pan, making 12 mounds. Sprinkle scones with granulated sugar.

4. Bake for 12 to 15 minutes, or until lightly browned. Transfer to a wire rack to cool slightly before serving.

DARE TO COMPARE: At a hefty 460 calories, a Starbucks Blueberry Scone has twice the calories and fat and three times the carbs of your average glazed donut.

*See page 81 for sweetener options.

NUTRITION INFORMATION PER SERVING: (1 scone) Calories 120 | Carbohydrate 19g (Sugars 2g) | Total Fat 3g (Sat Fat 1g) | Protein 3g | Fiber 1g | Cholesterol 15mg | Sodium 230 mg | Food Exchanges: 1 Starch, ½ Fat | Carbohydrate Choices: 1 | Weight Watcher Plus Point Comparison 3

Savory Southern Biscuits

THE TECHNIQUE FOR MAKING THESE BISCUITS comes by way of legendary food scientist and cookbook author Shirley Corriher. Shirley explains that using ample liquid, in this case buttermilk, produces more steam, resulting in a deliciously soft and tender biscuit. My son Stephen says these savory biscuits remind him of stuffing—which he loves! I find them perfect for Savory Southern-Style Biscuits, Eggs, and Gravy (page 68).

MAKES 10 SERVINGS

1 cup plus 3 tablespoons all-purpose flour, divided

1 cup white whole wheat flour

2 teaspoons baking powder

½ teaspoon baking soda

¼ teaspoon salt

2 teaspoons sugar

⅛ teaspoon black pepper

½ teaspoon onion powder

1¼ teaspoons rubbed sage

2 tablespoons shortening

1⅓ cups low-fat buttermilk

1. Preheat the oven to 425°F. Lightly spray a 9-inch round cake pan with nonstick cooking spray.

2. In a large bowl, mix together the first 9 ingredients (1 cup of the all-purpose flour through sage).

3. Using your fingertips or a pastry blender, cut the shortening into the flour mixture until the shortening is thoroughly incorporated. Create a well in the center of the flour and pour in the buttermilk. Mix by hand or with a spatula until just moistened; do not over-mix. Dough will be very wet.

4. Place the remaining 3 tablespoons all-purpose flour in a small bowl. Using a scoop measure, spoon a scant ⅓ cup of dough onto the flour. Using your hands, roll the dough lightly across the flour, just to coat. Carefully lift up the biscuit, round it slightly, and place it in the prepared pan, nestling each biscuit next to each other. (Start with a circle around the edge and finish with two biscuits in the middle.) Touching each other helps the biscuits rise.

5. Bake for 20 to 22 minutes, or until golden brown.

Marlene Says: *These pair perfectly with chicken—baked, roasted, or fried! For a Southern-style slider, stuff them with the same, or sliced turkey.*

NUTRITION INFORMATION PER SERVING: Calories 90 | Carbohydrate 13g (Sugars 3g) | Total Fat 3g (Sat Fat 1g) | Protein 2g | Fiber 0g | Cholesterol 0mg | Sodium 250mg | Food Exchanges: 1 Starch, ½ Fat | Carbohydrate Choices: 1 | Weight Watcher Plus Point Comparison: 2

Quick Sour Cream and Onion Biscuits

IT'S IMPOSSIBLE TO HAVE A DISAPPOINTING MEAL when homemade biscuits are on the table. And with just a handful of ingredients and a few short minutes of hands on time, you can make any meal memorable with these tender sour cream and onion biscuits. The bubbles in the club soda are the trick to keeping them light.

MAKES 10 SERVINGS

⅓ cup minced green onion, green and white parts

2 cups reduced-fat baking mix (like Bisquick Heart Smart)

¼ teaspoon onion powder

½ cup light sour cream

½ cup club soda

1 tablespoon all-purpose flour

1 tablespoon melted margarine or butter

1. Preheat the oven to 450°F. Lightly spray an 8-inch round cake pan with nonstick cooking spray, and set aside. Place the green onions in a small, microwave-safe bowl, cover and microwave for 30 seconds.

2. In a large bowl, whisk together the baking mix and onion powder. With a fork, cut the sour cream into the dry ingredients. Stir in the green onions until evenly distributed, and add the club soda. Mix with a fork until just combined (mixture will be sticky).

3. Transfer the mixture from the bowl to a lightly floured board. Knead once with your hands, if needed, to finish combining. Divide the dough into 10 equal-size biscuits, and place them into the prepared cake pan. Brush the tops with margarine and bake for 16 to 18 minutes, or until golden brown.

NUTRITION INFORMATION PER SERVING: (1 biscuit) Calories 120 | Carbohydrate 18g (Sugars 2g) | Total Fat 3g (Sat Fat 1g) | Protein 3g | Fiber 0g | Cholesterol 5mg | Sodium 300mg | Food Exchanges: 1 Starch, ½ Fat | Carbohydrate Choices: 1 | Weight Watcher Plus Point Comparison: 3

Jalapeño Cheddar Muffins

WHOEVER SAYS THAT SAVORY MUFFINS aren't as much fun to eat as sweet muffins never tasted these! The savory pepper and cheese add just the perfect amount of zip to tingle your taste buds without overpowering them. I also love how quick and easy they are to whip up. Serve them with my Roasted Red Pepper and Tomato Soup (page 125) or to add a taste of homemade to a store-bought rotisserie chicken and bagged salad dinner.

MAKES 12 SERVINGS

1 cup low-fat buttermilk

3 large egg whites

3 tablespoons butter or margarine, melted

2 tablespoons granulated sugar

2 tablespoons canned jalapeño peppers, chopped

¾ cup grated reduced-fat sharp Cheddar cheese

1 cup all-purpose flour

¾ cup white whole wheat flour

2 teaspoons baking powder

¾ teaspoon baking soda

½ teaspoon garlic powder

1. Preheat the oven to 375°F. Lightly spray 12 muffin cups with non-stick baking spray (or line with paper or foil liners).

2. In a medium bowl, mix together the first six ingredients (buttermilk through cheese). Set aside.

3. In another medium bowl, whisk together the remaining ingredients (all-purpose flour through garlic powder). Make a well in the center and add the buttermilk mixture. Using a large spoon, stir until dry ingredients are just moistened.

4. Spoon the batter evenly into prepared muffin tins, filling each cup two-thirds full.

5. Bake for 14 to 16 minutes, or until the center springs back when lightly touched. Cool for 5 minutes before removing to a wire rack. Serve warm.

NUTRITION INFORMATION PER SERVING: Calories 120 | Carbohydrate 16g (Sugars 3g) | Total Fat 4g (Sat Fat 1.5g) | Protein 6g | Fiber 1g | Cholesterol 5mg | Sodium 280mg | Food Exchanges: 1 Starch, ½ Lean Meat | Carbohydrate Choices: 1 | Weight Watcher Plus Point Comparison: 3

Pumpkin Banana Miniloaves

THIS DELICIOUS QUICK BREAD marries the wonderful flavors of two all-time classics, pumpkin and banana, with a subtle spicing that allows the flavors of each to ring true. I find this moist bread perfect for giving to friends and loved ones. For plenty of gift-giving options, I have included baking times for a full loaf, miniloaves, and muffins. Baked big or small, it will be loved by all. (To add wholesomeness, replace ¾ cup all-purpose flour with white whole wheat.)

MAKES **12** SERVINGS

1 cup canned 100% pure pumpkin

1 large banana, mashed

¼ cup canola oil

2 large eggs

1 teaspoon vanilla extract

2 tablespoons molasses

¾ cup granulated no-calorie sweetener*

1¾ cups all-purpose flour

2 teaspoons baking powder

½ teaspoon baking soda

1 teaspoon cinnamon

½ teaspoon ground nutmeg

½ teaspoon ground ginger

1. Preheat the oven to 350°F. Lightly coat 3 small loaf pans (or one 9 x 5-inch loaf pan or 12 muffin cups) with nonstick cooking spray.

2. In a medium bowl, whisk together the first seven ingredients (pumpkin through sweetener). In a large bowl, stir together the flour, baking powder, baking soda, and spices. Make a well in the center and pour in the pumpkin mixture. With a large spoon or spatula, stir until dry ingredients are just moistened.

3. Spoon about 1 cup of the batter into each of the miniloaf pans and smooth the surface.

4. Bake the loaves for 30 minutes, or until a dry crack appears on top or a toothpick or cake tester inserted into the center comes out clean. Cool on rack for 10 to 15 minutes and then remove from pans.

Marlene Says: *For muffins, use ¼ cup of batter for each muffin, and bake for 16 to 18 minutes. For one large 9 x 5-inch loaf, use all of the batter, and bake 50 to 55 minutes.*

*See page 81 for sweetener options.

NUTRITION INFORMATION PER SERVING: Calories 140 | Carbohydrate 20g (Sugars 5g) | Total Fat 5g (Sat Fat 0g) | Protein 4g | Fiber 2g | Cholesterol 20mg | Sodium 200mg | Food Exchanges: 1 Starch, 1 Fat | Carbohydrate Choices: 1 | Weight Watcher Plus Point Comparison: 4

Classic Zucchini Bread

THIS RECIPE IS FOR JOANNE who wrote and asked me how she could make a "plain," nonchocolate version of the Chocolate Zucchini Loaf in my book Eat More of What You Love. *I thought a simple swap of flour for the cocoa powder might do it, but it took four different trials to get the new ingredient mix just right. This is everything a classic zucchini bread should be—wonderfully moist, with a nice firm crumb, and infused with just the right amount of spice and nuts. Enjoy!*

MAKES 12 SERVINGS

3 tablespoons canola oil

3 tablespoons brown sugar

⅔ cup granulated no-calorie sweetener*

2 large eggs

½ cup unsweetened applesauce

1½ teaspoons vanilla extract

1½ cups coarsely grated zucchini

1 cup all-purpose flour

¾ cup white whole wheat flour

1 teaspoon baking powder

1 teaspoon baking soda

1½ teaspoons cinnamon

¾ teaspoon allspice

⅓ cup chopped pecans

1. Preheat the oven to 350°F. Lightly spray a 9 x 5-inch loaf pan with nonstick baking spray.

2. In a medium bowl, whisk together the first six ingredients (oil through vanilla extract). Stir in the grated zucchini with a large spoon, and mix until well combined.

3. In a medium bowl, combine the remaining ingredients. Create a well in the center and add the zucchini mixture. Stir until the dry ingredients are just moistened. Spoon mixture into prepared pan and smooth the surface.

4. Bake for 50 to 55 minutes, or until a toothpick inserted into the center comes out clean. Cool on rack for 10 to 15 minutes and then remove from pan.

DARE TO COMPARE: With up to a cup each of oil and sugar per loaf, traditional zucchini breads can have *three* times the calories and four times as much fat as this lovely loaf.

*See page 81 for sweetener options.

NUTRITION INFORMATION PER SERVING: Calories 150 | Carbohydrate 18g (Sugars 4g) | Total Fat 7g (Sat Fat 0.5g) | Protein 4g | Fiber 2g | Cholesterol 35mg | Sodium 160mg | Food Exchanges: 1 Starch, 1 Fat | Carbohydrate Choices: 1 | Weight Watcher Plus Point Comparison: 4

Apples and Cinnamon Quick Cake

THIS APPLE UPSIDE-DOWN-STYLE CAKE is dangerously delicious. Reduced-fat baking mix keeps it healthy and super quick to make, while buttermilk ensures a moist and delectable cake. I find it just as good served after dinner or as a late night snack, as it is for breakfast. A drizzle of warm maple syrup drizzled over each piece is delightful.

MAKES 8 SERVINGS

2 tablespoons brown sugar

¾ cup granulated no-calorie sweetener, divided*

2 teaspoons cinnamon, divided

2 tablespoons margarine or butter

1 large apple, peeled and thinly sliced

1 large egg, beaten

1 cup buttermilk

1 teaspoon vanilla extract

1½ cups reduced-fat baking mix (like Bisquick Heart Smart)

¼ teaspoon nutmeg

1. Set oven rack to lower third of oven. Preheat the oven to 350°F. Lightly spray an 8-inch round cake pan with nonstick baking spray.

2. In a small bowl, combine the brown sugar, ¼ cup of sweetener, and 1 teaspoon cinnamon. Melt the margarine in the prepared pan in the oven. Remove, and evenly sprinkle the bottom with the brown sugar mixture. Arrange the apple slices on top of the sugar in a circular pattern.

3. In a small bowl, combine the egg, buttermilk, and vanilla. In a medium bowl, combine the baking mix, nutmeg, ½ cup sweetener, and 1 teaspoon cinnamon. Make a well in the center of the dry ingredients and pour in the buttermilk mixture. With a large spoon or spatula, stir just until blended; do not overmix.

4. Spoon the batter over the apples and bake for 25 to 30 minutes, or until a toothpick inserted into the middle comes out clean. Cool the cake 5 minutes in the pan. Run a knife around the edges of the pan and invert onto a plate. Serve warm.

Marlene Says: *A sweet baking apple like a golden delicious works well with this cake.*

*See page 81 for sweetener options.

NUTRITION INFORMATION PER SERVING: Calories 160 | Carbohydrate 25g (Sugars 8g) | Total Fat 4.5g (Sat Fat 1.5g) | Protein 4g | Fiber 1g | Cholesterol 30mg | Sodium 360mg | Food Exchanges: 1½ Starch, ½ Fat | Carbohydrate Choices: 1½ | Weight Watcher Plus Point Comparison: 4

Cinnamon Sour Cream Coffee Cake

WHEN MOST PEOPLE THINK OF COFFEE CAKE, this is what they are dreaming about. Tender, moist cake with cinnamon streusel inside and on top. To make it easy, here you simply add ½ of the streusel mix to the batter and give it a very light swirl of the spoon before dumping it into the pan. Sprinkling the remaining streusel mix on top ensures the cinnamon-y goodness you crave in a cake that's perfect for every occasion.

MAKES 16 SERVINGS

½ cup graham cracker crumbs

1¾ cups granulated no-calorie sweetener, divided*

¼ cup chopped walnuts

2 tablespoons cinnamon

3 cups cake flour

1 tablespoon baking powder

¾ teaspoon baking soda

⅓ cup plus 1 tablespoon margarine, or butter, divided

2 large eggs

2 large egg whites

2 teaspoons vanilla extract

½ cup unsweetened applesauce

1½ cups light sour cream

1 tablespoon brown sugar

1. Preheat the oven to 350°F. Lightly spray a 13 x 9-inch baking dish with nonstick baking spray. In a small bowl, combine the crumbs, ½ cup sweetener, walnuts and cinnamon. Set aside. In a medium bowl, sift together the cake flour, baking powder, and soda. Set aside.

2. In a large bowl, with an electric mixer, cream ⅓ cup margarine. Add remaining 1¼ cups sweetener and eggs, and beat until well mixed. Beat in the egg whites and vanilla, and then the apple-sauce. Add the flour mixture, and mix on low speed just until smooth. Stir in the sour cream. Add ⅔ cup of the streusel mix to the batter, and give it one *very* light swirl with the spoon or a spatula (DO NOT uniformly mix streusel in).

3. Dump the swirled batter from the bowl into the prepared pan, and lightly smooth. Add the tablespoon of margarine and brown sugar to the remaining streusel, and sprinkle on top of the cake. Bake for 23 to 28 minutes, or until a toothpick inserted near the center comes out clean.

DARE TO COMPARE: A piece of classic coffee cake at the local coffee shop packs 440 calories and 19 grams of fat. With cups of butter and sugar, most homestyle recipes are equally rich.

*See page 81 for sweetener options.

NUTRITION INFORMATION PER SERVING: (1 piece) Calories 170 | Carbohydrate 21g (Sugars 5g) | Total Fat 7g (Sat Fat 2.5g) | Protein 5g | Fiber less than 1g | Cholesterol 35mg | Sodium 240mg | Food Exchanges: 1½ Starch, 1 Fat | Carbohydrate Choices: 1½ | Weight Watcher Plus Point Comparison: 5

All-Star Dips and Appetizers

Deviled Eggs—Two Ways

Fruit Salsa with Cinnamon-Sugar Crisps

Two-Minute Fire-Roasted Salsa

Red Pepper Hummus

Buffalo Chicken Dip

Barbecued Black Bean Dip

Baked Pita Strips

Chicken Fajita Nachos

Creamy Crab Dip on a Crispy Crust

Sweet 'n Spicy Pickled Green Beans

Oven-Fried Mozzarella Sticks

Garlicky Grilled Shrimp

Easy Baked Egg Rolls

Moo-Shu Lettuce Wraps with Asian Peanut Sauce

SINCE APPETIZERS KICK-START A PARTY or evening of dining out, no one wants to spoil the mood by thinking about un-fun things like fat and calories, but unfortunately, appetizers are usually heavy hitters in more than just taste. Take Applebee's popular Appetizer Sampler, an all-star line up of creamy, cheesy, crispy, and fried appetizers that manages to rack up 2,530 calories, 167 fat grams, and almost three days' worth of sodium! Perhaps more staggering is that the appetizers that comprise such a plate, when ordered individually, average 1,200 calories and a full day's worth of fat and sodium. (Not a fun *start* to a healthy meal.)

But do not despair, this chapter boasts a dozen cheesy, fried, crunchy, creamy all-star appetizers that'll get your party started with only a mere fraction of the usual fat, calories, and sodium. And, because every one of them is easy and fuss-free, the cook can join the party!

For the wing-loving crowd, I suggest the crazy good Buffalo Chicken Dip. Ooey, gooey, warm, and creamy, it clocks in with 75% less fat of a traditional "wing" dip, but retains 100% of the spicy Buffalo flavor. For fried food lovers, no one will miss the deep fryer—or the calories and fat—when you serve up extra cheesy "Fried" Mozzarella Sticks or Easy Baked Egg Rolls. And for those who love things crispy, Baked Pita Strips will settle the score. Looking for something fresh and new? Check out such colorful healthy nibbles like the gorgeous Fruit Salsa with Cinnamon-Sugar Crisps, zingy Sweet 'n Spicy Pickled Green Beans, or festive Red Pepper Hummus. Appetizers such as these are not only low in fat and high in flavor, but they are nutritional all-stars to boot!

Deviled Eggs–Two Ways

IF YOU ARE A DEVILED EGG LOVER, I have good news for you. Packed with protein and low in calories, these deviled eggs are one of the most nutritious—and slimming—appetizers you can eat. Enjoy them "classic-style," or for an eggstra-ordinary devilish twist, try my Devilish Deviled Eggs variation. The extra flavor and subtle zing from the jalapeños make them one of my most popular appetizers.

MAKES 12 DEVILED EGGS

6 large eggs

2 tablespoons light mayonnaise

2 tablespoons low-fat Greek yogurt (or light sour cream)

1 teaspoon prepared yellow mustard

½ teaspoon cider vinegar

1 pinch of each salt and black pepper, or to taste

Paprika, for sprinkling

1. To hard-boil the eggs, place them in a saucepan in a single layer, and cover them with cold water. Bring the water to a boil, cover, reduce heat, and simmer on low for 12 minutes. Drain the water from the saucepan (leaving eggs inside), and run cold water over the eggs. Drain and give the pan a hard shake to crack the eggs. Add more cold water, and let set 5 minutes.

2. Peel eggs, and cut in half lengthwise. Remove yolks from whites, place 3 of them in a small bowl, and mash well with a fork (discard the remaining yolks). Add the remaining ingredients, except paprika, and mix until very smooth.

3. Fill the whites evenly with the filling, and garnish the tops with a sprinkle of paprika. Refrigerate until serving.

Marlene Says: *To make DEVILISH DEVILED EGGS, place 6 jarred jalapeño pepper rings onto a cutting board, and mash them with a fork. Add the mashed jalapeño and ½ teaspoon of the jarred juice to the egg yolk mixture. Instead of paprika, top deviled eggs with minced green onion tops and/or bacon bits.*

NUTRITION INFORMATION PER SERVING: (each half) Calories 35 | Carbohydrate 0g (Sugars 0g) | Total Fat 2g (Sat Fat 0.5 g) | Protein 3g | Fiber 0g | Cholesterol 45 mg | Sodium 85 mg | Food Exchanges: ½ Lean Meat | Weight Watcher Plus Point Comparison: 1

Fruit Salsa with Cinnamon-Sugar Crisps

THIS FRUITY AND VIBRANT TWIST on traditional chips and salsa is a true crowd pleaser. Put it out for a party or brunch, and watch it disappear. Yes, it's that good. The apple, strawberry, and kiwi combination gives you crunchy, sweet, and fresh flavor in every colorful bite, and the homemade cinnamon sugar crisps are downright addictive. For best presentation, cut all the fruit to a uniform size.

MAKES 8 SERVINGS

1 tablespoon low-sugar apricot preserves

½ medium apple, diced

1 tablespoon fresh lime juice

2 medium kiwi fruit, peeled and diced

1½ cups chopped fresh strawberries

2 tablespoons sugar

1½ teaspoons cinnamon

4 (8-inch) reduced-carb high-fiber flour tortillas (like Mission Carb Balance)

1. Preheat the oven to 350°F.

2. In a small, microwave-safe cup or ramekin, combine the preserves with 1 tablespoon of water and microwave for 30 seconds, or until the preserves melt. Place the diced apple in a medium bowl and toss with the lime juice. Add the kiwi and strawberries, and gently toss to combine. Add the melted preserves and stir to evenly coat.

3. In a small bowl, combine the sugar and cinnamon. Working on a cutting board, spray both sides of a tortilla with nonstick cooking spray. Lay the tortilla flat, and sprinkle with 1½ teaspoons of the cinnamon-sugar mix. Spray lightly once more with cooking spray, and cut into 8 triangular wedges (like a pizza). Repeat with remaining tortillas.

4. Place the tortilla chips on a baking sheet and bake for 10 minutes (in two batches if necessary). Serve with fruit salsa.

Marlene Says: *This chopped apple, kiwi, and strawberry fruit salsa is also a great topping for yogurt or ice cream, with or without the crisps.*

NUTRITION INFORMATION PER SERVING: (¼ cup salsa + 4 cinnamon crisps) Calories 100 | Carbohydrate 18g (Sugars 8g) | Total Fat 2g (Sat Fat 1g) | Protein 3g | Fiber 7g | Cholesterol 0mg | Sodium 170mg | Food Exchanges: ½ Starch, ½ Fruit | Carbohydrate Choices: 1 | Weight Watcher Plus Point Comparison: 2

Two-Minute Fire-Roasted Salsa

A BIG THANK YOU GOES TO MY KITCHEN ASSISTANT MEGAN for this recipe. Fire-roasted tomatoes lend premium flavor to salsas, but store-bought brands also come with a premium price. When I explained that I was looking to create a quick and easy salsa using far more economical canned fire-roasted tomatoes, Megan shared hers. Unlike most jarred varieties, this salsa actually looks and tastes like those in Mexican restaurants and markets—and it's ready in minutes. Olé!

MAKES 8 SERVINGS

1 (14.5-ounce) can diced fire-roasted tomatoes

1 garlic clove, roughly chopped (or 1 teaspoon minced)

¼ cup roughly chopped onion

¼ cup fresh cilantro

1 tablespoon jarred jalapeño peppers

1 tablespoon fresh lime juice

⅛ teaspoon salt

1. Place all of the ingredients in a blender. Blend in short pulses to mix. Place in a container, cover, and store in the refrigerator. Salsa will keep for about one week.

DARE TO COMPARE: While all jarred salsas are low in fat, most are high in sodium, with some brands having as much as 480 milligrams in each ¼ cup. To keep the sodium level of your home-made salsa moderate, look for fire-roasted tomatoes that have less than 280 milligrams of sodium per half cup.

NUTRITION INFORMATION PER SERVING: (¼ cup) Calories 15 | Carbohydrate 3g (Sugars 2g) | Total Fat 0g (Sat Fat 0g) | Protein 0g | Fiber less than 1g | Cholesterol 0mg | Sodium 180mg | Food Exchanges: ½ Vegetable | Carbohydrate Choices: 0 | Weight Watcher Plus Point Comparison: 0

Red Pepper Hummus

SINCE MY HEALTHY HUMMUS RECIPE first appeared in Eat What You Love, *America's love affair with this creamy spread has skyrocketed. This very popular flavor couldn't be easier to make, as jarred red peppers actually taste better in this dip than roasting your own. Serve it with raw veggies and my rosemary-topped Baked Pita Strips (page 111), or jazz up sandwiches with a smear.*

| | MAKES 7 SERVINGS

1 (15-ounce) can garbanzo beans

2 tablespoons fresh lemon juice

2 tablespoons tahini

½ teaspoon cumin

¼ teaspoon salt

Pinch of cayenne pepper

⅓ cup jarred red pepper, no juice, divided

1 tablespoon olive oil

2 garlic cloves, minced

Sprig of fresh basil (optional)

1. Reserve 2 tablespoons of garbanzo bean liquid and set aside. Drain and rinse the garbanzo beans. Place the beans, lemon juice, tahini, cumin, salt, and cayenne pepper in a food processor, and begin to process. Add the reserved bean liquid, 1 tablespoon at a time and process until fairly smooth.

2. Remove 1 teaspoon of the red pepper, dice it, and set aside. Add the remaining red pepper to the food processor and process for 1 to 1½ minutes, or until almost smooth.

3. Combine the olive oil and minced garlic in a small, microwave-safe cup or ramekin, and cover with plastic wrap. Cook on high for 15 seconds. Remove, stir, and microwave another 15 seconds. Slowly stream in the olive oil and continue to process for 1 minute, or until completely smooth. Remove the hummus from the food processor and place in a bowl. Top with reserved chopped red pepper and sprig of basil. Cover and chill until ready to serve.

Marlene Says: *While hummus can be a healthy choice, some pre-made brands contain far more fat and calories than others. When purchasing hummus, look for a brand that has no more than 7 grams of fat in each 3-tablespoon serving.*

NUTRITION INFORMATION PER SERVING: (3 tablespoons) Calories 90 | Carbohydrate 0g (Sugars g) | Total Fat 5g (Sat Fat 0.5g) | Protein 3g | Fiber 3g | Cholesterol 0mg | Sodium 170mg | Food Exchanges: ½ Starch, 1 Fat | Carbohydrate Choices: ½ | Weight Watcher Plus Point Comparison: 1

Buffalo Chicken Dip

THERE IS A REASON THIS TYPE OF DIP IS SO POPULAR. *Warm and creamy and packed with tons of flavor, it's not just good, it's crazy delicious good! Staying true to the original, I kept the wonderful taste combination of Ranch dressing, hot sauce, cream cheese, and chicken, but then set out to make it even better. Grated carrot and crunchy celery add texture and sweetness to this buffalo dip, and brightly colored green onions and blue cheese adorn the top. Who said better-for-you can't simply be better?*

MAKES 16 SERVINGS

8 ounces tub-style reduced-fat cream cheese

2 tablespoons light mayonnaise

½ cup low-fat buttermilk

6 tablespoons hot wing sauce (like Frank's Red Hot Wings)

½ teaspoon garlic powder

½ teaspoon onion powder

2 cups shredded cooked chicken

½ cup finely grated carrot

⅓ cup finely diced celery

⅓ cup crumbled or grated blue cheese (about 1 ounce)

2 green onions, finely chopped

1. Preheat the oven to 350°F.

2. In a medium bowl, whisk together the cream cheese, mayonnaise, and buttermilk. Whisk in the hot sauce, garlic powder, and onion powder until well combined.

3. Fold in the chicken, carrot, and celery. Transfer mixture to a 1½ quart oven-safe dish and bake for 15 minutes. Remove from the oven, top with blue cheese, and bake for 5 minutes. Garnish with chopped green onions and serve.

DARE TO COMPARE: The traditional recipe for this dip had a hefty 210 calories, 17 grams of fat, and 690 milligrams of sodium per quarter cup serving. This dip boasts half the sodium, ⅓ of the calories, and 75% less fat than the original recipe.

NUTRITION INFORMATION PER SERVING: (scant ¼ cup) Calories 70 | Carbohydrate 2g (Sugars 2g) | Total Fat 4 g (Sat Fat 2g) | Protein 7g | Fiber 0g | Cholesterol 25mg | Sodium 320 mg | Food Exchanges: 1 Lean Meat, ½ Fat | Carbohydrate Choices: 0 | Weight Watcher Plus Point Comparison: 2

Barbecued Black Bean Dip

BRING ON THE BIG GAME. Here's another crowd-pleasing dip you can whip up in mere minutes using pantry staples. A family favorite, I find the secret is in the sauce—the barbecue sauce that is! It's one of those sneaky ingredients no one can quite put their finger on, but that elevates this bean dip above the rest. I prefer it served warm with the cheese melted, but it is also good at room temperature, or even cold, straight from the fridge.

MAKES 9 SERVINGS

1 teaspoon canola oil

½ cup diced onion

2 garlic cloves, minced

1 (15-ounce) can black beans, rinsed and drained

⅔ cup diced fire-roasted tomatoes (or salsa)

½ teaspoon ground cumin

½ teaspoon chili powder

2 tablespoons barbecue sauce

¼ cup chopped fresh cilantro

1 tablespoon fresh lime juice

¼ cup reduced-fat shredded Mexican blend cheese

1. Heat the oil in medium saucepan over medium heat. Add the onion and sauté for 3 to 4 minutes, or until translucent. Add garlic and sauté for another minute.

2. Add the next 5 ingredients (black beans through barbecue sauce) to the saucepan, and mash with a potato masher or large fork until most of the beans are smashed. Stir in cilantro and lime juice, and cook over medium heat for 1 minute.

3. Remove from heat, transfer dip to a medium bowl, and top with cheese.

NUTRITION INFORMATION PER SERVING: (3 tablespoons) Calories 60 | Carbohydrate 9g (Sugars 2g) | Total Fat 1.5g (Sat Fat 0g) | Protein 3g | Fiber 3g | Cholesterol 0mg | Sodium 230mg | Food Exchanges: ½ Starch | Carbohydrate Choices: ½ | Weight Watcher Plus Point Comparison: 1

Baked Pita Strips

THESE SAVORY PITA "STRIPS" ARE SURE TO COME IN HANDY when serving any of the four great dip recipes in this book, and also many of your own. Choose from the savory Southwestern seasoning blend—perfect for salsas and Barbecued Black Bean Dip (opposite page)—or the rosemary and garlic flavored mix for digging into Red Pepper Hummus (page 107).

MAKES 4 SERVINGS

2 (8-inch) whole wheat or regular pita pockets

Southwest Seasoning:

1 teaspoon chili powder

¼ teaspoon ground cumin

⅛ teaspoon salt

Rosemary Garlic Seasoning:

1 teaspoon finely minced rosemary

½ teaspoon garlic salt with parsley

1. Preheat the oven to 350°F.

2. Stack 2 pita rounds and cut in half. Using a sharp knife, cut each half into four strips by cutting from rounded edge to pocket. Separate each strip into 2 strips.

3. Place the pita strips on a baking sheet, rough side up, and spray with an even coating of cooking spray. Mix desired seasoning blend together, and sprinkle over the chips. Bake for 6 to 8 minutes, or until the strips are crisp and golden brown.

Marlene Says: *Look for garlic salt with parsley where you find the other spices. It offers a nice garlicky taste with less sodium than plain garlic salt.*

NUTRITION INFORMATION PER SERVING: (8 strips) Calories 90 | Carbohydrate 18g (Sugars 1g) | Total Fat 1g (Sat Fat 0g) | Protein 3g | Fiber 3g | Cholesterol 5mg | Sodium 240mg | Food Exchanges: 1 Starch | Carbohydrate Choices: 1 | Weight Watcher Plus Point Comparison: 2

Chicken Fajita Nachos

ON GAME DAY AT OUR HOUSE, we are serious about our nachos. And after readers raved about my Cheesy Chili Nachos in Eat More of What You Love, *I knew I had to deliver again. The result is what I'd like to think is a touchdown of Tex-Mex eating and I predict a big win when you serve these to your sporting crowd. Optional garnishes include cilantro, sour cream, and salsa.*

MAKES 4 SERVINGS

1 teaspoon oil

1 small onion, diced

½ large green pepper, diced

2 garlic cloves, minced

8 ounces boneless, skinless chicken breast, cubed

1 teaspoon cumin

½ teaspoon chili powder

⅛ teaspoon salt

Juice of 1 lime

2 teaspoons margarine or butter

2 teaspoons all-purpose flour

½ cup reduced-sodium chicken broth

1 cup shredded reduced-fat Cheddar cheese

½ (4-ounce) can diced green chiles

3 ounces reduced-fat tortilla chips (about 25 chips)

1. Spray a medium skillet with nonstick cooking spray, and place over medium-high heat. Add the onion and sauté 3 to 4 minutes. Add bell pepper and cook 2 minutes, or until peppers are softened, and add the garlic. Stir in chicken, cumin, chili powder, and salt, reduce the heat to medium, and cook 3 to 4 minutes, or until chicken is done. Add the lime juice and cook for 30 seconds. Set aside.

2. In a small saucepan over low heat, melt margarine and flour, and whisk until smooth. Add chicken broth and bring to a low boil, stirring continuously for about 1 minute. Stir in cheese and whisk until smooth. Lower heat, stir in green chiles, and remove from heat.

3. Spread out the chips onto a serving platter. Spoon fajita mixture evenly onto chips, and then drizzle cheese sauce over fajita mixture. Top with your favorite garnishes and serve.

DARE TO COMPARE: Chicken nachos often have more calories than beef. An order of Baja Fresh Charbroiled Chicken Nachos has 2,020 calories, over 100 grams of fat, and almost 3,000 milligrams of sodium!

NUTRITION INFORMATION PER SERVING: Calories 190 | Carbohydrate 15g (Sugars 2g) | Total Fat 5g (Sat Fat 1.5g) | Protein 21g | Fiber 1g | Cholesterol 45mg | Sodium 390mg | Food Exchanges: 1 Starch, 2½ Lean Meat | Carbohydrate Choices: 1 | Weight Watcher Plus Point Comparison: 5

Creamy Crab Dip on a Crispy Crust

THIS RECIPE MAKES ENTERTAINING OH-SO-EASY. With all of the ingredients on hand, you're never more than minutes away from having a showstopping hot appetizer ready to feed a crowd. Creamy, cheesy, hot crab dip, served on a crispy pizza crust—need I say more? The dip topping can even be prepared ahead of time. Spread it on the crust just before baking, and you're good to go!

MAKES 12 SERVINGS

¼ cup light mayonnaise

¼ cup plain low-fat Greek yogurt (or light sour cream)

½ teaspoon Old Bay Seasoning

Dash or two of Tabasco sauce (optional)

¾ pound crab meat (lump or imitation)

¾ cup shredded reduced-fat Swiss cheese

1 large thin-crust style pizza crust (like Boboli)

2 green onions, sliced thinly at an angle

1. Preheat the oven to 425°F. In a medium bowl, combine mayonnaise, yogurt, Old Bay, and Tabasco, if desired. Fold in the crab and cheese.

2. Evenly spread the crab mixture on the crust, place on a baking sheet, and bake for 10 to 15 minutes, or until puffed and brown. Top with sliced green onion, cut into wedges, and serve.

Marlene Says: *Imitation, "mock," crab meat works well in this recipe, but feel free to use lump crab meat as well. When using "mock" crab meat, shred the meat with your fingers before adding it to the dip.*

NUTRITION INFORMATION PER SERVING: (1 wedge) Calories 120 | Carbohydrate 15g (Sugars 0g) | Total Fat 4g (Sat Fat 1g) | Protein 7g | Fiber 2g | Cholesterol 10mg | Sodium 310mg | Food Exchanges: 1 Starch, 1 Lean Meat | Carbohydrate Choices: 1 | Weight Watcher Plus Point Comparison: 2

Sweet 'n Spicy Pickled Green Beans

PICKLING AND CANNING ARE BACK IN FASHION—but they can be time-consuming and messy. Here's an easy way to enjoy the sweet, sour, and salty flavor of old-fashioned pickled vegetables without slaving away in the kitchen as Grandma once did. Use these slim pickings to perk up any appetizer tray, or serve them as a bar snack with mixed drinks. Sliced red onions are a pretty addition.

MAKES 8 SERVINGS

1 cup distilled white vinegar

2 garlic cloves

⅔ cup no-calorie granulated sweetener*

2 tablespoons granulated sugar

1 tablespoon salt

2 teaspoons dill weed

¼ teaspoon cayenne powder

1 pound fresh green beans, trimmed

1. In a medium saucepan, combine the first 7 ingredients (vinegar through cayenne) and ¾ cup water. Bring to a simmer over medium heat, add the green beans, and return to a boil. Simmer for 3 minutes (or 2 minutes if you prefer crunchier beans), and remove from heat.

2. Cool to room temperature, cover, and refrigerate (preferably overnight). Serve cold or at room temperature.

Marlene Says: *Many factors affect how much of the salt and sugar is absorbed when pickling or brining. The highest expert opinion is 15%, so it is what was used for the nutrition calculations.*

*See page 81 for sweetener options.

NUTRITION INFORMATION PER SERVING: (10 beans) Calories 20 | Carbohydrate 5g (Sugars 2g) | Total Fat 0g (Sat Fat 0g) | Protein 1g | Fiber 2g | Cholesterol 0mg | Sodium 125mg | Food Exchanges: 1 Vegetable | Carbohydrate Choices: ½ | Weight Watcher Plus Point Comparison: 0

Oven-Fried Mozzarella Sticks

A CRISPY, CRUNCHY CRUST ON THE OUTSIDE, with melt-in-your-mouth cheesy goodness inside—it's no wonder that mozzarella sticks are one of America's favorite gut-busting appetizers. Luckily, my oven-baked version delivers the same taste sensations for one-third of the calories. My boys and their friends devoured these right off the baking sheet. Serve if desired with my Easy All-Purpose Marinara (page 188) or your favorite pizza sauce.

MAKES 8 SERVINGS

8 part-skim mozzarella string cheese sticks

2 tablespoons all-purpose flour

1 large egg, beaten

⅓ cup panko breadcrumbs

¼ cup dry breadcrumbs

2 tablespoons Parmesan

1 teaspoon dried parsley

½ teaspoon garlic salt

¼ teaspoon dried oregano

1. Preheat the oven to 400°F. Line a baking sheet with foil, and spray lightly with cooking spray. Cut the mozzarella sticks in half crosswise (you will have 16 short sticks).

2. Place the flour in a small bowl. Place the beaten egg in another small bowl. Combine remaining ingredients (panko through oregano) in a medium shallow bowl, and toss to combine.

3. Roll the mozzarella sticks in the flour (I do four at a time), and then in the egg. Let excess drip off and drop the sticks in the crumb mixture. With clean hands sprinkle the crumbs evenly over the sticks. Transfer to prepared baking sheet, and repeat with remaining sticks.

4. Lightly spray mozzarella sticks with cooking spray and bake 7 to 8 minutes, or until lightly browned and edge or two shows sign of melted cheese. (Note: Cheese will melt further when sticks are removed from the oven.)

DARE TO COMPARE: An order of fried mozzarella sticks at a restaurant averages twice as many calories, three times the fat, and five times the carbohydrates as these cheesy, protein-packed sticks.

NUTRITION INFORMATION PER SERVING: (2 sticks) Calories 80 | Carbohydrate 3g (Sugars 0g) | Total Fat 4.5g (Sat Fat 2.5g) | Protein 8g | Fiber 0g | Cholesterol 35mg | Sodium 220mg | Food Exchanges: 1 Lean Meat, ½ Fat | Carbohydrate Choices: 0 | Weight Watcher Plus Point Comparison: 2

Garlicky Grilled Shrimp

NO NEED FOR COCKTAIL SAUCE HERE, these shrimp have all the magical flavors of the Mediterranean built right in! Akin to a traditional shrimp cocktail sauce, the thick marinade base is chili sauce. From there, olive oil, basil, and plenty of garlic chime in. Best of all, this recipe is as simple as can be for entertaining. Skewer the shrimp and pop them on the outdoor grill, or grill them without the skewers on your favorite indoor grill—the choice is yours.

MAKES 6 SERVINGS

1 pound extra-large shrimp (about 24) cleaned and peeled

¼ cup chili sauce (like Heinz)

2 tablespoons olive oil

2 tablespoons fresh lemon juice

3 garlic cloves, minced

2 tablespoons fresh basil, or 2 teaspoons dried basil

¼ teaspoon salt

⅛ teaspoon cayenne pepper

1. In a flat bowl, or gallon zip lock bag, combine all of the ingredients and 1 tablespoon water and refrigerate for 1 hour.

2. If using bamboo skewers, soak 6 skewers in water while the shrimp marinates.

3. Preheat the grill to medium-high. Remove shrimp from the marinade and transfer to skewers, placing about 4 shrimp on each skewer.

4. Grill the shrimp for 2 minutes on each side, or until cooked through.

Marlene Says: *The small loss of marinade coating during grilling has been taken into account in nutritionals.*

NUTRITION INFORMATION PER SERVING: (4 shrimp) Calories 110 | Carbohydrate 4g (Sugars 0g) | Total Fat 3.5g (Sat Fat 1g) | Protein 16 g | Fiber 0g | Cholesterol 115mg | Sodium 130 mg | Food Exchanges: 2 Lean Meat, ½ Fat | Carbohydrate Choices: 0 | Weight Watcher Plus Point Comparison: 2

Easy Baked Egg Rolls

IN THE TIME IT TAKES TO GET CHINESE TAKE-OUT, you can roll up your own authentic egg rolls. Don't be intimidated by the process—if you can wrap a sandwich, you can make these. To save time, I use bagged coleslaw mix for the filling. If you don't have egg roll wrappers on hand or simply want to enjoy the delicious filling lettuce wrap-style, you can use leafy greens instead, as I do with my Moo-Shu Lettuce Wraps with Asian Peanut Sauce (page 120).

| MAKES 10 SERVINGS

Filling:

8 ounces lean ground pork (or turkey)

3 cups bagged coleslaw mix

4 green onions, thinly sliced

1 teaspoon jarred or freshly minced ginger

2 tablespoons reduced-sodium soy sauce

½ cup chopped water chestnuts

1 tablespoon hoisin sauce

Black pepper to taste

10 egg roll wrappers

1. Preheat the oven to 400°F.

2. Spray a large, nonstick skillet with cooking spray, and set over medium-high heat. Crumble in the meat and cook for 8 to 10 minutes, breaking it into small pieces until the meat is almost cooked through. While the meat is cooking, place the coleslaw and green onions in a medium, microwave-safe bowl. Cover and microwave on high for 3 minutes.

3. In a small bowl, combine the ginger and soy sauce, and add to the skillet. Simmer 3 minutes and remove from heat. Stir in slaw mix, water chestnuts, hoisin sauce, and black pepper.

4. Fill a small bowl with water. Working on a flat surface, place an egg roll wrapper with a point toward you. Place ⅓ cup of filling across the center. Using your finger, apply a small amount of water to the edges of the wrapper. Fold the bottom corner up over the filling, fold in both sides, and roll the egg roll toward the top point. Spray the egg roll lightly with cooking spray and place on a baking sheet. Repeat with remaining egg roll wrappers.

5. Bake for 12 minutes, turn the egg rolls, and bake another 4 minutes, or until crispy and golden brown.

NUTRITION INFORMATION PER SERVING: (1 egg roll) Calories 135 | Carbohydrate 21g (Sugars 1g) | Total Fat 2g (Sat Fat 0.5g) | Protein 8g | Fiber 1g | Cholesterol 20mg | Sodium 340mg | Food Exchanges: 1 Starch, ½ Vegetable, ½ Lean Meat | Carbohydrate Choices: 1½ | Weight Watcher Plus Point Comparison: 3

Moo-Shu Lettuce Wraps with Asian Peanut Sauce

FOR THOSE OF YOU WHO ASK how I come up with new recipes, here's one way. When testing the recipe for my Easy Baked Egg Rolls (page 119), one of my kitchen assistants suggested that a simple way to enjoy the tasty filling would be to wrap it in lettuce leaves. I love lettuce wraps, so I wholeheartedly agreed. The testing of several sauces ensued, and an Asian-style peanut sauce was deemed the winner. After eating several wraps each, we agreed that this was indeed a recipe unto itself that needed to be shared.

MAKES 8 SERVINGS

1 recipe Egg Roll Filling (page 119)

¼ cup rice vinegar

2 tablespoons creamy peanut butter

1 tablespoon hoisin sauce

1 tablespoon reduced-sodium soy sauce

1 teaspoon sesame oil

Pinch red pepper flakes, or to taste

16 butter or iceberg lettuce leaves

1 medium carrot, peeled and coarsely grated

Cilantro (optional garnish)

1. Prepare the egg roll filling according to recipe directions.

2. For the peanut sauce, blend or whisk together the next 6 ingredients (vinegar through pepper flakes), until smooth (or place them in a small plastic container with a lid and vigorously shake).

3. For each wrap, spoon 3 tablespoons of the meat mixture onto a lettuce leaf, top with 1 heaping teaspoon of peanut sauce, and add a sprinkle of carrot and fresh cilantro, if desired. Alternately, place the filling on a platter with garnishes and serve with lettuce leaves and sauce.

Marlene Says: *This lettuce wrap recipe is my easiest yet. For an even more Moo-Shu experience, omit the sauce and smear each lettuce leaf with ½ teaspoon of hoisin sauce before adding the filling (subtracts 15 calories and 2 grams of fat per serving). Filling can also be used with flour tortillas.*

NUTRITION INFORMATION PER SERVING: (2 lettuce wraps + 1 tablespoon sauce) Calories 105 | Carbohydrate 8g (Sugars 3g) | Total Fat 5g (Sat Fat 1g) | Protein 8g | Fiber 2g | Cholesterol 40mg | Sodium 290mg | Food Exchanges: 1 Lean Meat, 1 Vegetable, ½ Fat | Carbohydrate Choices: ½ | Weight Watcher Plus Point Comparison: 2

Everyday Soups and Sandwiches

Roasted Red Pepper and Tomato Soup

Weeknight Chicken and Dumplings

Outback-Style Creamy Onion Soup

Quickie Kale and Calico Bean Soup

Sweet Potato Pumpkin Harvest Soup

Mushroom Bisque

Game Day No-Chop Chili

Hearty Lasagna Soup

Turkey Avocado 'wich on Wheat

Curried Chicken Salad Sandwich Three Ways

Cheesy Toasty Veggie Hero

Beef "Fil-A" Sandwich

Southern-Style Grilled Cheese

Buffalo Chicken Burger

Chicago-Style Hot Dogs

Simple Southwest Veggie Burgers

Bodacious "50-50" Bacon 'n Beef Burgers

San Francisco Patty Melt

WHEN IT COMES TO EVERYDAY FOODS, it's hard to rival the versatility, convenience, and utter satisfaction provided by soothing soups and scrumptious sandwiches. They're a duo that never disappoints, while offering endless options for mixing, matching, and modifying them to your own tastes.

I think soups are, well, super, and I assure you that every pot full in this chapter is infused with enticing aromas, exceptional taste—and great nutrition! Weeknight Chicken and Dumplings will fill your kitchen with the smell of home-style goodness in just 30 minutes. Slimmed down yet rich-tasting Mushroom Bisque will compliment any meal, and nothing will satisfy your dipping needs like my new Roasted Red Pepper and Tomato Soup (which also delivers a full days' worth of vitamin A and C!). Speaking of good nutrition, superfood kale is featured in my Quickie Kale and Calico Bean Soup. Packed with antioxidants and boatloads of Vitamin K, a single bowl also offers a whopping 12 grams of fiber. Fix a pot on the weekend, and you'll be well-nourished all week. (Soups store well for four to five days in the fridge, and even longer in the freezer.)

Enjoy pairing your soup with a sandwich? You'll find over a dozen scintillating sandwiches to choose from. Just like those at a sandwich shop or restaurant, my sandwiches and burgers are dressed to the nines with crave-worthy fillings, add-ons, and toppings. And while they taste the same as your favorites, the fat and calories aren't; my irresistible Buffalo Chicken Burger served with ranch topping clocks in at a slim 270 calories, not the 1,210 calories of the Chili's version, and the big Bodacious "50-50" Bacon 'n Beef Burgers are just 350 calories with 11 grams of fat, instead the usual 1,220 calories and 73 fat grams! Prefer something meatless? I guarantee my Cheesy Toasty Veggie Hero will make your day.

GLUTEN-FREE FOODS

If you or someone you love is on a gluten-free diet, the good news is that many of nature's finest foods, such as fruits, vegetables, meats, seafood, beans, nuts, and eggs—along with nutrient-rich dairy products and oil, are naturally gluten-free. And while foods made with wheat-based flour (or barley or rye), like bread, cakes, and cookies can be challenging, luckily, today's vast array of gluten-free products has made it easier to cook and eat gluten-free. One of the easiest and least expensive ways to ensure meals and baked goods are good-for-you, great-tasting, and gluten-free is to prepare them yourself. Here are a few tips to help you eat gluten-free the "everyday" way:

- For pancakes and waffles a 50/50 combo of buckwheat flour and oat flour works well as does Pamela's brand which can be found at most health-focused stores such as Whole Foods.

- For sandwiches use gluten-free bread or go "bunless" by wrapping sandwich fillings in lettuce leaves. Buy, or process toasted or stale gluten-free bread for gluten-free breadcrumbs.

- Gluten-free pastas are easy-to-find and can be used anywhere I specify pasta. Alternately, pour pasta sauces over cooked rice, spaghetti squash, or even baked potatoes halves.

- Most corn tortillas are gluten-free as are 100% corn tortilla chips.

- Buy, or make, gluten-free broths and your own dressings and sauces. The dressings and sauces in this book are gluten-free, or can easily be made so. Use Tamari sauce for light soy sauce.

- For thickening and dredging, cornstarch, tapioca flour, and gluten-free flour work well. When replacing flour with cornstarch or tapioca flour, to thicken, simply use half as much.

- For muffins, quick breads and baked goods, store-bought gluten-free flours and baking mixes are the easy way to go, but taste and texture vary considerably. For baking, Cup4Cup gluten-free "flour" is the best replacement for all-purpose flour I have found (see page 30).

- Apple Pie Oatmeal (page 59), Gluten-Free Oatmeal Spice Bars (page 90), Peanut Butter Oatmeal Chocolate Chip Cookies (page 310), and My Unbelievable Chocolate Cake (with Cup4Cup flour, page 301) are gluten-free sweet treats, as are the recipes on pages 312, 313, 317, 322, 323, and 327. Use gluten-free graham crackers or cookie crumbs to make gluten-free cheesecakes or pies. Sugar-free pudding, ice cream, whipped topping, cream cheese, and sweeteners are all gluten-free.

- For better flavor, double extracts, bump up the spices, and opt for flavorful additions like lemon and orange zest, nuts, or chocolate chips when creating your own gluten-free goodies.

Roasted Red Pepper and Tomato Soup

WHEN IT COMES TO PRODUCE, red peppers and tomatoes make a glorious pair. Not only are they complimentary in color, but the sweetness of the pepper also tempers the acid in the tomato, making them a perfect culinary couple. Add a handful of spinach and topping of feta, and you have a gorgeously simple soup with a sophisticated flair. From start to finish, this nutrient-packed soup is done in less than 30 minutes.

⊣ MAKES 4 SERVINGS

2 teaspoons olive oil

½ cup chopped onion

2 garlic cloves, minced

1 medium carrot, finely grated

⅔ cup roasted red peppers, chopped

1 (14-ounce) can no-salt diced tomatoes

1 (14-ounce) can reduced-sodium chicken broth

1 teaspoon dried basil

¼ teaspoon black pepper

¾ teaspoon cornstarch

1 cup fresh spinach leaves, cut into ½-inch ribbons

¼ cup crumbled reduced fat feta cheese

1. Heat the oil in a medium soup pot over medium heat. Add the onion and sauté 3 to 4 minutes, or until translucent. Add the garlic and carrot, sauté another 2 minutes, and then add the red peppers, tomatoes, broth, basil, and black pepper. Bring to a boil, reduce heat, and simmer for 10 minutes.

2. Transfer the hot soup to a blender, or use an immersion blender, and blend until smooth. Mix the cornstarch with one 1 tablespoon of water, return the pureed soup to the pot if using a blender, and stir in the cornstarch mixture. Bring the bisque to a low simmer for 1 to 2 minutes until thickened and warm. Stir in the spinach, and simmer one additional minute to wilt spinach.

3. Crumble feta on top of soup just before serving.

Marlene Says: *Jars of roasted red peppers come in many sizes. An 8-ounce jar, drained, yields about ⅔ cup. Leftover peppers can be used in salads or in the Red Pepper Hummus (page 107), Antipasto Pasta Salad (page 161), or Cheesy Toasty Veggie Hero (page 141).*

NUTRITION INFORMATION PER SERVING: (1 generous cup) Calories 90 | Carbohydrate 12g (Sugars 7g) | Total Fat 3.5g (Sat Fat 1g) | Protein 5g | Fiber 3g | Cholesterol 5mg | Sodium 550mg | Food Exchanges: 2 Vegetable, ½ Fat | Carbohydrate Choices: 1 | Weight Watcher Plus Point Comparison: 2

Weeknight Chicken and Dumplings

ARGUABLY, THERE ARE AS MANY VERSIONS of this classic dish as there are Southerners, but there's no argument about the comfort it serves up. Fresh vegetables, fluffy homemade rosemary-scented dumplings, and a creamy full flavor give my version of this stew-like soup Southern style, while using canned broth and cooked chicken make it weeknight friendly. This dish is quick, easy, and hearty without being heavy. Leftovers, if you have any, are mighty tasty.

MAKES 4 SERVINGS

2 teaspoons olive oil

1 medium onion, chopped (about 1½ cups)

4 medium carrots, peeled and chopped (about 1⅓ cup)

3 medium celery stalks, chopped (1 cup)

1¼ teaspoons poultry seasoning

2 tablespoons all-purpose flour

2 (14-ounce) cans reduced-sodium chicken broth

½ plus ⅓ cup low-fat milk, divided

2 cups shredded cooked chicken breast

¼ teaspoon salt

⅔ cup reduced-fat baking mix

2 tablespoons cornmeal

½ teaspoon chopped fresh rosemary

1. In a large soup pot, heat the oil over medium heat. Add the onion and sauté for 3 minutes. Add the carrots, celery, and poultry seasoning, and sauté for 3 minutes. Stir in flour and cook for 1 minute. Stir in broth, ½ cup milk, chicken, and salt, and bring to a boil. Reduce the heat to medium-low, and simmer for 5 minutes.

2. While the soup simmers, in a medium bowl, combine baking mix, cornmeal, rosemary, and remaining ⅓ cup milk, until a stiff batter forms. Drop batter by 1½ tablespoon portions onto the soup, spacing evenly for 8 dumplings.

3. Cover the pot and steam the dumplings for 7 to 9 minutes, ensuring that the soup stays at a low simmer.

4. Turn off the heat, uncover pot, and let sit for 2 minutes. Stir the soup carefully, without disturbing the dumplings, and serve.

DARE TO COMPARE: The rich biscuits and cream in the original versions of this classic dish can send the calories soaring. All white meat chicken and a lighter dumpling equals 50% less fat and twice as much protein in your bowl.

NUTRITION INFORMATION PER SERVING: (1½ cups) Calories 240 | Carbohydrate 29g (Sugars 8g) | Total Fat 8g (Sat Fat 1g) | Protein 21g | Fiber 3g | Cholesterol 40mg | Sodium 690mg | Food Exchanges: 2 Lean Meat, 1½ Starch, 1 Vegetable | Carbohydrate Choices: 2 | Weight Watcher Plus Point Comparison: 6

Outback-Style Creamy Onion Soup

WHEN I ASKED MY READERS WHICH RECIPES they would love me to make over, not surprisingly, I got several requests for Outback Steakhouse's onion soup. A full two-thirds of the calories in each bowl of the creamy soup comes from fat—and not the healthy kind. I love that my version is also rich and creamy, and more so, I love how the onions shine brighter in this soup. A satisfying cup boasts a 90% reduction in fat, just as much protein, and 75% less sodium. Feel free to top it with another tablespoon of cheese as a garnish if you please.

MAKES 6 SERVINGS

1 teaspoon canola oil

3 cups thinly sliced sweet onions

1 (14-ounce) can reduced-sodium beef broth

1 (14-ounce) can reduced-sodium chicken broth

½ teaspoon black pepper

1 (12-ounce) can low-fat evaporated milk

¼ cup flour (instant, like Wondra recommended)

2 tablespoons reduced-fat cream cheese

⅓ cup shredded reduced-fat Cheddar cheese

⅛ to ¼ teaspoon salt

1. Heat the oil in a medium soup pot over medium-low heat. Add the onions and sauté 5 to 7 minutes, or until softened and translucent, but not browned.

2. Add the beef broth, chicken broth, and pepper. Cover and bring to a low boil.

3. In a small bowl, whisk together evaporated milk and flour until smooth. Stir into the pot. Cover and cook, stirring periodically, until thickened, about 5 minutes. Turn heat to low, add the cream cheese, and stir until smooth. Whisk in the Cheddar, stir until mostly melted, remove from heat, adjust salt to taste, and serve.

DARE TO COMPARE: There are 482 calories and 36 grams of fat—including an entire day's worth of saturated fat—in one bowl of Outback Steakhouse's creamy onion soup. A tablespoon of cheese as a garnish here will add just 20 calories to each cup.

NUTRITION INFORMATION PER SERVING: (1 cup) Calories 135 | Carbohydrate 16g (Sugars 11g) | Total Fat 4g (Sat Fat 2.5g) | Protein 10g | Fiber 1g | Cholesterol 15mg | Sodium 470mg | Food Exchanges: 1 Low-fat Milk, ½ Starch | Carbohydrate Choices: 1 | Weight Watcher Plus Point Comparison: 4

Quickie Kale and Calico Bean Soup

IF YOU ARE LOOKING FOR A PROTEIN-PACKED, fiber-filled, energy-boosting soup that eats like a meal, this one's for you. It's especially pleasing to note that a single bowl delivers over a day's worth of Vitamins A, C, and K, and it takes just minutes to throw together. A sprinkle of Parmesan, a squeeze of fresh lemon juice, or a dash or two of hot sauce are great soup bowl toppers.

MAKES 4 SERVINGS

1 teaspoon olive oil

1 small onion, chopped

4 cups chopped kale

1¼ teaspoons garlic powder

½ teaspoon onion powder

1 (15-ounce) can kidney beans, rinsed and drained

1 (15-ounce) can garbanzo beans, rinsed and drained

2 (14.5-ounce) cans stewed tomatoes

1 (14-ounce) can reduced-sodium chicken broth

1 large carrot, peeled and chopped

1½ teaspoons Italian seasoning

½ teaspoon black pepper

¼ teaspoon salt (or more to taste)

Grated Parmesan cheese (optional)

1. Heat the olive oil in a large soup pot over medium heat. Add the onions and sauté for 4 to 5 minutes, or until onions are soft and translucent.

2. Add remaining ingredients to the pot (kale through salt), plus 1 cup of water. Bring the soup to a boil, reduce the heat to low, cover, and simmer 1 hour, or until vegetables are tender and flavors have melded. Serve with Parmesan cheese or other add-ins, as desired.

Marlene Says: *If you are really in a hurry, skip browning the onions and add all the ingredients into the soup pot at once, and simmer as directed. This soup is also great in a slow cooker. Add everything to the slow cooker, stir, and cook for 3 to 4 hours on high, or 7 to 8 hours on low.*

NUTRITION INFORMATION PER SERVING: (1½ cups) Calories 240 | Carbohydrate 42g (Sugars 9g) | Total Fat 2.5g (Sat Fat 0g) | Protein 13g | Fiber 12g | Cholesterol 0mg | Sodium 420mg | Food Exchanges: 2 Starch, 1½ Lean Meat, 1 Vegetable | Carbohydrate Choices: 2½ | Weight Watcher Plus Point Comparison: 5

Sweet Potato Pumpkin Harvest Soup

ANOTHER NATURAL MATCH MADE BY MOTHER NATURE is sweet potato and pumpkin. While these are often associated with fall recipes, I find them worthy of enjoying all year long. As proof, every time I make this soup, I'm amazed at how something so sweet, smooth, and comforting can be so low in calories, carbs and fat. If you like a little zing in your soup, add the pinch of cayenne. Just a tiny pinch, or it will be too spicy.

MAKES 5 SERVINGS

2 teaspoons canola oil

1 medium onion, diced

1 medium sweet potato

1 (15-ounce) can 100% pure pumpkin

2 (14-ounce) cans reduced-sodium chicken broth

1 tablespoon brown sugar

¾ teaspoon dried thyme, crushed

¼ teaspoon salt, or to taste

Pinch black pepper

Pinch of cayenne pepper (optional)

Light sour cream (optional garnish)

1. Heat the oil in a large soup pot over medium heat. Add the onion and sauté for 8 to 10 minutes, or until well softened and starting to caramelize.

2. While the onion is cooking, pierce the sweet potato with a fork, and place it in the microwave. Cook on high for 6 to 7 minutes, or until soft when pierced with a fork. Let cool for 2 minutes.

3. Add the pumpkin, broth, brown sugar, thyme, salt, black pepper, optional cayenne, and flesh of the cooked sweet potato to the soup pot. Stir to combine, gently mashing the sweet potato. Cover and simmer for 10 to 15 minutes, stirring occasionally.

4. Transfer the hot soup to a blender, or use an immersion blender, and puree the soup until smooth. If using a blender, return the pureed soup to the pot, and bring to a low simmer for 1 to 2 minutes until warm. Serve garnished with a swirl of sour cream, if desired.

NUTRITION INFORMATION PER SERVING: (1 cup) Calories 100 | Carbohydrate 18g (Sugars 10g) | Total Fat 2g (Sat Fat 0g) | Protein 3g | Fiber 4g | Cholesterol 0mg | Sodium 330mg | Food Exchanges: 1 Starch | Carbohydrate Choices: 1 | Weight Watcher Plus Point Comparison: 2

Mushroom Bisque

ACCORDING TO THE FOOD COMPANION DICTIONARY, *a "bisque" is a soup made with cream that usually includes seafood. This soup has neither seafood nor cream, but it does have a rich, creamy texture and outstanding mushroom flavor that simply cannot be found in a canned soup. After the first spoonful, my husband said, "This tastes like a bisque." So Mushroom Bisque it is. (P.S.—The sherry wine is optional, but I highly recommend it for classic bisque-like flavor.)*

MAKES 4 SERVINGS

1 teaspoon olive oil

1 cup chopped onion

1 garlic clove, minced

4 cups sliced mushrooms

½ teaspoon dried thyme

3 tablespoons flour, divided

1 (14-ounce) reduced-sodium beef broth

1 teaspoon Worcestershire sauce

½ teaspoon salt

½ cup nonfat half-and-half

1 cup low-fat milk

⅛ teaspoon black pepper

2 tablespoons dry sherry wine (optional)

1. Heat the oil in large soup pot over medium heat. Add the onions and garlic to the pot. Cook, stirring occasionally, for 4 to 5 minutes or until the onions are soft and translucent. Add the mushrooms, stirring occasionally for 5 minutes, or until they release all of their liquid.

2. Add the thyme to the pot by crushing it between your fingers, sprinkle in 2 tablespoons flour, stir, and cook for 1 minute. Stir in the broth, Worcestershire, and salt. Bring the soup to a boil, reduce to a simmer, cover, and cook for 10 minutes.

3. In a small bowl, stir remaining tablespoon of flour into the half-and-half. Add it to the soup, along with the milk and black pepper, and cook for 2 to 3 minutes, or until the soup thickens. Adjust the salt and pepper to taste. Remove from heat and stir in the sherry, if desired.

DARE TO COMPARE: While most restaurant seafood bisques average around 300 calories per cup, the richest ones contain over 450 calories (yes, in just one cup!).

NUTRITION INFORMATION PER SERVING: (about 1 cup) Calories 140 | Carbohydrate 20g (Sugars 10g) | Total Fat 3g (Sat Fat 1g) | Protein 8g | Fiber 2g | Cholesterol 0mg | Sodium 370mg | Food Exchanges: 1 Starch, 1 Vegetable, ½ Fat | Carbohydrate Choices: 1 | Weight Watcher Plus Point Comparison: 4

Game Day No-Chop Chili

YES, THIS RECIPE FOR CHILI ALSO INCLUDES canned chili. The idea came from a friend, and while I was skeptical at first, canned chili works brilliantly as a thickener and a base, especially in the slow cooker, where I prefer to cook this game-friendly chili. The add-ins of lean turkey and beans up the protein and fiber content (and dilute the sodium content), while additional spices elevate the taste. Serve with chopped green onions and cilantro to add fresh-from-the-fridge goodness.

MAKES 10 SERVINGS

1¼ pounds lean ground turkey

1 (28-ounce) can diced tomatoes with juice

2 (15-ounce) cans no-beans chili (Hormel brand)

1 ½ tablespoons chili powder

1 teaspoon ground cumin

½ teaspoon garlic powder

1 (15-ounce) can reduced-sodium red kidney beans, rinsed and drained

1 (15-ounce) can reduced-sodium black beans, rinsed and drained

1. Spray a large, nonstick skillet (for the slow cooker) or large soup pot (for the stove top) with cooking spray, and set over medium-high heat. Crumble in the turkey and cook, breaking up the meat into small chunks and stirring often. Cook until the pink color is gone, 6 to 7 minutes. (For slow cooking, transfer to a 4- to 6-quart slow cooker.)

2. Add the tomatoes and their juices, the chili, chili powder, cumin, and garlic powder, and mix well. Gently stir in the beans.

3. Cover and cook for 3 hours on a very low setting on the stovetop, or 8 hours on low, or 4 hours on high in a slow cooker, stirring once halfway through, if you can. If chili looks a little saucy to your taste, uncover and cook for 10 to 15 more minutes before serving.

Marlene Says: *This is a hearty meat and bean chili. To add some veggies to the mix, "no-chop" frozen onions or peppers can be added with the tomatoes. A cup or two of fresh chopped peppers and/or onions are, of course, equally welcome.*

NUTRITION INFORMATION PER SERVING: (1 cup) Calories 260 | Carbohydrate 22g (Sugars 4g) | Total Fat 8g (Sat Fat 2.5g) | Protein 22g | Fiber 6g | Cholesterol 40mg | Sodium 580mg | Food Exchanges: 2½ Lean Meat, 1 Starch, ½ Vegetable | Carbohydrate Choices: 1 | Weight Watcher Plus Point Comparison: 6

Hearty Lasagna Soup

WHILE MANY SOUPS say they eat like a meal, this one truly delivers! Cheesy, beefy, and rich in tomato flavor, it's quickly become a family favorite. Campanelle pasta is more spoon-friendly, but lasagna noodles are fun, so I leave that choice up to you. To add even more cheesy goodness, mix 6 ounces of low-fat ricotta with a pinch of each salt and pepper, and spoon two tablespoons into each bowl before adding the soup.

MAKES 6 SERVINGS

1 teaspoon olive oil

1 medium onion, chopped

1 small red pepper, chopped

4 garlic cloves, minced

1 teaspoon Italian seasoning

½ teaspoon oregano

1 pound lean ground beef

1 (28-ounce) can crushed tomatoes

1 teaspoon granulated sugar

1 (14-ounce) can, or 2 cups reduced-sodium beef broth

¼ teaspoon crushed red pepper

1 cup dry campanelle pasta or 4 lasagna noodles

3 tablespoons grated Parmesan cheese

¼ teaspoon salt (optional)

½ cup reduced-fat shredded mozzarella cheese

1. In a large soup pot over medium-high heat, heat the oil. Add the onion and cook for 4 minutes or until translucent. Add the red pepper, sauté for 2 minutes, then add the garlic, Italian seasoning, and oregano and cook for 1 minute. Crumble in the beef and cook until the beef is no longer pink.

2. Add the crushed tomatoes, sugar, beef broth, red pepper, and 2 cups of water. Bring to a boil. Reduce the heat, cover, and simmer on low for 10 minutes. Add the pasta (breaking the lasagna noodles into pieces), and bring to a boil. Reduce the heat, cover, and simmer for 10 minutes, or until pasta is tender. Stir in the Parmesan.

3. Ladle 1½ cups of soup into bowls, top each with 1½ tablespoons cheese.

> **DARE TO COMPARE:** The lasagna soup recipe that inspired this makeover packs 625 calories and 900 milligrams of sodium in each one-cup serving!

NUTRITION INFORMATION PER SERVING (1½ cups) Calories 260 | Carbohydrate 25g (Sugars 7g) | Total Fat 9g (Sat Fat 4g) | Protein 28g | Fiber 5g | Cholesterol 55mg | Sodium 510mg | Food Exchanges: 4 Lean Meat, 2 Vegetable 1 Starch | Carbohydrate Choices: 1½ | Weight Watcher Plus Point Comparison: 7

Turkey Avocado 'wich on Wheat

FANCY SANDWICH COMBINATIONS COME AND GO, but a turkey sandwich on whole wheat bread is a classic that never loses its appeal, especially one with bacon! This version marries the best of a classic turkey cobb salad with a California-style turkey avocado sandwich. The result is a sandwich that has it all, but with only half the usual sodium and a fraction of the fat. The creaminess from the mayo-blend and avocado makes cheese not required.

MAKES 1 SERVING

1 tablespoon light mayonnaise

1 tablespoon plain nonfat yogurt

2 teaspoons real bacon bits

2 slices light wheat bread

2 lettuce leaves

2 ounces lean deli-style turkey, thinly sliced

1 slice tomato

⅙ avocado, thinly sliced

2 to 3 tablespoons alfalfa sprouts

1. In a small bowl, mix together the mayonnaise, yogurt, and bacon bits.

2. Spread 1 tablespoon of the mayonnaise mixture on each slice of bread. Top one slice with the lettuce, then the turkey slices, tomato, and avocado slices, and finish with the sprouts. Top with remaining slice of bread, cut in half, and take a big bite.

DARE TO COMPARE: A deli-style turkey avocado sandwich with bacon averages 550 calories, 25 grams of fat, and 1600 milligrams of sodium. Order one at a full-service restaurant, and you will find a similar calorie and sodium count in just *half* of a sandwich! To lower the sodium of this sandwich, use Juicy Herb Turkey Breast (page 207), low-sodium deli-sliced turkey, or omit the bacon bits.

NUTRITION INFORMATION PER SERVING: (1 sandwich) Calories 250 | Carbohydrate 26g (Sugars 3g) | Total Fat 11g (Sat Fat 2g) | Protein 18g | Fiber 5g | Cholesterol 30mg | Sodium 842mg | Food Exchanges: 1½ Starch, 2 Lean Meat, 2 Fat | Carbohydrate Choices: 1½ | Weight Watcher Plus Point Comparison: 7

Curried Chicken Salad Sandwich
Three Ways

I LOVE IT WHEN AN EASY AND DELICIOUS RECIPE is also versatile. Within seconds of tasting this amazing chicken salad tucked between two slices of white bread, I was conjuring up the other great chicken salad sandwich combos you'll find on the next two pages. It's hard to say which one is the tastiest because they are all so good—so I leave that decision up to you.

Filling

2 cups diced cooked chicken breast

2 stalks celery, diced

1 small carrot, shredded

2 tablespoons golden raisins

3 tablespoons minced green onion

¼ cup plain nonfat Greek yogurt

3 tablespoons light mayonnaise

1½ teaspoons curry powder

1 teaspoon sugar

8 slices light white bread or French bread

4 leaves of green or red-leaf lettuce

¼ cup sliced almonds

1. In a medium bowl, combine the chicken, celery, carrot, raisins, and green onion, and stir.

2. In a small bowl, mix together the yogurt, mayonnaise, curry powder, and sugar, and add to the chicken mixture. Stir well to combine.

3. To assemble the sandwiches, take four slices of bread and place a lettuce leaf on each. Top each with ½ cup of chicken salad, 1 tablespoon of sliced almonds, and a remaining slice of bread.

Marlene Says: *One-half cup of the chicken salad alone topped with 1 tablespoon of sliced almonds has 185 calories, 8 grams of fat, 2 grams of fiber, and 8 grams of carbohydrate.*

NUTRITION INFORMATION PER SERVING: (1 sandwich) Calories 280 | Carbohydrate 26g (Sugars 5g) | Total Fat 9g (Sat Fat 0.5g) | Protein 26g | Fiber 6g | Cholesterol 55mg | Sodium 460mg | Food Exchanges: 2½ Lean Meat, 1½ Starch, ½ Fat | Carbohydrate Choices: 1½ | Weight Watcher Plus Point Comparison: 7

Curried Chicken Salad in Warm Pita Pockets

FOR THIS SANDWICH, I heat the pita bread like I do tortillas. The result is warm, sumptuously soft pita that is easier to stuff and a delight to eat. If you are not going to eat this immediately, wrap it in foil.

MAKES 4 SERVINGS

1 recipe Curried Chicken Salad filling (page 137)

2 whole pita pockets

12 spinach leaves, washed and dried

¼ cup sliced almonds

1. Sprinkle each pita lightly with water, and wrap each in a paper towel. Place in the microwave and cook on high power for 30 seconds, or until the pita are warm.

2. To assemble the pita pockets, cut pitas in half, open and place 3 spinach leaves in each pocket. Spoon in ½ cup of chicken salad and top with 1 tablespoon of sliced almonds.

NUTRITION INFORMATION PER SERVING: (1 sandwich) Calories 270 | Carbohydrate 25g (Sugars 5g) | Total Fat 8g (Sat Fat 0.5g) | Protein 25g | Fiber 4g | Cholesterol 55mg | Sodium 380mg | Food Exchanges: 2½ Lean Meat, 1½ Starch, ½ Fat | Carbohydrate Choices: 1½ | Weight Watcher Plus Point Comparison: 7

Curried Chicken Salad Wraps

THIS WRAP-STYLE SANDWICH is perfect for on-the-go lunches. The iceberg lettuce adds a satisfying crunch, and the tortillas fortify the sandwich with body-slimming fiber.

MAKES 4 SERVINGS

1 recipe Curried Chicken Salad filling (page 137)

¼ cup sliced almonds

4 (8-inch) reduced-carb, high-fiber flour tortillas

1 to 1⅓ cups shredded iceberg lettuce

1. Stir the sliced almonds into the chicken salad.

2. Place ½ cup of chicken salad on each tortilla; top with approximately ¼ cup of shredded lettuce. Fold the bottom 1½ inches of the tortilla upward to cover filling, and then fold in the sides and roll up. Place a toothpick in the center of the wrap to hold it shut. Repeat procedure for remaining wraps.

NUTRITION INFORMATION PER SERVING: (1 wrap) Calories 270 | Carbohydrate 24g (Sugars 5g) | Total Fat 10g (Sat Fat 0.5g) | Protein 25g | Fiber 8g | Cholesterol 55mg | Sodium 460mg | Food Exchanges: 1½ Starch, 2½ Lean Meat, 1 Fat | Carbohydrate Choices: 1½ | Weight Watcher Plus Point Comparison: 7

Cheesy Toasty Veggie Hero

THIS ITALIAN-STYLE HERO SANDWICH could turn a meat lover into a vegetarian. Kudos to chef Rachael for suggesting and creating it with me. From the Parmesan garlic spread to the sweet and tangy roasted vegetables, you'll savor a fantastic array of textures and flavors in every creamy, cheesy, crunchy bite. Fresh mozzarella takes this hero to heroic heights, but regular sliced mozzarella will work just fine.

MAKES 2 SERVINGS

1 tablespoon light mayonnaise

1 tablespoon plain nonfat yogurt

2 teaspoons grated Parmesan cheese

¼ teaspoon garlic powder

2 French rolls

½ medium eggplant, sliced into ½-inch rounds

1 medium zucchini, sliced lengthwise

½ small red onion, sliced

1 tablespoon balsamic vinegar

2 teaspoons Italian seasoning

1 teaspoon garlic powder

Black pepper to taste

½ cup quartered artichoke hearts, drained

¼ cup roasted red peppers, drained and sliced

2 ounces fresh mozzarella, thinly sliced

1. Preheat the broiler. In a small bowl, combine the first 4 ingredients (mayonnaise through garlic powder). Set aside. Open French rolls and carefully remove about one-half of the bread from the inside top and bottom of the rolls. Spread the rolls open and place insides down on a baking sheet. Broil for 2 minutes to lightly toast the outsides. Set aside.

2. Spray a nonstick grill pan with cooking spray, and place over medium-high heat. Place the eggplant, zucchini, and onion slices onto the pan, reduce heat slightly, and grill for 3 minutes (working in batches if necessary), until the vegetables are browned and softened on the underside. Turn with tongs; brush the tops with balsamic vinegar. Sprinkle with Italian seasoning, garlic powder, and black pepper to taste. Grill for another 2 minutes, or until vegetables are tender.

3. To assemble, spread 1 tablespoon Parmesan spread on the inside top half of each roll. Pile the grilled vegetables into the hollowed bottom halves, top with artichokes and red pepper, and finish with cheese. Place sandwiches open-faced on a baking sheet (both cheese and Parmesan spread sides should be exposed), and broil for 3 minutes, or until cheese melts and Parmesan spread is warm. Remove, and press sandwiches closed. Eat while warm!

NUTRITION INFORMATION PER SERVING: (1 sandwich) Calories 315 | Carbohydrate 42g (Sugars 12g) | Total Fat 10g (Sat Fat 1g) | Protein 14g | Fiber 9g | Cholesterol 30mg | Sodium 600mg | Food Exchanges: 3 Vegetable, 1½ Starch, 1 Lean Meat, 1 Fat | Carbohydrate Choices: 2½ | Weight Watcher Plus Point Comparison: 8

Beef "Fil-A" Sandwich

IF YOU HAVE EVER EATEN A CHICK-FIL-A SANDWICH, you know that the only thing more beloved than the chicken sandwiches themselves is the sauce. This open-faced features my version of the crave-worthy sauce. Feel free to use it as a sandwich spread wherever it suits you, or for a more "chick-fillet" experience, slather it onto the Crispy, Spicy Chicken Sandwich as found in Eat What You Love.

MAKES 2 SERVINGS

1 tablespoon light mayonnaise

1 tablespoon low-fat yogurt

1 teaspoon hickory smoke barbecue sauce

1 teaspoon sugar

½ teaspoon honey

1 teaspoon prepared mustard

¼ teaspoon white vinegar

2 slices light bread

¼ cup fresh spinach leaves

2 slices tomato

4 ounces thinly sliced roast beef

1. In a small bowl, combine the first 7 ingredients (mayonnaise through vinegar).

2. To assemble the sandwich, put half the spinach leaves on each slice of bread. Top each with a tomato slice and half of the beef. Spread each sandwich with 1½ tablespoons of Fil-A-style sauce.

Marlene Says: *Deli-style roast beef tends to be high in sodium, and the amount varies greatly. Look for those marked reduced-sodium, or to reduce the sodium even further, use the No-Fail Roast Beef on page 269.*

NUTRITION INFORMATION PER SERVING: (1 sandwich) Calories 160 | Carbohydrate 16g (Sugars 6g) | Total Fat 4g (Sat Fat 1g) | Protein 4g | Fiber 2g | Cholesterol 35mg | Sodium 590mg | Food Exchanges: 4 Lean Meat, 1 Starch | Carbohydrate Choices: 1 | Weight Watcher Plus Point Comparison: 4

Southern-Style Grilled Cheese

PIMENTO CHEESE IS EVERY BIT AS SOUTHERN as fried chicken and biscuits. And in true Southern fashion, it's about as rich as it can be. I am pleased that this recipe offers it up in a drippy, creamy, oh-so-good waist-whittling grilled cheese sandwich that doesn't sacrifice its cheesy taste or creamy texture. Get a big napkin for this one—it will even have demure Southern belles rolling up their sleeves.

| MAKES 4 SERVINGS

3 tablespoons plain Greek yogurt

2 tablespoons light mayonnaise

¾ teaspoon Worcestershire sauce

¼ teaspoon onion powder

3 to 4 drops Tabasco sauce (optional)

1 cup grated reduced-fat Cheddar cheese

4 tablespoons canned pimientos, drained and chopped

8 slices sourdough bread

1. In a small bowl combine the first 4 ingredients (yogurt through onion powder), plus Tabasco, if using. Add the cheese and pimientos, stirring to combine ingredients evenly.

2. Spread ¼ cup of the cheese mixture on each of four slices of bread, and top with remaining bread.

3. Heat a medium, nonstick pan over very low heat. Spray both sides of the sandwiches with cooking spray. Heat in the pan for about 5 minutes per side, or until the bread is crispy, golden brown, and the cheese is completely melted.

Marlene Says: *This recipe makes one cup of pimento cheese, or enough for four sandwiches. Feel free to make one, two, or three instead. The pimento cheese makes a great dip or spread.*

NUTRITION INFORMATION PER SERVING: (1 sandwich) Calories 190 | Carbohydrate 24g (Sugars 0g) | Total Fat 4g (Sat Fat 2g) | Protein 13g | Fiber 1g | Cholesterol 10mg | Sodium 460mg | Food Exchanges: 1½ Starch, 2 Lean Meat | Carbohydrate Choices: 1½ | Weight Watcher Plus Point Comparison: 5

Buffalo Chicken Burger

IF YOU ARE A BUFFALO CHICKEN LOVER, you're sure to love these Buffalo burgers with a Ranch-style spread. To make your own ground chicken breast, simply cube one pound of boneless, skinless breast meat, place in the freezer for 30 minutes, and pop it into the food processor until coarsely ground. A crumble of blue cheese, sliced tomato, and red onion are also great toppers for this crazy-good burger.

MAKES 4 SERVINGS

3 tablespoons light mayonnaise

3 tablespoons plain nonfat Greek yogurt

¾ teaspoon onion powder, divided

½ teaspoon garlic salt, divided

¼ teaspoon black pepper, divided

1 pound ground chicken breast

3 tablespoons dry breadcrumbs

1 large egg white

3 tablespoons hot wing sauce (like Frank's Red Hot Buffalo Wing Sauce)

2 teaspoons butter

4 wheat hamburger buns

4 green leaf lettuce leaves

¼ cup grated carrot

1. In a small bowl, whisk together the mayonnaise, yogurt, ¼ teaspoon each of onion powder and garlic salt, and ⅛ teaspoon black pepper. Set aside.

2. In a large bowl, combine the chicken, breadcrumbs, egg white, ½ teaspoon onion powder, ¼ teaspoon garlic salt, and ⅛ teaspoon black pepper. Do not overmix. Divide mixture into four portions, and flatten to form patties.

3. Spray a large, nonstick skillet with cooking spray, and place over medium-high heat. Add the patties to the pan, and cook for 4 to 5 minutes on each side, or until almost cooked through. Add hot sauce, butter, and 2 tablespoons water to the skillet and stir (around burgers) to combine. Cover the pan, and cook over medium heat for 2 minutes. Uncover, flip the burgers, and cook until burgers are glazed with sauce.

4. Warm buns, place a lettuce leaf on the bottom of each half, add a burger, top with 1½ tablespoons of spread, and garnish with grated carrot. Cover and enjoy!

DARE TO COMPARE: The Buffalo Chicken Ranch sandwich plate served at Chili's restaurant clocks in with 1,210 calories, 54 grams of fat, and 3,970 milligrams of sodium. Fries can be found on page 232.

NUTRITION INFORMATION PER SERVING: (1 burger) Calories 270 | Carbohydrate 24g (Sugars 1g) | Total Fat 6g (Sat Fat 1g) | Protein 33g | Fiber 4g | Cholesterol 70mg | Sodium 440mg | Food Exchanges: 4 Lean Meat, 1½ Starch | Carbohydrate Choices: 1½ | Weight Watcher Plus Point Comparison: 7

Chicago-Style Hot Dogs

WHEN IT COMES TO HOT DOGS, there is none more beloved than a Chicago-style dog. My Chicago dogs come with all of the classic toppers—tomatoes, cucumbers, onions, peppers, and sweet relish—only in the form of a delicious, chopped-style topping. To minimize the sodium, I include dill weed in the topping mix. Its pickle-like flavor provides the perfect antidote for the sodium-loaded spear customarily served on the bun (but I won't tell if you add it as well).

MAKES 4 SERVINGS

Relish

²/₃ cup chopped, seeded tomatoes

¹/₃ cup peeled, seeded, and chopped cucumber

3 tablespoons diced red onion

2 tablespoons pepperoncini peppers, drained and chopped

1 teaspoon pepperoncini juice

1 tablespoon sweet pickle relish

¼ teaspoon dried dill weed

4 hot dogs, like Hebrew National 97% Fat Free Beef Franks

4 hot dog buns

4 teaspoons prepared mustard

1. To prepare relish, in a medium bowl, combine the first 7 ingredients (tomatoes through dill weed). Set aside.

2. Cook the hot dogs according to package directions.

3. Warm the buns and spread each with 1 teaspoon of the mustard. Add a hot dog and top with ¹/₃ cup relish.

DARE TO COMPARE: A typical Chicago-style fast-food hot dog clocks in with 430 calories, 20 grams of fat, 14 grams of protein, and 2,500 milligrams of sodium.

NUTRITION INFORMATION PER SERVING: (1 topped dog) Calories 165 | Carbohydrate 28g (Sugars 4g) | Total Fat 2.5g (Sat Fat 0.5g) | Protein 12g | Fiber 4g | Cholesterol 15mg | Sodium 840mg | Food Exchanges: 1½ Starch, 1½ Lean Meat, 1 Vegetable | Carbohydrate Choices: 2 | Weight Watcher Plus Points: 4

Simple Southwest Veggie Burgers

BEEF BURGERS HAVE MET THEIR MATCH! These better-for-you, great tasting, easy-to-make veggie burgers are fashioned after the most popular ones you can buy ready-made. Top these in classic burger style with lettuce, tomato, and onion, veggie style with avocado and sprouts, or go fully Southwestern style with barbecue sauce.

MAKES 8 SERVINGS

1 medium onion, finely diced

1 medium green bell pepper, finely diced

2 teaspoons chopped jarred jalapeño peppers

1 (15-ounce) can black beans, rinsed and drained

1 (15-ounce) can pinto beans, rinsed and drained

½ cup cooked instant brown rice

1 teaspoon cumin

1½ teaspoons chili powder

1 teaspoon garlic powder

½ teaspoon salt

½ cup corn niblets

1 large egg, lightly beaten

¼ cup dry breadcrumbs

8 whole wheat hamburger buns

1. Spray a medium, nonstick skillet generously with cooking spray, and place over medium-high heat. Add the onions, bell pepper, and jalapeño, and cook for 5 to 7 minutes, or until the vegetables are soft and starting to brown. Set aside to cool.

2. Place the beans and rice in medium bowl. Mash them with a potato masher, leaving about one-fourth of the beans whole. Mix in the next 7 ingredients (cumin through breadcrumbs), and then the cooked vegetables. Use your hands to shape the mixture into 8 patties, about ½ inch thick.

3. Coat a large, nonstick sauté pan with cooking spray, and place over medium heat. Add the patties and cook for 2 to 3 minutes on each side, or until lightly browned and cooked through. Serve on buns with your favorite toppings.

Marlene Says: *The patties can be cooked immediately, but will hold together better if refrigerated for about 20 minutes. To freeze, place individual patties on waxed paper and freeze until frozen, remove from waxed paper, and wrap airtight.*

NUTRITION INFORMATION PER SERVING: (1 burger) Calories 220 | Carbohydrate 43g (Sugars 3g) | Total Fat 2.5g (Sat Fat 0g) | Protein 12g | Fiber 11g | Cholesterol 25mg | Sodium 280mg | Food Exchanges: 2 Starch, 1 Vegetable, 1 Lean Meat | Carbohydrate Choices: 2½ | Weight Watcher Plus Point Comparison: 6

Bodacious "50-50" Bacon 'n Beef Burgers

IF YOU LOVE BACON, these are for you! This recipe was inspired by the burgers served at Slater's 50/50, a restaurant famous for its big, juicy burgers made with a "50/50" blend of ground bacon and beef. (Yep, they're 50% bacon.) Creating an equally bodacious burger took several attempts, but I guarantee, this big ⅓ pound burger topped with creamy barbecue sauce does the 50/50 proud! Get ready to say "WOW."

MAKES 4 SERVINGS

2 tablespoons barbecue sauce

2 tablespoons light mayonnaise

3 slices center-cut bacon, diced

½ cup minced onion

1 cup minced fresh mushrooms

3 tablespoons dry breadcrumbs

½ teaspoon black pepper

¼ teaspoon salt

½ teaspoon liquid smoke

1 large egg white

1 pound lean ground beef

4 whole grain hamburger buns (like Pepperidge Farm)

Lettuce and tomato (optional)

1. In a small bowl, whisk together the first 2 ingredients. Set aside.

2. Place a medium, nonstick skillet over medium heat, add bacon, and cook for 3 minutes, or until the bacon starts to render some fat. Add the onions and sauté until soft (bacon should be meaty, not crisp). Remove skillet from heat, and stir in next 6 ingredients (mushrooms through egg white). Add the beef, and mix gently to combine. Divide the beef mixture into 4 portions, and flatten to form patties.

3. Heat a grill or grill pan over medium-high heat. Add the patties and cook for 3 to 4 minutes on each side, or until cooked through. Warm the buns. On the bottom of each bun, place a lettuce leaf and slice of tomato, if desired, and a burger. Top with 1 tablespoon of the barbecue spread and top half of the bun.

DARE TO COMPARE: The famous bacon-packed signature burger at Slater's 50/50 also comes packed with 1,220 calories and 73 grams of fat, including an entire day's worth of saturated fat.

NUTRITION INFORMATION PER SERVING: (1 hamburger) Calories 350 | Carbohydrate 29g (Sugars 6g) | Total Fat 11g (Sat Fat 5g) | Protein 38g | Fiber 5g | Cholesterol 75mg | Sodium 460mg | Food Exchanges: 4 Lean Meat, 1½ Starch, ½ Vegetable | Carbohydrate Choices: 2 | Weight Watcher Plus Point Comparison: 9

San Francisco Patty Melt

I STILL HAVE FOND MEMORIES of the first time I tasted a Patty Melt sandwich. My mother was away, and my father, who rarely cooked, prepared them for dinner. One bite was all it took to realize that this was no ordinary sandwich; it was special. With seasoned caramelized onions, a moist flavorful burger, and melted cheese, this too is a Patty Melt to remember. (The fact that it has one third of the usual calories is a bonus!)

MAKES 4 SERVINGS

1 large onion, thinly sliced (about 3 cups)

2 tablespoons sherry

3 teaspoons Worcestershire sauce, divided

½ teaspoon dried thyme

¼ teaspoon plus pinch salt, divided

12 ounces lean ground beef

½ cup minced fresh mushrooms

3 tablespoons dry breadcrumbs

1 large egg white

½ teaspoon black pepper

4 slices reduced-fat Swiss cheese

8 slices sourdough bread (like Francisco)

4 teaspoons Dijonnaise

1. Spray a large, nonstick skillet with cooking spray, and place over medium heat. Add the onion and cook for 6 to 7 minutes, stirring occasionally, until they begin to brown. Add the sherry, 1 teaspoon Worcestershire sauce, and 2 tablespoons water. Crush in thyme with your fingers, add a pinch of salt, and cook until the onions are soft and golden brown. Set aside.

2. While the onions are cooking, in a medium bowl, mix together the ground beef, mushrooms, breadcrumbs, egg white, 2 teaspoons Worcestershire sauce, pepper, and ¼ teaspoon salt. Divide the mixture into 4 portions, and flatten to fit the size of the bread. Spray a nonstick skillet with cooking spray, and place over medium-high heat. Add the patties and cook for 2 minutes per side, or until barely cooked through. Transfer patties to the onion pan, top each with a slice of cheese, and cover.

3. Wipe out the empty skillet, spray with cooking spray, and place over medium heat. Spread 1 teaspoon Dijonnaise on each of 4 slices of bread, top with patty and ¼ of the onions. Top with remaining bread and grill each sandwich about 2 minutes per side, or until nicely browned, using additional cooking spray if necessary.

NUTRITION INFORMATION PER SERVING: (1 sandwich) Calories 350 | Carbohydrate 35g (Sugars 6g) | Total Fat 9g (Sat Fat 4.5g) | Protein 32g | Fiber 3g | Cholesterol 55mg | Sodium 680mg | Food Exchanges: 4 Lean Meat, 2 Starch, ½ Vegetable, | Carbohydrate Choices: 2½ | Weight Watcher Plus Point Comparison: 9

Side and Entrée Salad Sensations

Garden Salad with Thousand Island Dressing

Italian "House" Salad with Cheesy Italian Dressing

Three-Minute Tomato and Avocado Salad

Spectacular Steakhouse Wedge Salad with Blue Cheese Dressing

Balsamic, Beet, and Orange Salad

Crunchy Cucumbers with Creamy Fresh Dilled Ranch Dressing

Antipasto Pasta Salad

Apple Poppy Seed Slaw

Guilt-Free Watergate Salad

Superfood Fruit and Grain Salad

Sweet Potato Salad with Warm Bacon Dressing

Hand-Tossed Pizza Salad for Two

Barbecued Chicken Chopped Salad

Chicken Waldorf Salad

Seafood Louie Salad

F YOU OWN EITHER OF MY EARLIER BOOKS, *Eat What You Love* or *Eat More of What You Love*, you already know that I am a tried-and-true salad lover; I love creating them, preparing them for family and friends, and I especially love eating them! The only thing I don't love is the excess fat and calories that most prepared salads contain. Most ready-to-eat and restaurant salads tend to be light in vegetables and heavy in accoutrements such as dressing, cheese, bacon, and nuts. Moreover, since a cup of mayonnaise contains 1,440 calories, a cup of nuts 800, and a cup of cheese 500, it's not surprising that a side salad can have the calories of a meal, or that the tasty entrée salads at restaurants average 1,000 calories or more!

This chapter brings you plenty of marvelous makeovers for the salads you love, along with plenty of healthy new creations. One of my favorite makeovers is the Garden Salad with Thousand Island Dressing. For me, it's *all* about the dressing, and with only 25 calories per tablespoon, this "thousand" is perfect for spreading around. Blue cheese and bacon take center stage on the Spectacular Steakhouse Wedge with Blue Cheese Dressing. This sensational Outback Steakhouse makeover weighs in at an astoundingly slim 120 calories (instead of the usual 1,000), leaving plenty of room in your calorie budget for the rest of your meal (see page 332 for menu suggestions). Makeover magic also pays off with the Food Network celebrity chef-inspired Sweet Potato Salad with Warm Bacon Dressing. I've brought the sodium down by 50% and the fat even more!

Of my new creations, the Superfood Fruit and Grain Salad, Three-Minute Tomato and Avocado Salad, and Balsamic, Beet, and Orange Salad are three of my favorites. All are vibrant in color, chock full of vitamins and minerals, and of course, taste great!

Garden Salad with Thousand Island Dressing

AS A POPULAR TOPPING FOR SALADS AND SANDWICHES ALIKE, Thousand Island is one of America's most beloved dressings, but with over 1,000 calories a cup, it's a healthy diet killer. As a big Thousand Island lover, I am thrilled that the dressing on this salad delivers the same traditional sweet and tangy flavor, with fresh homemade creamy goodness—for a whole lot less.

MAKES 4 SERVINGS

Dressing

¼ cup light mayonnaise

¼ cup plain nonfat Greek yogurt

2 tablespoons chili sauce

2 teaspoons granulated sugar (or packet sweetener)

¼ teaspoon onion powder

⅛ teaspoon black pepper

2 tablespoons minced celery

Salad

1 bag butter lettuce, about 6 cups

1 large carrot, peeled and shredded

½ cucumber, seeded and chopped

¼ cup chopped fresh parsley

3 to 4 radishes, sliced

1. For the dressing, whisk together all of the ingredients in a small bowl (thin, if desired, by adding 1 to 2 teaspoons of water). Set aside.

2. For the salad, place the lettuce in a large bowl. Top with carrot, cucumber, parsley, and radish slices. Drizzle the dressing over the salad, toss lightly, and serve.

DARE TO COMPARE: A tablespoon of restaurant Thousand Island dressing averages 70 calories (and the average serving size is 4 tablespoons!). Each tablespoon of this dressing has just 25 calories and a mere 2 grams of fat. Feel free to smear it on your favorite burger and make it your own special sauce.

NUTRITION INFORMATION PER SERVING: (1¾ cups) Calories 90 | Carbohydrate 12g (Sugars 7g) | Total Fat 4g (Sat Fat .5g) | Protein 3g | Fiber 2g | Cholesterol 5mg | Sodium 250mg | Food Exchanges: 1 Vegetable, ½ Starch, 1 Fat | Carbohydrate Choices: 1 | Weight Watcher Plus Point Comparison: 2

Italian "House" Salad with Cheesy Italian Dressing

AS ITALIAN RESTAURATEURS KNOW, a fresh green salad is the perfect partner to a rich Italian entrée. This salad is fashioned after what most Italian restaurants call a "house" salad, a simple mixture of greens garnished with tomato and tossed with an Italian-style dressing. Creamy, cheesy Italian dressing and toothsome garbanzo beans make this simple salad super.

MAKES 4 SERVINGS

Dressing

2 tablespoons light mayonnaise

2 tablespoons grated Parmesan cheese

1 tablespoon olive oil

1½ teaspoons Dijon mustard

1 teaspoon red wine vinegar

¾ teaspoon dried oregano, crushed

¾ teaspoon minced garlic

¼ teaspoon black pepper

Salad

4 generous cups chopped romaine lettuce

2 medium Roma tomatoes, chopped

½ cup garbanzo beans, drained and rinsed

¼ cup thinly sliced red onion

1. For the dressing, place the ingredients plus 2 tablespoons water in a medium bowl or lidded container. Whisk, or cover and shake well, to combine.

2. For the salad, place the romaine, tomatoes, garbanzos, and onions in a large bowl. Pour on the dressing and toss lightly to coat.

Marlene Says *Love the dressing? Feel free to toss it with pasta or a favorite salad mix. A 2-tablespoon serving has just 50 calories.*

NUTRITION INFORMATION PER SERVING: (1½ cups) Calories 105 | Carbohydrate 10g (Sugars 2g) | Total Fat 6g (Sat Fat 1.5g) | Protein 5g | Fiber 3g | Cholesterol 5mg | Sodium 180mg | Food Exchanges: 1 Vegetable, 1 Fat, ¼ Starch | Carbohydrate Choices: 1 | Weight Watcher Plus Point Comparison: 2

Three-Minute Tomato and Avocado Salad

THIS IS MY NEW FAVORITE ACCOMPANIMENT to any Mexican meal. Cool, crunchy, creamy, and slightly sweet, it's the perfect last-minute side, garnish, or topper. Don't be tempted to toss it like a traditional mixed salad; after trying it both ways, drizzling the dressing over the vibrantly colored tomato-avocado mix is essential to keep it looking fresh. Any Day Chicken Enchiladas (page 248) and Chipotle Beef Barbacoa (page 206) are perfect plate partners.

MAKES 4 SERVINGS

Dressing

Juice of 1 lime

1 tablespoon rice vinegar

1½ teaspoons granulated sugar

1 teaspoon olive oil

Pinch salt

Salad

3 cups shredded iceberg lettuce

2 cups chopped tomatoes

¾ cup chopped avocado (about 1 small avocado)

¼ cup chopped green onions, green and white parts

2 tablespoons chopped cilantro

1. For the dressing, whisk together all the ingredients in a small bowl. Set aside.

2. For the salad, place the lettuce on a large platter. Arrange tomatoes and avocado over the lettuce. Sprinkle with green onions and chopped cilantro. Drizzle the dressing over the salad and serve.

Marlene Says: *Creamy avocados not only deliver amazing flavor, but they are also one of the few fruits that are a good source of the heart-healthy monounsaturated fats. Also low in carbs, one-fifth of an avocado provides nearly 20 essential vitamins and minerals.*

NUTRITION INFORMATION PER SERVING: (1½ cups) Calories 90 | Carbohydrate 10g (Sugars 6g) | Total Fat 6g (Sat Fat 1g) | Protein 2g | Fiber 3g | Cholesterol 0mg | Sodium 15mg | Food Exchanges: 1 Vegetable, 1 Fat | Carbohydrate Choices: ½ | Weight Watcher Plus Point Comparison: 3

Spectacular Steakhouse Wedge Salad with Blue Cheese Dressing

THE STEAKHOUSE WEDGE SERVED AT OUTBACK STEAKHOUSE inspired this dazzling salad. A cool, crispy wedge of iceberg lettuce is topped with creamy blue cheese dressing, loaded with diced tomatoes, red onion, and smoky bacon bits, and then drizzled with a sweet balsamic glaze. A resounding hit among all who have tasted it, I think you will find the salad—and the amazingly slim nutrition stats—spectacular.

MAKES 4 SERVINGS

Dressing and Drizzle

¼ cup low-fat buttermilk

2 tablespoons light mayonnaise

2 tablespoons plain nonfat Greek yogurt

4 tablespoons crumbled blue cheese

1½ teaspoons white wine vinegar

¼ teaspoon black pepper

¼ cup balsamic vinegar

2 teaspoons brown sugar

Salad

1 medium head iceberg lettuce

1 cup chopped tomatoes

¼ cup medium diced red onion

8 teaspoons real bacon bits

1. To make the blue cheese dressing, whisk the first 6 ingredients together in a small bowl (buttermilk through pepper). To make the balsamic drizzle, stir the vinegar and brown sugar together in a small pot, and simmer over medium heat for 4 to 6 minutes, or until thick and syrupy and reduced by one-half (watch carefully near the end of cooking—once reduced, the syrup can quickly burn). Remove from heat. Set aside.

2. Cut the head of lettuce into quarters lengthwise, and cut the core out of each wedge. Place wedges on plates, remove a small amount of lettuce to make a slightly rounded well, and pour 3 tablespoons of dressing over each wedge. Top with ¼ cup tomatoes and 1 tablespoon diced onion. Sprinkle 2 teaspoons of bacon bits across each salad, and finish by drizzling 2 teaspoons of the balsamic syrup back and forth across the salad (if the balsamic drizzle has gotten too thick, add a small amount of water and/or re-warm).

DARE TO COMPARE: In a Tuft's University study of restaurant nutrition accuracy, the classic blue cheese wedge side salad served at Outback Steakhouse had 1,035 calories (not the 396 that was listed). In fact, 20 percent of all foods tested, had at least 100 calories more than reported by restaurants.

NUTRITION INFORMATION PER SERVING: (1 wedge) Calories 120 | Carbohydrate 13g (Sugars 10g) | Total Fat 5g (Sat Fat 2.5g) | Protein 7g | Fiber 2g | Cholesterol 10mg | Sodium 370mg | Food Exchanges: 1½ Vegetable, 1 Fat | Carbohydrate Choices: 1 | Weight Watcher Plus Point Comparison: 3

Balsamic, Beet, and Orange Salad

BEETS ARE BACK! Considered an old-fashioned vegetable by some, beets have newfound popularity as they star in sensational eye-popping salads. And while fresh beets are fantastic, this easy salad proves that canned can be just as delicious—and they come with the bonus of no messy peeling! Paired with sunny oranges, tangy feta cheese, and nutrient-rich spinach, this salad offers a restaurant-level presentation in both color and taste. (P.S.—Fresh beets already prepped for you as found in some markets are excellent.)

MAKES 4 SERVINGS

Dressing

3 tablespoons orange juice

3 tablespoons balsamic vinegar

1 tablespoon plus 1 teaspoon olive oil

2 teaspoons Dijon mustard

1½ teaspoons orange zest (zest entire orange)

Black pepper to taste

Salad

4 cups fresh spinach leaves

1 (15-ounce) can whole beets, drained and quartered

1 medium orange, peeled, sectioned, sections cut in half

¼ cup crumbled reduced-fat feta cheese

Orange zest, for garnish

1. For the dressing, whisk together all the ingredients in a small bowl. Set aside.

2. In a medium bowl, combine the spinach with ¼ cup of dressing and gently toss. Transfer to a serving platter. In the same bowl, gently toss the beets and oranges with 2 tablespoons of dressing. Arrange the dressed beets and oranges on top of spinach.

3. Drizzle the remaining 2 tablespoons of dressing over the salad. Top with feta and remaining orange zest, if desired.

Marlene Says: *The pigments that give beets their dark purple color are packed with heart-healthy antioxidants. Convenient, cost-effective canned beets retain their nutrients for up to two years, so stock up next time they are on sale. Rinsing canned beets removes 40% of the sodium.*

NUTRITION INFORMATION PER SERVING: (1⅓ cups) Calories 115 | Carbohydrate 13g (Sugars 9g) | Total Fat 6g (Sat Fat 1.5g) | Protein 5g | Fiber 3g | Cholesterol 10mg | Sodium 340mg | Food Exchanges: 1 Vegetable, ½ Fruit, ½ Lean Meat | Carbohydrate Choices: 1 | Weight Watcher Plus Point Comparison: 3

Crunchy Cucumbers with Fresh Dilled Ranch Dressing

COOL, CREAMY, AND EXTREMELY VERSATILE, this salad pairs well with just about any entrée—from burgers and steak, to chicken and fish. For the prettiest presentation, use a carrot peeler to remove 3 to 4 lengthwise strips of cucumber peel, leaving thin green stripes of peel remaining, before slicing the cucumbers. To make Basic Ranch Dressing, instead of the dilled version, see below.

MAKES 6 SERVINGS

Dressing

¼ cup low-fat buttermilk

2 tablespoons light mayonnaise

2 tablespoons plain Greek yogurt

1½ teaspoons finely chopped fresh dill

1½ teaspoons finely chopped fresh parsley (or ½ dried)

1 teaspoon minced green onion

¼ teaspoon garlic powder

⅛ teaspoon salt

⅛ teaspoon black pepper

Salad

3 cups cucumber slices, about ⅛ inch (about 1 pound)

½ cup thinly sliced red onion (optional)

1. For the dressing, whisk together all the ingredients in a medium bowl. Set aside if using immediately, or cover and refrigerate. (Best used within 1 to 2 days.)

2. Within 30 minutes to 2 hours of serving, add the cucumbers, and red onion, if desired, and toss gently to coat. Place in the refrigerator to chill.

Marlene Says: *To make BASIC RANCH DRESSING, in a small bowl, combine the dressing ingredients, omitting the dill and green onions. Add ¼ teaspoon of onion powder. Thin with a teaspoon or two of water to reach desired consistency.*

NUTRITION INFORMATION PER SERVING: (½ cup) Calories 25 | Carbohydrate 2g (Sugars 2g) | Total Fat 1.5g (Sat Fat 0g) | Protein 1g | Fiber 0g | Cholesterol 0mg | Sodium 100mg | Food Exchanges: ½ Vegetable | Carbohydrate Choices: 0 | Weight Watcher Plus Point Comparison: 1

Antipasto Pasta Salad

BRIMMING WITH THE INGREDIENTS AND FLAVORS of an Italian antipasto platter, this hearty yet healthy crowd-pleasing pasta salad is perfect for summer entertaining. Pack it up and tote it to your next barbecue or picnic, or enjoy it with a whole grain roll as a light meal. Prepare it the same day you plan to serve it to ensure the best texture and visual appeal. Buon appetito!

MAKES 8 SERVINGS

Dressing

¼ cup white wine vinegar

3 tablespoons olive oil

1 teaspoon Dijon mustard

1 teaspoon dried oregano

1 teaspoon minced garlic

⅛ teaspoon black pepper or to taste

Pinch of salt, or to taste

Salad

2 cups dry penne pasta

2 cups sliced fresh mushrooms

1 (8-ounce) package frozen artichoke hearts, thawed and quartered

4 slices reduced-fat provolone cheese

2 ounces light Italian salami

½ cup roasted red peppers, drained and sliced

⅓ cup packed fresh basil leaves

1. In a small bowl, whisk together the first 7 ingredients (vinegar through salt). Cook the pasta according to the package directions, drain, rinse, place in a large bowl, and set aside.

2. Place the mushrooms in a medium, microwave-safe bowl, and cover with plastic wrap. Cook on high for 1½ minutes, or until mushrooms begin to soften. Uncover and pour off any liquid. Add the artichoke hearts to the mushrooms, and toss with 2 tablespoons of the dressing. Set aside.

3. Stack the provolone slices and cut like a pizza into eighths. Stack the salami slices and cut into quarters. Separate the provolone and salami pieces and add to the pasta, along with the red peppers.

4. Stack the basil leaves, roll them up, and slice into very thin strips. Top the pasta salad with the basil, marinated mushrooms, and artichokes. Quickly whisk the dressing, add to the salad, and toss. Garnish with additional fresh basil if desired.

NUTRITION INFORMATION PER SERVING: (about 1 cup) Calories 210 | Carbohydrate 25g (Sugars 1g) | Total Fat 9g (Sat Fat 2.5g) | Protein 11g | Fiber 4g | Cholesterol 15mg | Sodium 330mg | Food Exchanges: 1 Starch, 1 Vegetable, 1 Lean Meat, 1 Fat | Carbohydrate Choices: 1½ | Weight Watcher Plus Point Comparison: 6

Apple Poppy Seed Slaw

I ABSOLUTELY LOVE SUMMER, and crisp cool slaws are indispensable to my warm weather menus. Granny smith apples add natural sweetness to a mix of green cabbage, celery, and green onions in this creamy slaw. I love the appearance of the all-green mix, but you also swap in red apples or purple cabbage for more color. Either way, you'll get a healthy serving of fruit and vegetables in every sweet and tangy bite.

MAKES 8 SERVINGS

Dressing

6 tablespoons light mayonnaise

⅓ cup plain nonfat Greek yogurt

2 tablespoons granulated sugar (or 3 packets)

1 tablespoon white wine vinegar

1 teaspoon poppy seeds

¼ teaspoon salt

Salad

2 cups chopped green apples (about 2 apples with peel)

Juice of 1 medium lemon

5 cups shredded green cabbage

2 stalks celery, thinly sliced

2 medium green onions, thinly sliced

1. For the dressing, whisk together all of the dressing ingredients in a small bowl.

2. For the slaw, in a large bowl, place the apples and lemon juice, and toss to combine. Add the cabbage, celery, and green onions. Pour dressing over the salad and toss.

NUTRITION INFORMATION PER SERVING: (¾ cup) Calories 75 | Carbohydrate 12g (Sugars 9g) | Total Fat 3g (Sat Fat 0g) | Protein 2g | Fiber 2g | Cholesterol 0mg | Sodium 190mg | Food Exchanges: 2 Vegetable, ½ Starch, ½ Fat | Carbohydrate Choices: 1 | Weight Watcher Plus Point Comparison: 2

Guilt-Free Watergate Salad

THIS SPECIAL OCCASION SALAD became popular in the 1970s when the Watergate scandal was front page news. With so many goodies on most holiday tables, it's good to know you have a dish that tastes so yummy, yet can keep your conscious guilt-free. If marshmallows are a must for you, go ahead and add them. My suggestion would be to add half the normal amount (or 1 cup) to keep this light.

MAKES 8 SERVINGS

1 (20-ounce) can crushed pineapple, packed in unsweetened juice, drained with juice reserved

1 (4 serving–size) package sugar-free instant pistachio pudding mix

⅛ teaspoon almond extract (optional)

1 cup low-fat cottage cheese

1½ cups light whipped topping

3 tablespoons sliced almonds

1. In a large bowl, place the pineapple and 2 tablespoons of reserved juice. Stir the pudding mix into the pineapple until dissolved. Stir in optional almond extract and set aside.

2. Place the cottage cheese in a small food processor and process until smooth, or put it in a deep bowl to use an immersion blender. Stir into the pudding mixture. Gently fold in the whipped topping. Refrigerate for 1 hour or more.

3. When ready to serve, top with sliced almonds.

NUTRITION INFORMATION PER SERVING: (½ cup) Calories 100 | Carbohydrate 13 g (Sugars 10g) | Total Fat 3g (Sat Fat 2g) | Protein 5g | Fiber 1g | Cholesterol 10mg | Sodium 180mg | Food Exchanges: ½ Starch, ½ Fruit, ½ Protein | Carbohydrate Choices: 1 | Weight Watcher Plus Point Comparison: 2

Superfood Fruit and Grain Salad

WHILE I OFTEN FIND THE MADE-UP TERM "SUPERFOOD" OVERUSED, for this salad, the term definitely applies! Packed with super foods, including vitamin- and protein-packed quinoa, antioxidant-rich blueberries, and heart healthy avocado, this colorful salad serves up super nutrition—with super taste! No quinoa? No problem. It's also super when made with brown rice. (P.S.—But even quinoa haters love this salad.)

MAKES 4 SERVINGS

⅓ cup uncooked quinoa (or ½ cup instant brown rice)

2 tablespoons fresh orange juice

1 tablespoon fresh lime juice

1 teaspoon orange zest

½ teaspoon honey or sugar

Salt to taste

½ cup diced mango

¼ cup diced avocado

¼ cup diced tomato

¼ cup diced red bell pepper

2 tablespoons finely chopped green onion

½ cup blueberries

2 tablespoons chopped cilantro

Ground black pepper to taste

1. Place the quinoa in a strainer, rinse well, and prepare according to package directions (if using brown rice, prepare according to directions). When cooked, transfer to a medium bowl to cool.

2. In a small bowl, combine the orange and lime juices, zest, honey or sugar, and salt, stirring well to dissolve ingredients.

3. When the quinoa or rice is close to room temperature, or cooler, add the next 5 ingredients (mango through green onion), pour in the dressing, and toss to combine. Gently fold in the blueberries and cilantro, and add ground pepper and salt to taste. (If using brown rice, dress within 1 hour of serving.)

Marlene Says: *This nutrient-packed salad is perfect for a picnic. If you want to make it even more "super," top it with toasted walnuts for an extra punch of protein, heart healthy fats, and antioxidants.*

NUTRITION INFORMATION PER SERVING: (½ cup) Calories 125 | Carbohydrate 22g (Sugars 7g) | Total Fat 4g (Sat Fat 1g) | Protein 4g | Fiber 3g | Cholesterol 0mg | Sodium 20mg | Food Exchanges: 1 Starch, ½ Fruit, ½ Fat | Carbohydrate Choices: 1½ | Weight Watcher Plus Point Comparison: 4

Sweet Potato Salad with Warm Bacon Dressing

LOOKING FOR A NEW POTATO SALAD RECIPE that is sure to impress? Look no further. This recipe comes by way of a famous Food Network chef, only my version boasts less than half the calories, 75% less fat, and even more flavor. Reducing the oil while simultaneously adding caramelized onions and a touch of liquid smoke did the trick to place this roasted potato salad in prize-winning contention with all my testers.

MAKES 8 SERVINGS

2 pounds sweet potatoes, peeled and cut into 1 ½-inch chunks

Dressing

4 slices center-cut bacon

1 large red onion, chopped (1 ½ to 2 cups)

2 garlic cloves, minced

¼ cup cider vinegar

1 tablespoon olive oil

2 tablespoons brown sugar

⅛ teaspoon liquid smoke

⅛ teaspoon salt

⅛ teaspoon pepper

¼ chopped green onion tops (green part only, about 3 onions) for garnish

1. Preheat the oven to 425°F. Spray a baking sheet with cooking spray. Place sweet potatoes on the pan, and spray lightly with cooking spray. Bake for 15 minutes, spray again, stir, and bake another 10 to 15 minutes, or until soft when pierced with a fork.

2. While the sweet potatoes bake, in a medium skillet, cook the bacon until crisp. Transfer bacon to a paper-towel-lined plate, crumble, and set aside. Discard all but 1 tablespoon of the bacon drippings. Add the onion to the pan. Cook onion for 10 minutes, or until softened and lightly caramelized. Add garlic and cook for 1 minute. Add 2 tablespoons water and next 6 ingredients (vinegar through black pepper), and stir, scraping the pan to incorporate drippings. Bring to a low boil, and remove from heat.

3. Place the roasted sweet potatoes in a large bowl. Pour the hot dressing over the potatoes, and lightly toss to coat. Sprinkle with reserved bacon and green onion tops. Serve warm or at room temperature.

Marlene Says: *To make ROASTED GERMAN POTATO SALAD, swap unpeeled red potatoes for sweet potatoes, and reduce onions to 1 cup. When the onions have cooked for 5 minutes, add 2 cups sliced mushrooms to the skillet, and cook until the mushrooms are soft and onions lightly caramelized (about 5 minutes). Proceed as directed in step 3. (Subtract 15 calories and 4 grams of carbohydrates.)*

NUTRITION INFORMATION PER SERVING: (about ⅔ cup) Calories 160 | Carbohydrate 30g (Sugars 16g) | Total Fat 3.5g (Sat Fat 1g) | Protein 3g | Fiber 4g | Cholesterol 5mg | Sodium 55mg | Food Exchanges: 1½ Starch, 1 Vegetable, ½ Fat | Carbohydrate Choices: 2 | Weight Watcher Plus Point Comparison: 4

Hand-Tossed Pizza Salad for Two

MY HUSBAND CLAIMS THAT THE BEST WAY TO TOSS A SALAD is with your hands. Yep, dressing and all. Of course you are welcome to use whatever "utensils," natural or otherwise, that suit you best when tossing this delicious blend of fresh romaine lettuce, traditional pizza toppings, and zesty tomato dressing. Feel free to add a handful of one or more of your own favorite pizza toppers; sliced green or red peppers and mushrooms, thinly sliced red onion, and black olives all come to mind.

MAKES 2 SERVINGS

Dressing

1 tablespoon tomato paste

2 tablespoons balsamic vinegar

1 tablespoon olive oil

½ teaspoon garlic powder

½ teaspoon dried oregano

½ teaspoon granulated sugar

Salt and pepper to taste

Salad

4 generous cups chopped romaine lettuce

16 slices turkey pepperoni

⅓ cup shredded part-skim mozzarella cheese

¾ cup halved cherry tomatoes

2 tablespoons fresh chopped basil (optional)

¼ cup croutons

2 tablespoons fresh grated Parmesan

1. In a small bowl, whisk the tomato paste with 2 tablespoons water until smooth. Whisk in remaining dressing ingredients and add salt and pepper to taste. Thin with 1 to 2 teaspoons more water if desired. Set aside.

2. Place the lettuce in a large bowl. Cut 10 of the pepperoni slices in half and add to the bowl. Sprinkle in the mozzarella, tomatoes, and fresh basil, if desired. Pour the dressing over the salad, and toss lightly until coated. Divide salad onto two plates. Top with remaining pepperoni, croutons and Parmesan.

NUTRITION INFORMATION PER SERVING: (1 salad) Calories 240 | Carbohydrate 13g (Sugar 4g) | Total Fat 13g (Sat Fat 4g) | Protein 16g | Fiber 3g | Cholesterol 5mg | Sodium 580mg | Food Exchanges: 2 Vegetable, 2 Lean Meat, 1½ Fat | Carbohydrate Choices: 1 | Weight Watcher Plus Point Comparison: 7

Barbecued Chicken Chopped Salad

SINCE 1985, THE ORIGINAL BBQ CHICKEN CHOPPED HAS REIGNED as California Pizza Kitchen's most popular salad. With this filling homemade version you still get the ingredients that made it famous—including juicy barbecue-sauced chicken, corn, black beans, and cheese, along with creamy Ranch-style dressing —for less than one-third of the original calorie price. For extra crunch, garnish it with a few low-fat tortilla chips.

MAKES 4 SERVINGS

1 recipe Basic Ranch Dressing (page 159), or ½ cup bottled low-fat ranch dressing

8 cups chopped romaine lettuce

2 cups chopped tomato

1 cup chopped jicama

¾ cup canned black beans, drained and rinsed

½ cup corn niblets

½ cup shredded reduced-fat mozzarella cheese

4 boneless, skinless chicken breasts, about 1 pound

¼ cup barbecue sauce

¼ cup chopped green onions

¼ cup cilantro

1. Prepare the dressing (as found in the Marlene Says section) according to recipe directions. Refrigerate until ready for use.

2. Place 2 cups of lettuce onto each of 4 large plates. Top the lettuce with equal amounts of tomatoes, jicama, black beans, and corn. Sprinkle cheese around the outside edges and set aside.

3. Spray a large, nonstick skillet with cooking spray, and place over medium heat. Pound chicken to ¼-inch thickness and add to the skillet. Cook for 3 to 4 minutes, or until underside is brown. Turn the breasts, and top each with 1 tablespoon barbecue sauce. Continue to cook 3 minutes longer, or until the chicken is cooked through. Transfer the breasts to a cutting board, slice each into ¼ inch slices, turn, and cut again into cubes. Transfer the chicken onto the salads.

4. Top chicken with green onions and cilantro, and drizzle 2 tablespoons of ranch dressing onto the surrounding greens.

DARE TO COMPARE: The Original CPK Barbecue Chicken Chopped salad has 1,133 calories, including an entire day's worth of fat and the equivalent of 6½ carbohydrate servings. The half salad has 590.

NUTRITION INFORMATION PER SERVING: (1 salad) Calories 325 | Carbohydrate 29g (Sugars 11g) | Total Fat 8g (Sat Fat 2g) | Protein 35g | Fiber 8g | Cholesterol 80mg | Sodium 520mg | Food Exchanges: 4½ Lean Meat, 2 Vegetables, 1 Starch | Carbohydrate Choices: 1½ | Weight Watcher Plus Point Comparison: 8

Chicken Waldorf Salad

THERE'S NO BETTER COMBINATION of salad mix-ins than sweet fruit and crunchy nuts, but this isn't new news. With its mixture of apples and walnuts, the classic Waldorf salad, as originated at the Waldorf Hotel in New York City, has been around for over 100 years. The traditional salad uses a creamy sweet mayonnaise-based dressing. I have kept the tradition but updated it with balsamic vinegar, with delicious results.

MAKES 2 SERVINGS

Dressing

2 tablespoons light mayonnaise

2 tablespoons balsamic vinegar

1½ teaspoons Dijon mustard

1 garlic clove, minced

2 teaspoons olive oil

1 teaspoon granulated sugar

¼ teaspoon salt

¼ teaspoon black pepper

Salad

4 cups bagged Mesclun salad mix

½ cup diced celery

1 cup cubed cooked chicken breast

1 small apple, cored and chopped

½ cup red grape halves

3 tablespoons chopped walnuts

2 tablespoons crumbled Gorgonzola, or other blue cheese

1. For the dressing, in a measuring cup or small bowl, whisk the mayonnaise with 2 tablespoons water until smooth. Whisk in remaining ingredients and set aside.

2. To assemble the salad, place salad greens and celery in a medium bowl. Pour 2 tablespoons dressing over the greens, and toss lightly to coat evenly. Divide the salad between two plates. Place half of the chicken in the center of each salad, and divide the apple on the greens around the chicken. Top the salads with the grapes, walnuts, and Gorgonzola, and drizzle the remaining dressing over the salads.

DARE TO COMPARE: California Pizza Kitchen is known as much for their salads as their pizzas. Less well known is that their Waldorf Chicken Salad—with 1,290 calories and over 80 grams of fat—outweighs nearly every original crust pizza in both fat and calories.

NUTRITION INFORMATION PER SERVING: (1 salad) Calories 330 | Carbohydrate 25g (Sugars 17g) | Total Fat 16g (Sat Fat 2.5g) | Protein 25g | Fiber 4g | Cholesterol 65mg | Sodium 770mg | Food Exchanges: 3 Lean Meat, 1 Fruit, 1 Vegetable, 1 Fat | Carbohydrate Choices: 1½ | Weight Watcher Plus Point Comparison: 9

Seafood Louie Salad

I LOVE LOUIE-STYLE SEAFOOD SALADS. Unfortunately, ordering one at a seafood restaurant usually means paying a premium price for a salad weighed down with calorie-laden dressing. This salad makes enjoying a Louie salad a whole lot easier on the wallet—and the waistline. Creamy, healthy avocado is included, along with the customary hard-cooked egg and Thousand Island dressing. Feel free to vary your seafood toppers. Top-quality jumbo lump crab is always a treat.

MAKES 2 SERVINGS

4 cups romaine lettuce, chopped

1 (6-ounce) can lump crab, drained

4 ounces medium cooked shrimp

2 Roma tomatoes, quartered lengthwise

1 large hard-cooked egg, quartered lengthwise

½ medium avocado, sliced

6 tablespoons Thousand Island dressing (see page 153)

2 lemon wedges

Chopped fresh parsley

1. For the salad, divide the lettuce between two plates. For each salad, pile ⅓ cup crab and ⅔ cup shrimp on the center of the lettuce. Arrange 4 tomato quarters around the plate, and top the lettuce with 2 egg quarters and ½ of the avocado slices.

2. Spoon 3 tablespoons of dressing over the salad, and garnish with a lemon wedge and chopped parsley.

DARE TO COMPARE: You would need to walk for over 3 hours to burn off the 700 calories in a typical restaurant crab and shrimp Louie salad. The major calorie culprit is the Thousand Island dressing.

NUTRITION INFORMATION PER SERVING: (1 salad) Calories 300 | Carbohydrate 14g (Sugars 7g) | Total Fat 13g (Sat Fat 2.5g) | Protein 33g | Fiber 4g | Cholesterol 280mg | Sodium 600mg | Food Exchanges: 4½ Lean Meat, 1 Vegetable, 1 Starch, 2 Fat | Carbohydrate Choices: 1 | Weight Watcher Plus Point Comparison: 8

Easy Any Day
Pastas and Pizzas

Pasta with Chicken and Fresh Pomodoro Sauce

Chicken Enchilada Pasta Skillet

Better-for-You Three Cheese Baked Ziti

Stacked Macaroni and Cheese

Chicken Cheddar Bacon Ranch Mac 'n Cheese

Creamy Weeknight Spaghetti

American Chop Suey

Sneaky Stuffed Shells

Pasta Carbonara

Panda-Style Chicken Chow Mein

Lemony Shrimp and Spinach Fettuccine in Cream Sauce

Easy All-Purpose Marinara

Light and Luscious All-Purpose Alfredo Sauce

Linguine with Red Clam Sauce for Two

Individual Mexican Pizza(s)

Chicken Alfredo Pizza

WHEN IT COMES TO FOOD PASSIONS, it's common to hear people name chocolate, wine, or even cheese. My passion is pasta, and you are likely to find it on my table any day of the week. According to the National Pasta Association, I'm not alone; Americans eat over 6 billion pounds of pasta each year!

Yet for all the pasta we eat, pasta often gets a bad rap. The truth is, pasta is a good source of protein, B vitamins, and minerals, and when served up right, it's moderate in calories. Moreover, with all the wonderful pastas on the market today, including whole grain blends, gluten-free pastas, and those that are higher in fiber, there's a perfect pasta for everyone, and every body.

My easy, any day pastas have the same glorious creamy, cheesy, smoky, and spicy elements of crave-worthy pasta dishes. Ranging from a healthy home-baked favorite like Better-for-You Three Cheese Baked Ziti, or a stovetop wonder like my Chicken Enchilada Pasta Skillet, to what may be the ultimate comfort food, Chicken Cheddar Bacon Ranch Mac 'n Cheese, you'll find them all, amazingly, with less than 350 calories per serving! You'll also save time, money, and oodles of calories when you enjoy restaurant-style pasta dishes at home. I'm delighted to say that I've cracked the code to creating a slim but sinfully tasty Pasta Carbonara, and my spin on Applebee's popular Lemony Shrimp and Spinach Fettuccine in Cream Sauce (with 90% less sodium!) is sure to please.

And if you are looking to create your own healthy pasta sensations, I'm here to help. Pair the quick-fix Light and Luscious All-Purpose Alfredo Sauce with your preferred pasta shape, add a lean protein and veggies (see the Marlene Says on page 244), and dinner is on the table. Oh, and be sure to use the leftover sauce to make an irresistible Chicken Alfredo Pizza. I could eat that *every* day!

Pasta with Chicken and Fresh Pomodoro Sauce

BELIEVE IT OR NOT, EVEN A HEALTHY-SOUNDING PASTA entrée like Pasta Pomodoro (pasta with fresh tomatoes, olive, and garlic), can have over 1,000 calories when ordered out. The secret to creating this simple, but wonderfully fragrant pasta entrée, is fresh ingredients and very little cooking time—just 2 minutes for the sauce. To make Caprese Pomodoro, add 8 ounces of bite-sized fresh mozzarella pieces with the basil in lieu of the chicken. Garnish either dish with additional fresh basil.

MAKES 4 SERVINGS

6 ounces dry spaghetti

4 teaspoons olive oil, divided

4 garlic cloves, thinly sliced

12 ounces boneless, skinless chicken breast, sliced very thin

2 cups cherry tomatoes, halved

2 tablespoons sweet vermouth (or chicken broth)

1 tablespoon balsamic vinegar

¼ teaspoon salt

½ cup fresh basil, leaves stacked, rolled, and thinly sliced

¼ cup shredded Parmesan cheese

Black pepper to taste

1. Cook the pasta according to the package directions (because the sauce goes so quickly, be sure to start the pasta first). Drain, place in serving bowl, and cover. (Tip: Use the hot pasta water to warm the bowl before adding the pasta to it.)

2. While pasta is cooking, heat 2 teaspoons oil in a large, nonstick skillet over medium heat. Add the garlic and sauté about 30 to 45 seconds, or until lightly browned. Add the chicken and cook for 3 to 4 minutes, or until browned on the underside. Turn the chicken, and cook 1 more minute, or until just cooked through.

3. Stir in the tomatoes, vermouth, vinegar, and salt, and cook for 2 minutes. Pour the mixture over the pasta and toss. Add the basil, Parmesan, and remaining olive oil, and toss again lightly to evenly coat the pasta. Season with pepper to taste and serve immediately.

DARE TO COMPARE: The Tomato Basil Spaghettini entrée with fresh tomato sauce and chicken at California Pizza Kitchen serves up 1,200 calories, 125 grams of carbs, and 58 grams of fat.

NUTRITION INFORMATION PER SERVING: (1½ cups) Calories 320 | Carbohydrate 38g (Sugars 4g) | Total Fat 9g (Sat Fat 2g) | Protein 27g | Fiber 6g | Cholesterol 60mg | Sodium 390mg | Food Exchanges: 3 Lean Meat, 2 Starch, 1 Vegetable, 1 Fat | Carbohydrate Choices: 2½ | Weight Watcher Plus Point Comparison: 8

Chicken Enchilada Pasta Skillet

THIS PASTA DISH IS FUSION CUISINE at its best. Tender chicken and a zesty, tomato-rich, homemade enchilada sauce mingle with melted cheese and perfectly cooked pasta. You're sure to be putting this one on your dinner menu often when you see how quickly it comes together and how delicious a Mexican-Italian combination can be. Family-friendly? You bet!

MAKES 4 SERVINGS

1½ cups dry penne pasta

1 medium onion, chopped

1 medium red bell pepper, chopped

2 garlic cloves, minced

1½ tablespoons chili powder

1 teaspoon ground cumin

1 teaspoon sugar

¼ teaspoon dried oregano

⅛ teaspoon salt, or to taste

1 (8-ounce) can tomato sauce

2 cups shredded cooked chicken breast

½ cup reduced-fat Cheddar cheese

2 tablespoons cilantro, minced for garnish

1. While preparing the sauce, cook the pasta according to the package directions. Drain the pasta and set aside.

2. Spray a large, nonstick skillet with cooking spray, and place over medium-high heat. Add the onion and bell pepper and sauté for 3 to 4 minutes, or until slightly softened. Push the vegetables to one side of the skillet, and reduce heat to medium. On the empty side of the skillet, add the garlic, chili powder, cumin, sugar, oregano, and salt, and stir until fragrant, about 30 seconds. Pour the tomato sauce and 1 cup of water over the spice mixture, stir well, and simmer 2 minutes to blend the spices into the sauce. Stir to mix the onions and pepper with the sauce, cover, and simmer another 5 minutes.

3. Add the chicken to the sauce, and stir to coat. Add the pasta and toss to combine. Reduce the heat to low, sprinkle on the cheese, and cover for 1 minute. Remove from heat and garnish with cilantro.

Marlene Says: *A dollop of light sour cream and black olives are great as additional garnishes for this dish.*

NUTRITION INFORMATION PER SERVING: (1½ cups) Calories 250 | Carbohydrate 32g (Sugars 6g) | Total Fat 3.5g (Sat Fat 0.5g) | Protein 26g | Fiber 5g | Cholesterol 55mg | Sodium 630mg | Food Exchanges: 3 Lean Meat, 1½ Starch, 1½ Vegetable | Carbohydrate Choices: 2 | Weight Watcher Plus Point Comparison: 6

Better-for-You Three Cheese Baked Ziti

MELT-Y CHEESE, PERFECTLY COOKED PASTA, and bubbling tomato sauce—who can resist eating baked ziti? Now no one has to with this better-for-you bake. Made with savory sausage, tender sauteed zucchini, and three types of cheese, the only thing missing in this hearty dish is half the calories and 75% of the usual fat. Double the recipe (or split a single recipe into two dishes) and freeze one for a fresh-from-the-freezer, no-fuss family meal.

MAKES 6 SERVINGS

8 ounces dry penne pasta

4 ounces Italian turkey sausage

1 medium onion, diced

2 large garlic cloves, minced

2 medium zucchini, sliced into rounds and quartered

1 (28-ounce) can tomato puree

2 teaspoons dried basil leaves

1 teaspoon dried oregano

¼ teaspoon salt

¾ cup low-fat ricotta cheese

1 cup shredded reduced-fat mozzarella cheese

½ cup grated Parmesan cheese.

1. Preheat the oven to 400°F. Lightly spray a 9 x 13-inch baking dish with cooking spray.

2. Cook the pasta for 1 minute less than the minimum cooking time on package directions. Drain the pasta and set aside.

3. While the pasta cooks, spray a large, nonstick skillet generously with cooking spray, and place over medium heat. Add the sausage and onions and cook for 3 to 5 minutes, breaking up the sausage into crumbles. Add the garlic and zucchini and cook for another 3 minutes, stirring frequently. Add the tomato puree, basil, oregano, and salt, and cook another 5 minutes. Remove the skillet from heat, and gently stir in the ricotta and pasta.

4. Spoon the mixture into the prepared baking dish. Sprinkle evenly with mozzarella and top with Parmesan. Bake for 20 minutes, or until the sauce is bubbly and the cheese begins to brown.

DARE TO COMPARE: If you ever grabbed a plate of pasta at the mall or airport, chances are it was at Sbarro's. You would have to walk 7 miles to burn off the 700 calories (and 40 grams of fat) in their ever-popular Baked Ziti.

NUTRITION INFORMATION PER SERVING: (1½ cups) Calories 295 | Carbohydrate 38 g (Sugars 6g) | Total Fat 9g (Sat Fat 4g) | Protein 20g | Fiber 6g | Cholesterol 40mg | Sodium 630mg | Food Exchanges: 2 Starch, 1 Vegetable, 2 Lean Meat | Carbohydrate Choices: 2½ | Weight Watcher Plus Point Comparison: 8

Stacked Macaroni and Cheese

A WHILE BACK, MY FRIEND NANCIE took me to a restaurant named Stacks whose have-it-your-way concept allows you to "stack" your dish with ingredients you enjoy best. One of the items on the menu was a macaroni and cheese entrée "stacked" with caramelized onions, rosemary, and chicken (all ingredients I love). Unfortunately, although packed with plenty calories, the dish was disappointing. This creamy, cheesy, super flavor-stacked mac 'n cheese, however, delivers all I had hoped for, and more.

MAKES 4 SERVINGS

1¾ cups dry penne pasta

1 large carrot, peeled and cut in half rounds

1 teaspoon olive oil

1 large onion, sliced into strips

8 ounces boneless, skinless chicken breast, cut into 1-inch pieces

½ teaspoon fresh rosemary, minced

Black pepper to taste

Cheese Sauce:

¾ cup low-fat evaporated milk

½ cup reduced-sodium chicken broth

1 tablespoon cornstarch

¾ teaspoon dry mustard

½ teaspoon garlic salt with parsley

1 cup reduced-fat shredded sharp Cheddar cheese, divided

1. Cook the pasta according to the package directions, adding the carrots to the pot the last 3 minutes. Drain, rinse with cool water, and set aside.

2. Heat the oil in a large, nonstick skillet over medium heat. Add the onions and sauté for 8 minutes, or until they begin to caramelize and soften, stirring occasionally. Add the chicken and cook for 2 minutes. Sprinkle in the rosemary, and cook until chicken is cooked and onions are well caramelized. Season with pepper to taste.

3. Combine the first five sauce ingredients (evaporated milk through garlic salt) in a small saucepan over medium heat, and whisk until the mixture comes to a low boil and thickens. Turn off the heat, add ¾ cup cheese, and whisk until the sauce is smooth.

4. Add the pasta to the chicken and toss to combine. Pour in the cheese sauce, stir to combine for 1 minute, or until the pasta is hot. Lightly stir in or top the dish with remaining ¼ cup cheese.

NUTRITION INFORMATION PER SERVING: (1½ cups) Calories 325 | Carbohydrate 38g (Sugars 5g) | Total Fat 9g (Sat Fat 4g) | Protein 28g | Fiber 5g | Cholesterol 60mg | Sodium 430mg | Food Exchanges: 3 Lean Meat, 2 Starch, 1 Vegetable | Carbohydrate Choices: 2½ | Weight Watcher Plus Point Comparison: 7

Chicken Cheddar Bacon Ranch Mac 'n Cheese

THIS DISH WAS ORIGINALLY SET AS A FOOTNOTED VARIATION of my Stacked Macaroni and Cheese recipe (see previous page) but after one bite, I knew it deserved a recipe of its own. Creamy, cheesy, and oh-so-smoky, this is a Cheddar bacon lover's dream. Believe me; no one will ever notice that it has less than half the calories and 75% less fat when compared to traditional Cheddar bacon mac 'n cheese recipes.

MAKES 4 SERVINGS

1¾ cups dry penne pasta (like Dreamfields)

1 large carrot, peeled and cut into coins

1 teaspoon olive oil

1 large onion, chopped

8 ounces boneless, skinless chicken breast, cut into 1-inch pieces

½ teaspoon dried dill

⅛ teaspoon black pepper

1 Cheese Sauce recipe from page 179

½ teaspoon onion powder

¼ teaspoon liquid smoke

1 tablespoon real bacon bits

¼ cup chopped green onions

1. Cook the pasta according to package directions. When the pasta has 3 minutes of cook time remaining, add the carrots to the pasta water and continue cooking. Drain and rinse with cold water. Set aside.

2. Heat the oil in a large, nonstick skillet over medium heat. Add the onions and sauté for 8 minutes, or until they begin to caramelize and soften, stirring occasionally. Toss the chicken with dill and pepper; add to the skillet. Cook for 5 to 6 minutes, or until the chicken is cooked, and onions are well caramelized.

3. While the chicken is cooking, in a small saucepan over medium heat, make the cheese sauce, using ¾ cup of cheese in the sauce as directed, adding the onion powder and liquid smoke. Add the pasta to the chicken, toss to combine, and the cheese sauce, and mix well. Garnish with the remaining ¼ cup cheese, bacon bits, and green onions.

NUTRITION INFORMATION PER SERVING: (1½ cups) Calories 320 | Carbohydrate 41g (Sugars 11g) | Total Fat 6g (Sat Fat 2.5g) | Protein 28g | Fiber 5g | Cholesterol 55mg | Sodium 550mg | Food Exchanges: 3 Lean Meat, 2½ Starch, 1 Vegetable | Carbohydrate Choices: 2½ | Weight Watcher Plus Point Comparison: 8

Creamy Weeknight Spaghetti

JARRED OR PREMADE MARINARA (see page 190 for my Easy All-Purpose Marinara), gets a quick taste and texture boost from fresh produce, lean turkey, and luscious cream cheese in this simple home-style spaghetti dish that comes together in 20 minutes. Pile it into a 9 x 13-inch dish, and it's perfect for potluck suppers. Leftovers reheat beautifully the next day for lunch. A simple green salad is the perfect accompaniment.

MAKES 6 SERVINGS

8 ounces dry spaghetti

1 teaspoon olive oil

1 small onion, chopped

1 pound lean ground turkey

1 (24 to 28-ounce) jar marinara sauce (or about 3 cups)

2 medium tomatoes, seeded and chopped

3 tablespoons light tub-style cream cheese

Chopped fresh parsley, for garnish

Parmesan cheese (optional)

1. Cook the pasta according to the package directions. Drain the pasta and set aside.

2. While pasta is cooking, heat the oil in a large, nonstick sauté pan over medium-high heat. Add onion and sauté for 2 to 3 minutes, or until softened. Add the turkey and cook, breaking up the meat, for 5 to 7 minutes, or until browned.

3. Stir in the marinara sauce and ¼ cup water, cover, and simmer for 5 minutes. Add the tomatoes and cream cheese, stirring until the cheese melts and the sauce is creamy. Add the pasta, and toss to coat well with meat sauce. Garnish with parsley, and top with Parmesan cheese, if desired.

NUTRITION INFORMATION PER SERVING: (1½ cups) Calories 310 | Carbohydrate 39g (Sugars 7g) | Total Fat 9g (Sat Fat 2.5g) | Protein 21g | Fiber 5g | Cholesterol 60mg | Sodium 450mg | Food Exchanges: 2½ Lean Meat, 2 Starch, 2 Vegetable | Carbohydrate Choices: 2½ | Weight Watcher Plus Point Comparison: 8

American Chop Suey

WHETHER YOU CALL IT GOULASH, Johnny Marzetti, or as they do in New England, American Chop Suey, this economical-yet-nourishing pasta dish has been gracing the dinner tables of American families for decades. I lighten it up with lean ground beef and extra chopped veggies cooked into a savory tomato sauce flavored with soy sauce for a bit more "chop suey" flair. Chopsticks not required.

6 ounces (about 2 cups dry) rotini pasta

1 teaspoon olive oil

3 celery stalks, chopped

1 medium yellow onion, chopped

1 large green bell pepper, chopped

1 pound lean ground beef

3 garlic cloves, minced (or 1 tablespoon)

1 (15-ounce) can diced tomatoes

1 cup reduced-sodium chicken broth

2 teaspoons cornstarch

2 tablespoons reduced-sodium soy sauce

1 teaspoon granulated sugar

1. Cook the pasta according to package directions and set aside.

2. While pasta cooks, heat the oil in a large, nonstick skillet over medium-high heat. Add the celery, and cook for 1 minute. Add the onion and bell pepper and cook 3 to 4 minutes, until slightly softened but still crisp-tender. Remove from pan and set aside.

3. Return the skillet to the heat, add ground beef, and cook for 5 minutes, or until barely browned (the meat will continue to cook). Add garlic and cook for 1 minute. Stir in tomatoes and chicken broth, and bring to a simmer.

4. In a small bowl, whisk together the cornstarch, soy sauce, and sugar, and add to the pan. Cook, while stirring, until sauce is thickened. Place the cooked pasta in a bowl, pour the meat mixture over the pasta, and stir to coat.

Marlene Says: *This dish is an easy, nutritionally well-rounded, one-pan supper. It is a good source of Vitamin A and an excellent source of thiamin, niacin, Vitamin B6, and Vitamin C.*

NUTRITION INFORMATION PER SERVING: (1½ cups) Calories 265 | Carbohydrate 31g (Sugars 4g) | Total Fat 6g (Sat Fat 2.5g) | Protein 25g | Fiber 3g | Cholesterol 45mg | Sodium 490mg | Food Exchanges: 2½ Lean Meat, 1½ Starch, 1 Vegetable | Carbohydrate Choices: 2 | Weight Watcher Plus Point Comparison: 7

Sneaky Stuffed Shells

THIS RECIPE WAS INSPIRED by a recipe that didn't come together quite as I had hoped. While several parts of the dish failed, the delicious, creamy filling was not one of them, and thus it now graces these luscious stuffed shells. Pureed cauliflower makes the double cheese filling extra creamy, but you'll never know it's there. There's no need to tell the kids (or the adults) that they're getting almost two servings of vegetables in every serving.

MAKES 6 TO 9 SERVINGS

24 jumbo dry pasta shells

1 teaspoon olive oil

1 cup onion, finely chopped, divided

2 garlic cloves, minced

10 ounces frozen cauliflower, thawed and well-drained

¾ cup low-fat cottage cheese

¼ cup shredded Parmesan cheese

1 large egg white

2 teaspoons dried basil

¼ teaspoon black pepper

1 (10-ounce) package frozen spinach, thawed and squeezed dry

2¼ cups marinara sauce (page 190, or jarred), divided

½ cup shredded part-skim mozzarella cheese

1. Preheat the oven to 400°F. Prepare the pasta shells according to the package directions, drain, and set aside.

2. Meanwhile, prepare the filling. In a large, nonstick skillet, heat the oil over medium heat. Add the onion and garlic and sauté about 5 minutes, or until translucent. Transfer to the bowl of a food processor, add the cauliflower and cottage cheese, and process until smooth and creamy. Add the Parmesan, egg white, basil, and pepper, and process to combine. Add the spinach, pulse a few times until fully incorporated, and set aside.

3. In a 13 x 9-inch baking dish, stir together and spread 1¼ cups marinara sauce and ½ cup water.

4. Open each shell (a forefinger and thumb work nicely), stuff with about 2 tablespoons filling, and place in the dish, cheese side up. Repeat with all of the shells, and top with the remaining cup of sauce. Sprinkle with mozzarella, cover with foil, and bake for 25 minutes.

Marlene Says: *Twenty-four shells fit nicely into a 13 x 9-inch dish and split evenly into either 6 or 8 servings. There will, however, be a small amount of filling leftover. Feel free to either cook a few more shells, or stir the leftover filling into a serving of pasta. (Each stuffed and topped shell has 66 calories.)*

NUTRITION INFORMATION PER SERVING: (3 shells) Calories 200 | Carbohydrate 29g (Sugars 6g) | Total Fat 5g (Sat Fat 2g) | Protein 12g | Fiber 4g | Cholesterol 30mg | Sodium 410mg | Food Exchanges: 1 Starch, 1 Lean Meat, 2 Vegetable, ½ Fat | Carbohydrate Choices: 2 | Weight Watcher Plus Point Comparison: 5

Pasta Carbonara

IT WASN'T EASY, BUT I'VE CONQUERED CARBONARA! When I asked my Facebook fans which pasta dish they love most, pasta carbonara quickly made it to the top of the nice-but-naughty list. So get ready to dig into this guilt-free version—made with real eggs, bacon, chicken, shrimp, and plenty of cheese. (Feel free to use an entire pound of either chicken or shrimp, instead of the combination.)

2 teaspoons cornstarch

½ cup low-fat evaporated milk

⅓ cup grated Parmesan cheese

¼ teaspoon each salt and pepper

1 large egg

1 large egg white

6 ounces dry spaghetti

1 teaspoon olive oil

3 garlic cloves, minced

8 ounces large raw shrimp, peeled and deveined

6 ounces boneless, skinless chicken breast, sliced very thin

1 cup frozen peas

2 tablespoons real bacon bits

¼ cup chopped fresh parsley

1. In a small bowl, whisk cornstarch into evaporated milk. Add Parmesan, salt, pepper, egg, and egg white, and whisk until well combined.

2. Cook the pasta according to the package directions, adding to the last minute of cooking time. While the pasta is cooking, heat the oil in a large, nonstick skillet over medium heat. Add garlic and cook for 30 seconds. Add the shrimp and chicken and sauté 3 to 4 minutes, turning until cooked.

3. When the pasta is cooked, drain and return to pot. Immediately add the sauce, peas, and bacon to the hot pasta, and toss for 2 minutes until the sauce begins to thicken. Stir in chicken and shrimp, and let pasta sit for an addition 2 to 3 minutes, or until sauce thickens to desired consistency. Place in serving bowls, sprinkle each with 1 tablespoon parsley, and serve immediately.

DARE TO COMPARE: More of an Alfredo-style pasta dish than a true carbonara, the Chicken and Shrimp Carbonara at Olive Garden comes with a whopping 1,440 calories, 88 grams of fat (including two days' worth of saturated fat), and 3,000 milligrams of sodium!

NUTRITION INFORMATION PER SERVING: (1½ cups) Calories 335 | Carbohydrate 40g (Sugars 6g) | Total Fat 7g (Sat Fat 1g) | Protein 32g | Fiber 6g | Cholesterol 150 mg | Sodium 500mg | Food Exchanges: 3½ Lean Meat, 2½ Starch | Carbohydrate Choices: 3½ | Weight Watcher Plus Point Comparison: 8

Panda-Style Chicken Chow Mein

SAY GOOD-BYE TO TAKE-OUT CHOW MEIN! This versatile recipe can be made with any lean meat or seafood, or a combination thereof. When made with just veggies, the result is a chow mein noodle side dish similar to the one offered at Panda Express. The tricky part of slimming down this recipe was to get the right texture for the noodles without frying them in loads of oil. You'll find my solution in step 1.

| MAKES 4 SERVINGS

5 ounces dry whole grain spaghetti or linguine

½ cup reduced-sodium chicken broth

2 tablespoons reduced-sodium soy sauce

1 tablespoon oyster sauce (optional)

2 teaspoons granulated sugar

1 teaspoon cornstarch

¼ teaspoon black pepper, or more to taste

2 teaspoons sesame oil

1 cup chopped celery

½ cup thinly sliced green onion (sliced on the diagonal)

1 tablespoon minced garlic (3 large cloves)

3 cups shredded green cabbage

2 cups shredded cooked boneless, skinless chicken breast

1. Preheat the oven to 425°F. Cook the pasta according to the package directions. Drain very well. Spray a baking sheet with nonstick cooking spray, spread the pasta on the prepared baking sheet, and spray the top of the pasta with cooking spray. Bake for 8 minutes, or until noodles look dry and a bit browned. Stir the noodles, and bake another 2 minutes. Remove and set aside.

2. While the noodles cook, whisk together the next 5 ingredients (soy sauce through pepper), and set aside.

3. Heat the sesame oil in a large, nonstick skillet or wok over medium-high heat. Add the celery and stir-fry for 2 minutes. Add the green onion and garlic, and cook for 1 minute. Stir in the cabbage and 1 tablespoon water, cover and cook for 2 minutes. Uncover, stir in the soy sauce mixture, and simmer for 1 minute. Add the chicken and pasta, toss well, and cook until all ingredients are hot.

Marlene Says: *As a side dish, each 1-cup serving has 160 calories (instead of the 390 at the "panda").*

NUTRITION INFORMATION PER SERVING: (1½ cups) Calories 260 | Carbohydrate 30g (Sugars 3g) | Total Fat 5g (Sat Fat 0g) | Protein 24g | Fiber 6g | Cholesterol 55mg | Sodium 500 mg | Food Exchanges: 2½ Lean Meat, 1½ Starch, 1 Vegetable | Carbohydrate Choices: 2 | Weight Watcher Plus Point Comparison: 6

Lemony Shrimp and Spinach Fettuccine In Cream Sauce

THIS IS MY TAKE ON THE UNDERSTANDABLY POPULAR Lemon Shrimp Fettuccine pasta at Applebee's. Just like theirs, mine features plump shrimp, ripe tomatoes, fresh spinach, and a creamy sauce— spiked with fresh lemon zest. What my dish does not have is oodles of calories and over two full teaspoons' worth of salt in each serving! Trust me, this is one makeover worth making over . . . and over . . . again.

MAKES 4 SERVINGS

6 ounces dry fettuccine

2 teaspoons olive oil

3 cups fresh baby spinach

1 cup seeded, diced fresh tomato

¾ cup chopped quartered artichokes (optional)

¾ cup nonfat half-and-half

1 tablespoon cornstarch

¼ cup chopped green onion

1 teaspoon minced garlic

1 pound large or extra-large shrimp (about 24 per pound), peeled and deveined

½ cup white wine (or chicken broth)

¾ teaspoon lemon zest

¼ cup grated Parmesan cheese

1. Cook the pasta according to the package directions. Drain the pasta and place it back in the pot. Toss with 1 teaspoon olive oil, stir in the spinach, tomato, and artichokes (if desired), and cover.

2. In a small bowl, whisk together the half-and-half and cornstarch. Set aside.

3. Heat the remaining teaspoon oil in a large, nonstick skillet over medium heat. Add green onions and garlic and sauté for 2 minutes, or until the onions are softened. Add the shrimp and cook for 2 minutes, turning halfway, until shrimp is pink on both sides but not cooked through. Stir in wine and zest.

4. Whisk the cornstarch mixture again and add to the sauté pan. Continue to cook, stirring, for 3 to 4 minutes, until sauce is thick and smooth. Add the shrimp and cream sauce to the fettuccine, and toss gently to coat. Top with Parmesan cheese.

DARE TO COMPARE: One order of Lemon Shrimp Fettuccine at Applebee's has 1,090 calories, more than a day's worth of saturated fat, and a startling 5,170 milligrams (or two to three days' worth!) of sodium.

NUTRITION INFORMATION PER SERVING: (1½ cups) Calories 320 | Carbohydrate 42g (Sugars 7g) | Total Fat 5g (Sat Fat 2g) | Protein 28g | Fiber 6g | Cholesterol 135mg | Sodium 360mg | Food Exchanges: 3 Lean Meat, 2½ Starch, 1 Vegetable | Carbohydrate Choices: 2½ | Weight Watcher Plus Point Comparison: 7

Easy All-Purpose Marinara

IN TODAY'S HECTIC WORLD, jarred marinara is a pantry staple for many of us. Yes, it's convenient and can be inexpensive, but few, if any, are as good as homemade. Add the fact that jarred sauces are also usually high in sodium and/or sugar, and an easy, all-purpose marinara recipe is indispensable. In Eat More Of What You Love, I included a very similar recipe for the slow cooker, and many readers have asked for a stovetop version. Here you go! This recipe makes the equivalent of two 28-ounce jars, keeps for up to two weeks in the fridge, (at least two months in the freezer,) and can be used anywhere I specify marinara.

MAKES 6 CUPS SAUCE

1 medium white onion, chopped, about 1¼ cups

1 tablespoon olive oil

3 garlic cloves, minced, or 1 tablespoon jarred

½ cup dry red wine or reduced-sodium beef broth

1 (28-ounce) can crushed tomatoes

1 (8-ounce) can tomato sauce

1 (6-ounce) can tomato paste

2 teaspoons sugar

1½ teaspoons dried basil leaves

1½ teaspoons dried oregano

1. In a large pot, heat the oil over medium-high heat. Add the onion and cook for 6 to 8 minutes, or until softened. Stir in the garlic and cook for 1 minute. Pour in the wine and cook for 4 to 5 minutes, or until most of the liquid is evaporated.

2. Stir in all of the remaining ingredients and 1 cup of water. Reduce the heat, cover, and cook for 20 to 30 minutes, stirring occasionally. Remove from heat and let cool completely before refrigerating.

Marlene Says: *This sauce can cook for as little as 20 minutes, but the flavor is richer if cooked longer. When time permits, I let simmer another 30 minutes over medium-low heat, adding extra water to thin. My Italian mother starts hers on the stove, partially covers the pot, and places it in a 350°F oven for 1½ to 2 hours.*

NUTRITION INFORMATION PER SERVING: (½ cup) Calories 60 | Carbohydrate 11g (Sugars 3g) | Total Fat 1.5g (Sat Fat 0g) | Protein 2g | Fiber2 g | Cholesterol 0 mg | Sodium 220mg | Food Exchanges: 1½ Vegetable | Carbohydrate Choices: ½ | Weight Watcher Plus Point Comparison: 1

Light Luscious All-Purpose Alfredo Sauce

NO, YOU READ THE TITLE CORRECTLY, and yes, the ever-popular Alfredo sauce can be light as well as luscious—and moderate in sodium, too. I tested and tweaked this until I got it right, and now it's a staple in my recipe repertoire (I prefer the lesser amount of garlic as a sauce, more for pizza). After tasting it, you'll be saying "arrivederci" to the jarred stuff. Toss with your favorite pasta, drizzle over chicken, use it to make Chicken Alfredo Pizza (page 194), or, jazz it up with minced rosemary, bacon bits, mustard, or lemon zest. The luscious possibilities are endless!

MAKES **2** CUPS SAUCE

1 cup low-fat evaporated milk

2 tablespoons instant flour (like Wondra)

1 cup reduced-sodium chicken broth

3 tablespoons light cream cheese

1 to 1½ teaspoons garlic powder

¼ teaspoon pepper, or more to taste

⅛ teaspoon salt

¼ cup grated Parmesan cheese

1. In a medium saucepan, whisk the evaporated milk and flour until smooth. Whisk in the broth and place over low heat.

2. Add the cream cheese, garlic powder, pepper, and salt. Bring to a low simmer and cook until the sauce thickens, about 4 minutes. Whisk in the Parmesan and cook for 1 to 2 more minutes, or until sauce is smooth.

DARE TO COMPARE: Simple homemade Alfredo sauce can have as much as 240 calories and 25 grams of fat, including 16 grams of saturated fat, in a mere quarter cup.

NUTRITION INFORMATION PER SERVING: (¼ cup) Calories 60 | Carbohydrate 5g (Sugars 4g) | Total Fat 2.5g (Sat Fat 2g) | Protein 4g | Fiber 0g | Cholesterol 10mg | Sodium 230mg | Food Exchanges: ½ Fat, ¼ Milk | Carbohydrate Choices: 0 | Weight Watcher Plus Point Comparison: 2

Linguine with Red Clam Sauce for Two

IF YOU'RE LOOKING FOR A ROMANTIC HOMEMADE DINNER FOR TWO, this seafood pasta-lover's delight is worthy of candlelight, cloth napkins, and a tablecloth setting. After testing several times, I found that the key to an unforgettable red clam sauce is to use good quality canned whole tomatoes (diced or puréed do not yield the same result). Enjoy this trattoria-worthy dish with someone you love.

MAKES 2 SERVINGS

3 ounces dry linguine pasta

2 teaspoons olive oil, divided

⅓ cup chopped onion

2 teaspoons minced garlic

1 (6.5-ounce) cans chopped clams (drain and reserve juice)

1 (14-ounce) can whole peeled plum tomatoes

1 tablespoon tomato paste

½ teaspoon dried basil

¼ teaspoon dried oregano

⅛ teaspoon black pepper, plus more to taste

1 to 2 tablespoons white wine or dry vermouth (optional)

2 tablespoons chopped parsley for garnish

1. Cook the pasta according to the package directions. Drain the pasta, and return to the pot.

2. While pasta cooks, heat 1 teaspoon oil in a large, nonstick skillet over medium-low heat. Add the onion and cook for 3 minutes, stirring. Stir in garlic and cook 1 minute. Add the reserved clam juice, bring to a boil, and simmer for 3 minutes, or until liquid has reduced by half and onions are soft.

3. Add the next 5 ingredients (tomatoes through pepper), crushing the tomatoes with your hand as you add them to the skillet. Reduce heat to medium-low and simmer for 7 to 10 minutes, or until mixture thickens slightly, stirring occasionally.

4. Add the reserved clams and wine, if desired, and simmer for 2 minutes. Season the sauce with additional pepper to taste and swirl in remaining teaspoon of olive oil. Serve the sauce over the pasta and garnish with chopped parsley.

NUTRITION INFORMATION PER SERVING: (~ 1¾ cups) Calories 315 | Carbohydrate 47g (Sugars 9g) | Total Fat 7g (Sat Fat 1g) | Protein 21g | Fiber 7g | Cholesterol 35mg | Sodium 460mg | Food Exchanges: 2 Starch, 2 Lean Meat, 2 Vegetable | Carbohydrate Choices: 3 | Weight Watcher Plus Point Comparison: 8

Individual Mexican Pizza(s)

TRAVEL SOUTH OF THE BORDER with my tasty Mexican take on pizza. Flour tortillas form the amazing cracker-like crusts and salsa steps in for pizza sauce. My kitchen assistant Megan says this pizza reminds her of one she used to order at Taco Bell—only ours has a lot less grease. Feel free to make one or two pizzas at a time over a couple of days, or all four at once.

MAKES 1 TO 4 SERVINGS

Meat Topping:

8 ounces lean ground beef

1 teaspoon chili powder

½ teaspoon ground cumin

¼ teaspoon garlic powder

2 green onions, chopped

1 teaspoon all-purpose flour

½ cup salsa or jarred fire-roasted tomatoes

4 high fiber tortillas (like Mission Carb Balance)

¾ cup reduced-fat shredded Mexican blend cheese, divided

1⅓ cups shredded lettuce

¾ to 1 cup chopped tomatoes

¼ cup light sour cream

Fresh cilantro for garnish (optional)

1. Preheat the oven to 425°F. Spray a medium, nonstick skillet with cooking spray, and place over medium heat. Add the ground beef, spices, and green onions, and cook until meat is browned, for 5 to 6 minutes. Sprinkle flour over beef, stir, and add salsa. Cook for 1 to 2 minutes or until thickened.

2. For each pizza, place a tortilla on a baking pan and spray lightly with cooking spray. Bake for 4 minutes, or until lightly crisped.

3. Remove the tortilla from the oven, spread with ⅓ cup meat mixture, top with 3 tablespoons cheese, and bake for 4 minutes or until cheese is melted. Top with ⅓ cup lettuce and 3 to 4 tablespoons tomatoes. Mix 1 tablespoon sour cream with a small amount of water to thin, and drizzle over pizza. Garnish with cilantro, if desired.

Marlene Says: *The meat mixture makes enough for 4 individual pizzas. If you don't use it all at once, it will keep (covered) in the refrigerator for at least 3 days.*

NUTRITION INFORMATION PER SERVING: (1 pizza) Calories 280 | Carbohydrate 25g (Sugars 4g) | Total Fat 10g (Sat Fat 5g) | Protein 24g | Fiber 13g | Cholesterol 45mg | Sodium 800mg | Food Exchanges: 1 | 3 Lean Meat, 1 Starch, 1 Vegetable, 1 Fat | Carbohydrate Choices: 1 | Weight Watcher Plus Point Comparison: 7

Chicken Alfredo Pizza

GOURMET PIZZA DOESN'T GET MUCH BETTER THAN THIS Chicken Alfredo pie. My Light and Luscious All-Purpose Alfredo Sauce is the base for tender baby spinach, juicy chicken, sweet cherry tomatoes, and a double cheese topper, creating the ultimate in pizza dining. Serve it to your friends, and they may start calling you for delivery!

MAKES 8 SERVINGS

1 thin-crust wheat pizza crust (like Boboli)

½ cup light Alfredo sauce (recipe on page 191, or jarred)

2 cups fresh baby spinach

⅔ cup cooked chicken breast, chopped

¾ cup cherry tomatoes, halved

½ cup shredded part-skim mozzarella cheese

2 tablespoons shredded Parmesan cheese

1 cup fresh baby spinach, thinly sliced (optional garnish)

Fresh basil, chopped (optional garnish)

1. Position a rack in the middle of the oven and preheat the oven to 450°F.

2. Place the crust on a baking sheet and spread the pizza sauce over the crust. Top evenly with the baby spinach, chicken, and tomato halves.

3. Sprinkle the mozzarella and Parmesan evenly on top, and bake in the middle of the oven for 15 minutes or until the cheese is melted and the crust is browned. Scatter fresh spinach and basil over top of pizza, if desired.

NUTRITION INFORMATION PER SERVING: (1 slice) Calories 160 | Carbohydrate 14g (Sugars 2g) | Total Fat 5g (Sat Fat 2g) | Protein 16g | Fiber 2g | Cholesterol 35mg | Sodium 290mg | Food Exchanges: 1½ Lean Meat, 1 Starch, Fat | Carbohydrate Choices: 1 | Weight Watcher Plus Point Comparison: 4

Cook It Fast or Slow: Pressure and Slow Cooker Favorites

Asian BBQ Drummies

Italian Sloppy Joes

Old-Fashioned Beef Stew

Citrus Salsa Chicken

Rigatoni and Meat Sauce

Chipotle Beef Barbacoa

Juicy Herbed Turkey Breast

Fabulous French Onion Chicken

Potato Leek Soup

Risotto Primavera

Turkey Taco Soup

Judy's All-Purpose Beans

Homemade Chicken Stock

O F ALL THE CHAPTERS IN THIS BOOK, this one is perhaps the most special. While pressure and slow cooker cookbooks abound, there is not one (that I have found) that offers what I do here—dual cooking instructions for both pressure and slow cooking. It took plenty of extra effort, but at the bottom of every fast-fix pressure cooker recipe, you will find the instructions on how to cook the same recipe in a slow cooker. It's like getting two recipes in one! So whether you have a pressure cooker or a slow cooker, need to get dinner on the table extra quick, or want to fix-it-and-forget it, I'm happy to say, "I've got you covered!"

Pressure and slow cooking are *similar* in that they both use a moist heat method of cooking in an enclosed environment. In a slow cooker, the temperature and timing is "low and slow" whereas in a pressure cooker it's "high and fast." Cooking with superheated pressurized steam at higher-than-normal temperatures produces flavor-infused foods that cook in about one-third of the usual time! (See page 198 for tips on cooking under pressure.)

When it comes to mouthwatering last-minute cooking, there is nothing more delicious than cooking under pressure. Fork-tender Old-Fashioned Beef Stew, once an all-day affair, cooks under pressure in 15 minutes, while Fabulous French Onion Chicken (with only 170 slim calories) and flavorful, meaty Rigatoni and Meat Sauce, resplendent with mushrooms and red peppers, cook in just 6! Family favorite Mexican dishes like Citrus Salsa Chicken and Chipotle Beef Barbacoa—perfect for tacos, burritos, and enchiladas—are now as quick as they are versatile, and the long stirring required for creamy risotto is long gone when you fix Risotto Primavera in just 10 minutes in a pressure cooker. Cook it fast, or cook it slow, now the choice is yours!

FOR THE LOVE OF
PRESSURE COOKERS

Pressure cookers have long been revered for delivering the rich taste of long simmered foods in record time, but ease of use and safety were often a concern. No longer! The simplicity of the modern electric pressure cookers takes the pressure out of pressure cooking—and today's stovetop models are safer than ever. Here are eight tips on how to achieve pressure cooker success with my recipes:

Pressure cooking is a moist method of cooking in a pressurized superheated closed environment. Foods that are delicate, or that cook best with dry heat, like tender steaks and stir fries, are not well-suited to pressure cooking.

Read the manual to familiarize yourself with your pressure cooker. All of the recipes in this chapter were tested with a *6-quart electric pressure cooker*. Cookers between 5- and 7-quarts are fine. Sizing, liquid, and and/or timing adjustments are required for smaller or larger cookers.

Expect to use at least one cup of liquid for most recipes. Liquid is required to create steam, which in turn creates the pressure in the cooker. If you downsize a recipe, the liquid amount should remain the same. Extra cooking liquid can be reduced with the browning function or thickened with a mixture of flour or cornstarch and water.

Size matters. Larger pieces of meat take longer to cook than smaller ones. Follow the recipe instructions or make adjustments accordingly (for example, Chipotle Beef Barbacoa uses large pieces of meat. If cubed stew meat is used, it will cook in about half the time).

Seasonings and flavors become concentrated. When converting a regular recipe for the pressure cooker, less dried herbs and spices are often required.

Use the release method indicated. The "quick release" allows all the steam to escape immediately, while a "natural release" allows the steam to dissipate on its own before the pressure cooker is opened (which can take 15 minutes or longer). Always release the steam carefully. Placing a kitchen towel over the steam valve is a great way to catch the steam.

Reduce or increase the time as needed. The recipes in this chapter were well tested, but adding or subtracting even a minute or two of cooking time in a pressure cooker can make a huge difference in the outcome. Calibrate your cooker to mine by taking note of any differences in cooking time and jotting them down so you can adjust the next recipe accordingly.

Enjoy! Pressure cooking is not only fabulously flavorful and fast, it's economical. Pressure cookers use less energy and keep your kitchen cool. If you're under pressure to deliver a fast delicious meal, pressure cooking is the solution.

Asian BBQ Drummies

THIS RECIPE DOES DOUBLE DUTY as a light entrée or a hearty appetizer. It's also a perfect example of how pressure- and slow-cooking can differ. When made in the pressure cooker, the barbecue sauce is added up front, and in only 8 minutes you get a tasty sauce that (with a slight reduction) gloriously coats the tender, meaty legs. In the slow cooker, the sauce is added much later; if not, the accumulated juices from the slow-cooked legs dilute it. With far more meat than chicken wings, these legs fly off the plate.

MAKES 4 TO 6 SERVINGS

Sauce

½ cup sugar-free apricot preserves

2 tablespoons ketchup

2 tablespoons reduced-sodium soy sauce

1 teaspoon minced garlic

1 teaspoon minced ginger

⅛ – ¼ teaspoon red pepper flakes

¾ teaspoon sesame oil

Chicken

1 teaspoon canola or peanut oil

8 skinless chicken drumsticks

1 teaspoon sesame seeds (optional)

1. To make the sauce, in a small, microwave-safe bowl, stir together the first 7 ingredients (apricot preserves through sesame oil). Microwave on high for 1 minute. Stir in 6 tablespoons of water and set aside.

2. Set the pressure cooker to the "brown" or high setting, place the oil in the cooker, add the drumsticks, and brown them on all sides. Pour the sauce over the drumsticks. Securely lock the lid into place, set the cooker to high, and cook for 7 minutes. While chicken is cooking, lightly toast sesame seeds in a sauté pan, if desired, and set aside.

3. Quick-release the pressure, and carefully remove the lid. Set the cooker to high or brown, and let the chicken and sauce simmer for several minutes, uncovered, until the sauce thickens and fully coats the chicken. Remove, and garnish with sesame seeds, if desired.

Marlene Says: *To **COOK IT SLOW**, make the sauce as directed in step 1. Use either the browning function or a skillet to brown the legs as in step 2, then add them to the slow cooker. Add ¼ cup of water or broth, and cook the legs on low for 4 hours or high for 2 hours. Remove the legs and drain the accumulated liquid. Return legs to the cooker, add the sauce, and continue to cook for 30 minutes on high or 1 hour on low, or until the legs are tender.*

NUTRITION INFORMATION PER SERVING: (2 drumsticks) Calories 205 | Carbohydrate 13g (Sugars 1g) | Total Fat 6g (Sat Fat 1g) | Protein 27g | Fiber 4g | Cholesterol 85mg | Sodium 450mg | Food Exchanges: 3½ Lean Meat, 1 Starch | Carbohydrate Choices: 1 | Weight Watcher Plus Point Comparison: 5

Italian Sloppy Joes

AS A LONG TIME SLOPPY JOE FAN, I didn't think I could improve on my previous recipes...until now. Here the traditional tangy tomato sauce gets an Italian flavor kick with seasoned turkey, oregano, and fennel. It's hard to believe, but these zesty and hearty Joes also weigh in at less than 250 calories a sandwich. Cooked fast or slow, you can't go wrong with this new family favorite.

MAKES 10 SERVINGS

½ pound Italian seasoned ground turkey (or Italian turkey sausage)

1 pound lean ground beef

1 cup chopped onion

1 large red pepper, chopped

3 large stalks celery, diced

1 (6-ounce) can tomato paste

2 tablespoons balsamic vinegar

3 large garlic cloves, minced

1 tablespoon molasses

1 teaspoon dried oregano

½ teaspoon fennel seed, crushed*

½ to ¾ teaspoon salt (or to taste)

10 whole grain hamburger buns

1. Set the pressure cooker to the "brown" or high setting, crumble the turkey into the cooker and brown for a minute or two, and then crumble in the ground beef. Cook for 3 to 4 minutes, breaking up the meat with a spoon, until it is no longer pink.

2. Stir 1⅓ cups of water into the meat, add the remaining ingredients (besides the buns), and stir well. Securely lock the lid into place, turn the cooker to high, and cook for 12 minutes.

3. Quick-release the pressure and carefully remove the lid. Stir the meat mixture, turn the temperature to brown or sauté, and simmer the meat mixture uncovered for 3 minutes, or until desired thickness. To serve, place ½ cup of the meat mixture on each bun.

Marlene Says: **To COOK IT SLOW,** *use either the browning function or large skillet to brown the ground turkey and beef over medium-high heat. Add the mixture to a 4- to 6-quart slow cooker and continue with step 2. Cook on low for 6 to 8 hours or 3 to 4 hours on high. Remove lid and cook for additional 10 to 15 minutes on high, stirring occasionally, or to desired thickness.*

* To "crush" fennel seed, place on cuting board and chop it with a large knife.

NUTRITION INFORMATION PER SERVING: (1 sandwich) Calories 235 | Carbohydrate 26g (Sugars 7g) | Total Fat 6g (Sat Fat 2g) | Protein 21g | Fiber 4g | Cholesterol 45mg | Sodium 430mg | Food Exchanges: 1 Starch, 2 Lean Meat, 1 Vegetable | Carbohydrate Choices: 1½ | Weight Watcher Plus Point Comparison: 6

Old Fashioned Beef Stew

AS MY KITCHEN ASSISTANT MEGAN CAN ATTEST TO—after cooking beef stew for days on end—getting potatoes and meat perfectly cooked in the pressure cooker, at the same time, can be challenging. But I'm sure you'll agree that the effort was well worth it when you taste this wonderfully delicious, weekday-friendly, one-pot beef stew. Follow the layering order, and you can have fork-tender, old-fashioned stew in 30 minutes.

MAKES 6 SERVINGS

1½ pounds lean beef, cut into 1½-inch chunks

1 large onion, chopped

3 stalks celery, cut into 1-inch pieces

2 medium carrots, peeled and cut into 1-inch pieces

1 pound small red potatoes, halved

1 (14.5-ounce) can reduced-sodium beef broth

½ cup dry red wine (or broth)

3 tablespoons tomato paste

2 teaspoons dried thyme, crumbled

1 ½ teaspoons minced fresh rosemary

1 ½ teaspoons Worcestershire sauce

¼ teaspoon salt

2 cups frozen green beans, thawed

3 tablespoons instant flour (like Wondra)

1. Layer the first 5 ingredients (beef through potatoes) in the pressure cooker, in the order listed. In a medium bowl, whisk together next 7 ingredients (beef broth through salt), and pour into the pressure cooker.

2. Securely lock the lid into place, turn the cooker to high, and cook for 15 minutes at high pressure. When the pressure cooker time has elapsed, let the pressure release naturally for 10 minutes, and then release any residual pressure with the quick release.

3. Carefully uncover the pressure cooker, and stir in the green beans. Set the pressure cooker to the "brown" or high setting. Sprinkle the flour into the cooker. Stir and cook for 2 minutes, or until the sauce thickens.

Marlene Says: *To* **COOK IT SLOW**, *place the potatoes, celery, and carrots in a 4- to 6-quart slow cooker, and top with the onions and beef. Continue as in step 1, pouring whisked liquid into the slow cooker. Cover and cook on low for 8 to 9 hours, or 4 to 5 hours on high. Stir in green beans, set cooker to high or brown, and continue as in step 3, cooking uncovered for up to 10 minutes for sauce to thicken.*

NUTRITION INFORMATION PER SERVING: (1¼ cups) Calories: 270 | Carbohydrate 22g (Sugars 6g) | Total Fat 9g (Sat Fat 3g) | Protein 31g | Fiber 4g | Cholesterol 65mg | Sodium 75mg | Food Exchanges: 3 ½ Lean Meat, 1 Starch, 1 Vegetable, ½ Fat | Carbohydrate Choices: 1½ | Weight Watcher Plus Point Comparison: 7

Citrus Salsa Chicken

IF I COULD ONLY USE MY ELECTRIC "COOKERS" FOR ONE THING, it would be to produce fork-tender, flavor-saturated chicken. The juice of orange and lime add a citrus twist to the fire-roasted salsa and infuse the chicken in this recipe with extra flavor and moisture. If shredded (and the slow cooker gets a slight edge here), the meat is perfect for tacos, burritos, and quesadillas. Only cooking for two? No worries, you can re-purpose the leftover meat all week long.

MAKES 6 SERVINGS

2 teaspoons chili powder

1 teaspoon ground cumin

½ teaspoon salt

½ teaspoon dried oregano

6 (5-ounce) boneless, skinless chicken breasts (about 2 pounds)

1 teaspoon canola oil

1 cup chopped onion

1 (14-ounce) can diced fire-roasted tomatoes

½ cup light orange juice (like Trop50)

Juice from 1 medium lime

2 garlic cloves, crushed

1. In a small bowl, combine the chili powder, cumin, salt, and oregano. Pat the chicken breasts dry, and sprinkle with spice mixture (about ¼ teaspoon each side). Set pressure cooker to the "brown" or high setting, and place oil in the cooker. Add chicken breasts and brown for 2 to 3 minutes per side. Remove chicken from cooker and set aside.

2. Add the onions to the cooker and sauté for 2 to 3 minutes. Add the remaining ingredients (tomatoes through garlic), stir, place rack in the cooker, and place chicken breasts on the rack.

3. Securely lock the lid into place, turn the cooker to high, and cook for 6 minutes at high pressure. Quick-release the pressure and carefully remove the lid. Transfer the chicken breasts to plates to serve, and top with salsa.

Marlene Says: *To **COOK IT SLOW**, season breasts as in step **1**. Place the chicken breasts in a 4- to 6-quart slow cooker, top with onions, and add remaining ingredients. Cover and cook for 5 to 6 hours on low, or 2½ to 3 hours on high. Remove chicken, drain excess liquid out of the salsa to serve, or shred the meat, combining it with the some of the cooker liquid for tacos and more.*

NUTRITION INFORMATION PER SERVING: (1 breast or ¾ cup shredded) Calories 190 | Carbohydrate 8g (Sugars 4g) | Total Fat 5g (Sat Fat 0g) | Protein 30g | Fiber 2g | Cholesterol 95mg | Sodium 240mg | Food Exchanges: 4 ½ Lean Meat, 1 Vegetable | Carbohydrate Choices: ½ | Weight Watcher Plus Point Comparison: 5

Rigatoni and Meat Sauce

THE ITALIAN PART OF ME DIDN'T THINK IT WAS POSSIBLE to achieve pasta perfection in the pressure cooker, but I was wrong. Simply brown the onions, garlic, and beef, dump in the rest of the ingredients, and presto, in ten minutes you have a complete rigatoni dinner that would make any Nonna say, "Bellissimo!" To make pizza rigatoni, use green peppers, add 1 teaspoon dried oregano, and cook per directions. After releasing pressure, stir in 1 ounce (17 slices) of turkey pepperoni, and top with ¼ cup part-skim mozzarella cheese.

MAKES 6 SERVINGS

1 medium onion, chopped

1 tablespoon minced garlic

12 ounces lean ground beef

1 teaspoon fennel seed, crushed, or more to taste

½ teaspoon black pepper

1 ½ cups jarred marinara sauce (or Easy All-Purpose Marinara, page 190)

8 ounces rigatoni

1 (14-ounce) can diced tomatoes

1 8-ounce package sliced mushrooms (about 3 cups)

2 medium red bell peppers, seeded and chopped in 1 ½-inch pieces

⅓ cup grated Parmesan cheese

1. Spray the pressure cooker insert with cooking spray, set to the "brown" or high setting, add onions, and brown for 3 minutes. Add garlic and cook for 1 minute. Crumble in ground beef and cook, breaking up the meat, for 3 minutes, or until nearly cooked through.

2. Stir in the fennel seed, pepper, marinara, and ¾ cup water. Add the rigatoni, top with tomatoes, mushrooms, and bell peppers, ensuring the pasta is covered; do not stir.

3. Securely lock the lid into place, turn the cooker to high, and cook for 6 minutes at high pressure. Quick-release the pressure and carefully remove the lid. Stir to combine ingredients, let set for 2 to 3 minutes, and then stir in the Parmesan.

Marlene Says: *To **COOK IT SLOW**, use either a browning function or large skillet to brown the ground beef over medium-high heat. Add the meat to a 4- to 6-quart slow cooker. Add the onions, garlic, and remaining ingredients, and layer as in step 2. Cover and cook for 3 ½ to 4 hours on low, or 2 to 2½ hours on high. Uncover and stir carefully, being sure to mix ingredients from bottom to top.*

NUTRITION INFORMATION PER SERVING: (1½ cups) Calories 310 | Carbohydrate 39g (Sugars 8g) | Total Fat 7g (Sat Fat 3g) | Protein 26g | Fiber 5g | Cholesterol 40mg | Sodium 410mg | Food Exchanges: 2 Lean Meat, 2 Starch, 2 Vegetable | Carbohydrate Choices: 2½ | Weight Watcher Plus Point Comparison: 8

Chipotle Beef Barbacoa

INSPIRED BY THE POPULAR BURRITO and taco filling at Chipotle Mexican Grill, I created this with my take-out-loving boys in mind. The chipotle flavor comes by way of canned chipotle peppers in adobo sauce, which are easily found in the Mexican food section at most supermarkets. I use three medium-sized peppers, which yield a slightly spicy beef; if you want a true "Chipotle-style" kick, add one or even two more. My sons can now satisfy their big burrito and taco cravings by eating in—instead of out.

MAKES 10 SERVINGS

3 to 4 canned chipotle peppers in adobo sauce

½ red onion, roughly chopped

1 tablespoon chopped garlic (about 3 cloves)

½ teaspoon ground cloves

1 tablespoon dried oregano

1 tablespoon cumin

Juice of 2 limes

2 tablespoons tomato paste, divided

2½ to 3 pounds eye of the round (or other lean roast)

¾ teaspoon salt

2 bay leaves

1 cup reduced-sodium beef broth

1. Place the first 7 ingredients (chipotle peppers through lime juice) plus 1 tablespoon tomato paste in a small food processor, and process to puree ingredients.

2. Cut the meat into 4 equal-sized pieces, sprinkle with salt, and place in the pressure cooker. Spoon the spice puree over the meat, and add the bay leaves and broth. Securely lock the lid into place, turn the cooker to high and cook for 45 minutes at high pressure. Let the pressure release naturally.

3. Transfer the meat to a cutting board. Discard bay leaves. Using two forks, shred the meat by pulling it apart, and place in a bowl. Remove 1 cup of the cooking liquid, and stir into the meat to moisten it; cover the meat with foil.

4. Stir the remaining tablespoon of tomato paste into the remaining liquid. Turn the cooker to brown and reduce the liquid by half. Return the meat back to the cooker, and gently toss to incorporate the sauce into the meat. Serve with warm corn tortillas and your choice of garnishes.

Marlene Says: *To **COOK IT SLOW**, follow steps 1 and 2, placing meat in a 4- to 6-quart slow cooker. Cover and cook for 8 to 9 hours on low, or 4 to 5 hours on high. Continue with step 3. If your slow cooker does not have a browning function, drain the cooking liquid into a saucepan, reduce it on the stovetop with the tomato paste, and continue as directed.*

NUTRITION INFORMATION PER SERVING: (½ cup) Calories 160 | Carbohydrate 4g (Sugars 1g) | Total Fat 4g (Sat Fat 1g) | Protein 27g | Fiber 0g | Cholesterol 0mg | Sodium 180mg | Food Exchanges: 3½ Lean Meat | Carbohydrate Choices: 0 | Weight Watcher Plus Point Comparison: 4

Juicy Herbed Turkey Breast

MOIST HEAT ENSURES MOIST MEAT, as is the case with this juicy, savory turkey breast. Perfect for Sunday dinner, this planned leftover recipe also yields great sandwich meat that clocks in with less than half of the usual sodium of deli turkey breast—for one half the price. To simultaneously make flavor-infused chicken stock, swap out the water with reduced-sodium chicken broth, and add ½ cup each of chopped onion, celery, and carrot to the bottom of the cooker. Strain before using.

MAKES 6 TO 8 SERVINGS

2 teaspoons prepared mustard

2 teaspoons olive oil

1½ teaspoons minced garlic

1 teaspoon rubbed sage

1 teaspoon dried oregano

1 teaspoon fresh rosemary, chopped

1 teaspoon black pepper

½ teaspoon salt

2½- to 3-pound bone-in turkey breast, with skin

1. In a small bowl, stir together the first 8 ingredients (mustard through salt). Gently loosen the skin of the turkey breast (do not detach), and rub the spice paste over the turkey breast meat. Replace the skin on the breast meat and set aside.

2. Place 2 cups of water in the bottom of the pressure cooker. Place the cooking rack (over the vegetables if desired), in the cooker and place the turkey breast on the rack. Securely lock the lid into place, turn the cooker to high, and cook for 25 minutes at high pressure. Quick-release the pressure and carefully remove the lid. Remove the turkey, and let rest at least 10 minutes. Remove the skin before slicing.

Marlene Says: *To **COOK IT SLOW**, prepare turkey breast as directed in step 1. Place one cup of water (or broth), in the bottom of a 4- to 6-quart slow cooker. Add vegetables, if desired, and place turkey breast in the cooker, skin-side up. Cook for 3 to 4 hours on low or 1½ to 2 hours on high, or until internal temperature reaches 165°F.*

NUTRITION INFORMATION PER SERVING: (4 ounces cooked) Calories 150 | Carbohydrate 0g (Sugars 0g) | Total Fat 2 g (Sat Fat 0g) | Protein 30g | Fiber 0g | Cholesterol 10mg | Sodium 220mg | Food Exchanges: 4 Lean Meat | Carbohydrate Choices: 0 | Weight Watcher Plus Point Comparison: 4

Fabulous French Onion Chicken

THIS ONE'S FOR YOU FRENCH ONION SOUP LOVERS. Whether you plan ahead or whip it up the last minute, for less than one-half of the fat and calories in a single cup of French onion soup, you get a hearty chicken entrée that's crave-worthy good. Talk about a soup-inspired dish that eats like a meal!

MAKES 5 SERVINGS

1 large onion, sliced (about 2 to 2½ cups)

4 boneless, skinless chicken breasts (about 1¼ pounds)

1 teaspoon olive oil

1 cup reduced-sodium beef broth, divided

1 teaspoon granulated sugar

1 garlic clove, minced

½ teaspoon dried thyme

1 ½ teaspoons Worcestershire sauce

2 tablespoons sherry

¼ teaspoon salt

¼ teaspoon black pepper

2 slices reduced-fat Swiss cheese, cut in half

2 teaspoons cornstarch

1. Place the onions in a medium, microwave-safe bowl and cover with plastic wrap. Cook on high for 5 minutes. While onions cook, set the pressure cooker to the "brown" or high setting and add the oil. Add the chicken breasts, and brown both sides.

2. Remove the chicken, and add 1 tablespoon of beef broth to the cooker. Add onions and sugar, stir, and cook for 6 to 8 minutes, stirring occasionally (adding a bit more broth if necessary), until they begin to brown. Add the garlic, thyme, and Worcestershire, and cook 1 minute. Stir in sherry, salt, pepper, and remaining broth. Place rack in cooker and place chicken on rack.

3. Securely lock the lid into place, turn cooker to high, and cook for 5 minutes at high pressure. Quick-release the pressure and carefully remove the lid. Place a piece of Swiss cheese on each chicken breast, and cover the cooker for 1 minute.

4. Transfer the chicken to a plate and keep warm. Set the cooker to the "brown" or high setting. Mix cornstarch with 1 tablespoon of water, and add to cooker. Cook, while stirring, until sauce thickens. To serve, top each chicken breast with ¼ cup French onion sauce.

Marlene Says: *To COOK IT SLOW, microwave onions as in step 1. Brown chicken either using the browning function of your slow cooker, or cook on the stovetop using a medium-sized skillet over medium-high heat. Brown the onions as directed in step 2, and place them in a 4- to 6-quart slow cooker. Add remaining ingredients and top with chicken. Cover and cook for 4 to 5 hours on low or 2 to 2½ hours on high.*

NUTRITION INFORMATION PER SERVING: (1 breast with sauce) Calories 170 | Carbohydrate 6g (Sugars 3g) | Total Fat 4g (Sat Fat 1g) | Protein 27g | Fiber 0g | Cholesterol 0mg | Sodium 95mg | Food Exchanges: 4 Lean Meat, ½ Vegetable | Carbohydrate Choices: ½ | Weight Watcher Plus Point Comparison: 4

Potato Leek Soup

WHEN YOU CRAVE CREAM SOUP but don't want the calories, this soup delivers. I purposely seasoned it lightly, as I like to jazz it up with different garnishes—like a handful of chopped chives, a teaspoon of bacon bits, a sprinkle of grated cheese, or a dollop of light sour cream. For a more rustic soup, leave the skins on the potatoes (scrub them well) and puree only a portion of the soup. Be sure to rinse the leeks thoroughly after slicing them lengthwise, as their roots tend to collect sand.

MAKES 6 SERVINGS

1 teaspoon olive oil

4 medium leeks, white and light green parts

¾ teaspoon dried thyme

1½ pounds russet potatoes, peeled, and thinly sliced

1 (14-ounce) can reduced-sodium chicken broth

¾ teaspoon seasoned salt

¼ teaspoon black or white pepper, or to taste

½ cup nonfat half-and-half

1. Set the pressure cooker to "sauté" or on medium setting, and add the oil. Slice the leeks lengthwise and then cut crosswise. Add them to the cooker and sauté for 2 minutes. Crumble in the thyme with your fingers and stir.

2. Add the next 4 ingredients (potatoes through pepper) plus 2 cups water to the cooker. Securely lock the lid into place, turn the cooker to high, and cook for 5 minutes at high pressure.

3. Quick-release the pressure and carefully remove the lid. Using an immersion blender, puree the soup just until smooth. (Do not overpuree the soup or it will become gummy.) Stir in the non-fat half-and-half, and add additional pepper to taste. Warm the soup for 5 minutes before serving.

Marlene Says: *To* **COOK IT SLOW,** *sauté the leeks using either the browning function of your slow cooker or the stovetop using a medium skillet over medium-low heat. Heat the oil, sauté the leeks as in step 1, and transfer to a 4- to 6-quart slow cooker, along with the crumbled thyme. Proceed as in step 2, using 1 ¾ cups water. Cover and cook on low for 2 ½ to 3 hours or on high for 1 ½ hours, or until potatoes are soft. Finish the soup as in step 3.*

NUTRITION INFORMATION PER SERVING: (1 cup) Calories 120 | Carbohydrate 24g (Sugars 5g) | Total Fat 2g (Sat Fat 0g) | Protein 4g | Fiber 3g | Cholesterol 0mg | Sodium 50mg | Food Exchanges: 1 Starch, 1 Vegetable | Carbohydrate Choices: 1½ | Weight Watcher Plus Point Comparison: 3

Risotto Primavera

I DOUBT THAT YOU NEED ME TO TELL YOU that creamy, comforting risotto is not usually "healthy" when you consider that the starch-laden dish—layered with oil, butter, and cheese, and finished with heavy cream—can serve up as many as 1,000 calories. The beauty of pressure and slow cooking risotto is that the required stirring is eliminated. The beauty of this recipe is how the cauliflower goes virtually undetected as it reduces the carb and calorie load. To make this easy-peasy recipe as an entrée, tuck some cleaned raw shrimp into the rice mixture in step 3, and cook for 5 minutes, or until done.

MAKES 8 SERVINGS

2 teaspoons olive oil

1 cup diced onion

2 teaspoons minced garlic

1 cup plus 2 tablespoons Arborio rice

3¼ cups reduced-sodium chicken broth, divided

1¼ cups frozen cauliflower, thawed and minced

1 cup frozen peas, thawed

¼ teaspoon black pepper, or more to taste

⅓ cup grated Parmesan cheese

2 teaspoons butter (optional)

1. Set the pressure cooker to the "brown" or high setting, place olive oil in the cooker, add the onions, and sauté for 2 to 3 minutes. Add the garlic and sauté for 30 seconds. Add the rice, stir well to coat the grains, and cook for 1 minute.

2. Carefully stir in 2¾ cups chicken broth, watching for spattering. Securely lock the lid into place, turn the cooker to high, and cook for 5 minutes at high pressure.

3. Quick-release the pressure and carefully remove the lid. Set the cooker to the "simmer" (or high) setting, stir in the cauliflower, peas, pepper, and ¼ to ½ cup of chicken broth (or enough for desired consistency). Cook until tender to bite. Stir in the cheese and optional butter, and serve immediately.

Marlene Says: *To* **COOK IT SLOW,** *sauté the onions and garlic using the browning function of your slow cooker or on the stovetop using a medium, nonstick skillet over medium-high heat. Complete step 1. Transfer to a 4- to 6-quart slow cooker, add 2½ cups broth, cover, and cook for 1½ hours on high, or until rice is slightly chewy and most of liquid is absorbed. Uncover, and complete step 3. (Note: rice will continue to soften, so should be very al dente when adding vegetables and remaining broth.*

NUTRITION INFORMATION PER SERVING: (⅔ cup) Calories 160 | Carbohydrate 26g (Sugars 3g) | Total Fat 5g (Sat Fat 2g) | Protein 7g | Fiber 3g | Cholesterol 5mg | Sodium 140mg | Food Exchanges: 1½ Starch, 1 Fat | Carbohydrate Choices: 1½ | Weight Watcher Plus Point Comparison: 5

Turkey Taco Soup

IT'S HARD TO ARGUE WITH CONVENIENCE when something so easy is so good. This is one of the easiest soups I have ever made, and it's also one of the best. Beyond the great taco taste, it's high in satiating protein and fiber and low in fat and calories. It also lends itself to lots of toppings—like baked tortilla chips, grated cheese, fresh cilantro, or slices of avocado. To top it off, everybody loves it. Did I mention it was easy?

MAKES 6 SERVINGS

1 teaspoon canola oil

1 medium onion, chopped

2 stalks celery, chopped

1 pound lean ground turkey

1 (4-ounce) can diced green chiles

1 (14-ounce) can diced tomatoes

1 (15-ounce) can black beans, drained and rinsed

1 (14-ounce) can reduced-sodium chicken broth

1 (1.5-ounce) package reduced-sodium taco seasoning mix

1 cup frozen corn

1. Set the pressure cooker to the "brown" or high setting, and add the oil to the cooker. Add the onion and celery and sauté for 2 minutes. Add the turkey, and cook, breaking up the meat, for 3 to 4 minutes, or until it is browned.

2. Stir in remaining ingredients, and 1 cup water. Securely lock the lid into place, turn the cooker to high, and cook for 5 minutes at high pressure.

3. When the pressure cooker time has elapsed, quick-release the pressure. Carefully remove the lid, stir the soup, and serve with your favorite garnish.

Marlene Says: *To **COOK IT SLOW**, heat the oil in a large, nonstick skillet over medium-high heat, and cook the onion, celery, and turkey, as directed in step 1. Transfer to a 4- to 6-quart slow cooker, and add remaining ingredients. Cook for 3 to 4 hours on high or 5 to 6 hours on low.*

NUTRITION INFORMATION PER SERVING: (1½ cups) Calories 235 | Carbohydrate 23g (Sugars 5g) | Total Fat 6g (Sat Fat 2g) | Protein 21g | Fiber 6g | Cholesterol 55mg | Sodium 520mg | Food Exchanges: 2 ½ Lean Meat, 1 Starch, 1 Vegetable | Carbohydrate Choices: 1 | Weight Watcher Plus Point Comparison:5

Judy's All-Purpose Beans

THIS RECIPE WAS CREATED BY MY FRIEND, CHEF JUDY LACARA, who has been making home-cooked beans for years. Judy tells me that pressure cookers and slow cookers are both excellent when it comes to making beans, but she loves the speed of the pressure cooker. When you cook dried beans, you'll notice how much better the texture and the flavor are compared to canned, plus the sodium is lower and they cost less. This recipe makes the equivalent of two drained 15-ounce cans of lightly seasoned all-purpose black beans. Serve them alone or wherever cooked black beans are required. (Small white or pinto beans can be substituted.)

MAKES 6 SERVINGS

½ pound dried black beans (about 1⅛ cups), picked over and rinsed

1 tablespoon canola oil

1½ teaspoons onion powder

¼ teaspoon garlic powder

¼ teaspoon baking soda

¼ teaspoon oregano

¼ plus ⅛ teaspoon salt, divided

1. Place the beans in a large bowl or saucepan and add 6 cups of water. Let the beans soak for 12 hours or overnight (or a minimum of 5 hours for best results). Drain, discarding soaking liquid, and transfer the beans to the pressure cooker.

2. Add next 5 ingredients (oil through oregano), ¼ teaspoon salt, and 4 cups of water to the pressure cooker. Securely lock the lid into place, turn the cooker to high, and cook for 7 minutes at high pressure. (Oil is required to reduce foaming.)

3. When the pressure cooker time has elapsed, let the pressure release naturally; this takes about 17 to 20 minutes. Carefully remove the lid and drain the beans in a sieve or colander, reserving 1 cup of the cooking liquid. Transfer beans to a medium bowl, stir in remaining salt, and add ½ cup to 1 cup of reserved cooking liquid, depending on how you like your beans.

Marlene Says: *To* **COOK IT SLOW,** *soak the beans as in step 1, drain, and transfer to the slow cooker. Add ingredients as in step 2, omitting the oil (oil is a requirement when cooking beans in a pressure cooker, but not needed in a slow cooker). Cook on high for 2½ to 3 hours, or on low for 5 to 6 hours, until beans are tender. Drain and season as in step 3.*

NUTRITION INFORMATION PER SERVING: (½ cup) Calories 125 | Carbohydrate 21g (Sugars 2g) | Total Fat 1g (Sat Fat 0g) | Protein 8g | Fiber 8 g | Cholesterol 5mg | Sodium 40 mg | Food Exchanges: 1 Starch, 1 Lean Meat | Carbohydrate Choices: 1 | Weight Watcher Plus Point Comparison: 2

Homemade Chicken Stock

WHETHER MADE EXTRA FAST, OR EXTRA SLOW, homemade chicken stock is great to have on hand—especially when watching your sodium. The pressure cooker has the edge with this recipe, as the higher temperature forces more flavor from the meat, bones, and vegetables into the broth, but low and slow cooking also makes a great stock. And, when using meaty parts like legs and thighs, you get the bonus of having extra meat to use in other recipes. Keep in mind this recipe has all of the flavor but half the sodium of canned reduced-sodium broth, so you may need to adjust the salt when using it in recipes.

MAKES 7 CUPS

2½ to 3 pounds bone-in chicken (like thighs, legs or wings), skin and fat removed

1 medium onion, roughly chopped

2 large stalks celery, roughly chopped

1 medium carrot, roughly chopped

1 bay leaf

¼ teaspoon dried thyme

4 black peppercorns (optional)

¾ teaspoon salt, or more to taste

1. Place all the ingredients in the pressure cooker. Add 6 to 7 cups of water, or enough to cover all of the ingredients, but not to exceed the maximum amount of liquid specified for your pressure cooker.

2. Securely lock the lid into place, turn the cooker to high, and cook for 45 minutes at high pressure. Quick-release the pressure and carefully remove the lid. Strain the stock through a fine strainer into another container. If desired, remove chicken meat from bones and refrigerate for another use. Let the stock cool, refrigerate, and skim off any fat before using. Season with additional salt to taste.

Marlene Says: *To* **COOK IT SLOW**, *place all ingredients, along with 6 to 7 cups of water, in a slow cooker, and cook on low for 12 hours (or overnight), or high for 6 to 7 hours. Strain the stock as directed in step 2.*

NUTRITION INFORMATION PER SERVING: (1 cup) Calories 15 | Carbohydrate 2g (Sugars 0g) | Total Fat 0g (Sat Fat 0g) | Protein 2g | Fiber 0g | Cholesterol 0mg | Sodium 260mg | Food Exchanges: Free Food | Carbohydrate Choices: 0 | Weight Watcher Plus Point Comparison: 0

Sides for Every Day and Every Occasion

Popcorn Cauliflower

Thyme for Honey Mustard Carrots

Cheesy Spinach Bake

Classic Green Bean "Casserole"

Balsamic Green Beans Almandine

Skillet-Roasted Smoky Brussels Sprouts

Jalapeño Popper Stuffed Zucchini Boats

Better Bean Succotash

Two-Minute Sugar Snap Peas

Terrific Tomato Tart

Extra Crispy Oven-Baked Steak Fries

Creamy Steakhouse Mashed Potatoes

30-Minute Twice-Baked Potatoes

10-Minute Mexican-Style Pintos

Instant Curried Rice and Pea Pilaf

Sweet Noodle Kugel

Quick 'n Easy Any Day Applesauce

Any Day Stuffin' Muffins

MOVE OVER MEAT, IT'S TIME FOR VEGETABLES to take center stage. The rise in popularity of plant-based diets and farmer's markets have helped to put veggies in the spotlight and—as a nutritionist, and as a cook—it couldn't make me happier! Not only are Mother Nature's finest creations loaded with vitamins, minerals, and fiber (see page 13), but vegetables put beautiful color, tantalizing texture, and a multitude of flavors on your plate.

This chapter will have you craving your veggies with super sides that taste so good, you'll forget they're good for you! For everyday meals, my kid-friendly, oven-roasted Popcorn Cauliflower, with its yellow hue, crispy brown edges, and pop of Parmesan flavor is so addictive, it could be eaten by the bucketful! Or add some excitement to your plate with creamy, crunchy, spicy, Jalapeño Popper Stuffed Zucchini Boats. The zip will do you good :). Special occasion and holiday meals are all about traditional favorites, so I included several, from a Classic Green Bean "Casserole," made weeknight-friendly in a skillet, to Creamy Steakhouse Mashed Potatoes (with spinach and caramelized onions mixed right in), to an elegant, 10-minute, Balsamic Green Beans Almandine. I dare you to make *these* "special occasion" dishes only once or twice a year.

To really put veggies center stage, why not make them *the* meal? Going meatless once a week not only saves energy and money, it adds extra nutrients and fiber to your diet. My protein-rich slimmed down 30-Minute Twice-Baked Potatoes, ooey gooey Cheesy Spinach Bake, and zesty Terrific Tomato Tart are all perfect for light meals and Meatless Mondays.

FOR THE LOVE OF
VEGETABLES

Let's face it, when it comes to the foods we love to eat, vegetables don't often make the list, but that doesn't mean there's not a lot to love. From artichokes to zucchini, colorful, flavorful vegetables are incredibly healthful and amazingly versatile. In fact, experts recommend up to half our plates be filled with vegetables! You will find lots of veggie love in this book, be it at breakfast, lunch, or dinner. To help you and yours enjoy an abundance of delicious, nutritious vegetables every day, here are some tasty veggie tips.

Seven Tasty Veggie Lover Tips:

1. **Take your pick.** While fresh is best, canned and frozen vegetables are quick, easy, and convenient. Processed at the peak of freshness, they're also often as nutritious as fresh!

2. **Pump 'em up.** Feel free to add extra vegetables to soups, salads, sandwiches and pasta dishes. Nonstarchy veggies like bell peppers, broccoli, mushrooms, carrots and tomatoes add color, texture, and bulk as well as additional fiber and flavor to dishes. Choose your family's favorites.

3. **Be sneaky.** If your family doesn't love vegetables, sneak them into favorite foods. You'll find hidden veggies in the Banana Berry Super Smoothie, Very Veggie Stuffed Shells, and Bodacious "50-50" Bacon 'n Beef Burgers.

4. **Try something new.** Spinach is a familiar go-to green for adding to soups, pastas, and many other dishes. But did you know that kale, escarole, and Swiss chard can be used similarly? Pasta Pomodoro is a perfect recipe to try new greens.

5. **Think sweet.** Adding a touch of sweetness tames the bitterness. A pinch of sugar, balsamic vinegar, or honey goes a long way. The sweet flavor of my Skillet Roasted Smokey Brussels Sprouts is sure to make new fans of this often side-lined vegetable.

6. **Go meatless.** Studies show swapping meat for vegetables once a week may reduce the risk for diabetes, cancer, heart disease and obesity. Simple Southwest Veggie Burgers, 30-Minute Twice Baked Potatoes and Sneaky Stuffed Shells.

7. **Eat veggies for dessert!** Why limit vegetables to savory dishes? Vegetables add delectable flavor and moisture to baked goods—without fat! Keep your eyes peeled for carrots, pumpkin, rhubarb and zucchini in the dessert chapters!

Popcorn Cauliflower

ONCE YOU'VE HAD ROASTED CAULIFLOWER, you may not want to prepare it any other way. This recipe renders roasted cauliflower into a family-friendly side by tapping into popcorn's appeal. Antioxidant-rich turmeric creates the buttery popcorn hue, while salt and Parmesan supply flavor. The result is tasty enough to be eaten by the bucketful.

MAKES 5 SERVINGS

1 medium head cauliflower (about 2 pounds)

2 teaspoons olive oil

¼ teaspoon turmeric

¼ teaspoon salt

2 tablespoons grated Parmesan cheese

1. Preheat the oven to 425°F. Remove and discard leaves from the cauliflower, and break into florets, about 1 ½ inches.

2. Place florets on a baking sheet, and toss with the oil. Sprinkle lightly with turmeric and salt.

3. Bake for 20 minutes, turn the florets, and cook 5 to 10 minutes more, or until tender and lightly browned. Remove from the oven, sprinkle with the Parmesan, and serve.

Marlene Says: *Studies show that curcumin, the compound that gives turmeric it's intense yellow color, has anti-inflammatory, anti-tumor, and antioxidant properties. In addition to curcumin, this dish is high in vitamin C, blood pressure-lowering potassium, and fiber.*

NUTRITION INFORMATION PER SERVING: (⅔ cup) Calories 65 | Carbohydrate 8g (Sugars 1g) | Total Fat 2g (Sat Fat g) | Protein 4g | Fiber 4g | Cholesterol 5mg | Sodium 220mg | Food Exchanges: 1 Vegetable, ½ Fat | Carbohydrate Choices: ½ | Weight Watcher Plus Point Comparison: 1

Thyme for Honey Mustard Carrots

SAVORY-SWEET CARROTS make a delicious elegant side that cooks up in no "thyme" at all. If you can boil water and operate a microwave, you'll be serving these orange beauties in fewer than 15 minutes. The honey mustard and thyme glaze is also delicious on grilled chicken or fish.

MAKES 6 SERVINGS

1 pound fresh carrots, peeled

1 tablespoon honey

1 tablespoon Dijon mustard

1 tablespoon butter

¼ teaspoon dried thyme

⅛ teaspoon salt

1. Cut carrots in half widthwise and then again lengthwise to create thick sticks (the large pieces from the end of the carrot will require an additional lengthwise cut). Place carrots and ½ cup of water in a medium sauté pan. Place over medium-high heat and bring to a boil. Cover, reduce the heat to medium-low, and cook for 6 to 8 minutes or until the carrots are crisp-tender.

2. While the carrots are cooking, combine remaining ingredients in a small bowl and microwave for 10 seconds on high, or until butter is melted. Uncover the pan (if pan is dry, add 1 tablespoon water), and add the honey mixture. Stir, and continue to toss until all water has evaporated and the carrots are glazed with honey mustard.

NUTRITION INFORMATION PER SERVING: Calories 60 | Carbohydrate 10g (Sugars 5g) | Total Fat 2g (Sat Fat 1g) | Protein 1g | Fiber 2g | Cholesterol 5mg | Sodium 160mg | Food Exchanges: 1 Vegetable, ½ Fat | Carbohydrate Choices: ½ | Weight Watcher Plus Point Comparison: 1

Cheesy Spinach Bake

CHEESY AND EASY, this scrumptious spinach bake seems almost sinful, yet it packs a nutritious punch that would thrill even Popeye. My husband says he could eat this every day. Plate a double portion, like I often do, and you have a satisfying meatless lunch entrée packed with 18 grams of protein to power you through the rest of your day. Have you noticed that "cheesy" makes eating veggies easy?

———————————————————————————————————| **MAKES 8 SERVINGS**

1 (10-ounce) package frozen chopped spinach

1 large egg

½ cup low-fat milk

½ cup seasoned breadcrumbs

½ teaspoon baking powder

¼ teaspoon black pepper

¾ cup shredded reduced-fat Cheddar cheese

4 tablespoons shredded Parmesan cheese, divided

2 large egg whites

1. Preheat the oven to 350°F. Spray an 8 x 8-inch baking dish with nonstick cooking spray and set aside.

2. Place the spinach in a large, microwave-safe bowl, add 1 tablespoon of water, cover, and microwave on high for 5 minutes. Place the spinach in a colander, and press out the cooking liquid until the spinach is almost dry. Set aside.

3. In a large bowl, whisk together the egg and milk. Whisk in breadcrumbs, baking powder, and pepper. Stir in the Cheddar cheese, 2 tablespoons Parmesan, and the spinach, and mix well. In a medium bowl, beat egg whites until soft peaks form, and fold into the spinach mixture.

4. Spread spinach evenly in the prepared pan, top with remaining 2 tablespoons Parmesan, and bake for 23 to 25 minutes, or until set and the top is golden brown.

NUTRITION INFORMATION PER SERVING: (½ cup) Calories 95 | Carbohydrate 8g (Sugars 0g) | Total Fat 4.5g (Sat Fat 2g) | Protein 9g | Fiber 2g | Cholesterol 35mg | Sodium 295mg | Food Exchanges: 1 Lean Meat, 1 Vegetable, ½ Fat | Carbohydrate Choices: ½ | Weight Watcher Plus Point Comparison: 3

Classic Green Bean "Casserole"

AFTER NUMEROUS *TRIALS ON THIS* take on the classic holiday side, nothing beat good old canned soup and frozen green beans for the ease and texture that has made it a tradition. But this is not your mother's green bean casserole. Made in a skillet, it's now weeknight fast and everyday friendly. Fresh onions, mushrooms, and Marsala wine make it fresher and more flavorful than ever, and nonfat half-and-half makes it extra creamy. Options for toppers, including, of course, fried onions, can be found below.

MAKES 8 SERVINGS

1 pound frozen French-cut green beans

1 small onion, thinly sliced

2 cups thinly sliced mushrooms

1 garlic clove, minced

¼ cup Marsala wine

1 (10.75-ounce) can reduced-fat cream of celery soup

½ cup nonfat half-and-half

¼ teaspoon black pepper

¼ teaspoon seasoned salt (optional)

1. Place the green beans in a large, microwave-safe dish, cover, and microwave for 4 minutes. Carefully uncover, stir the beans, re-cover, and microwave for 4 more minutes. Remove and set aside.

2. Spray a large, nonstick skillet with cooking spray, and place over medium-high heat. Add the onions and sauté for 3 minutes. Add mushrooms and garlic and cook for 3 minutes, stirring frequently. Deglaze the pan with Marsala, stirring it into the vegetables.

3. Stir in the green beans, and toss to combine. Stir in the soup, half and half, pepper, and optional seasoned salt. Cover and simmer over low heat for 5 to 10 minutes, stirring occasionally until the mixture is thickened and creamy. (If desired, place green bean mixture in a casserole dish and bake at 350°F for 20 to 25 minutes before serving.) Top as desired below.

Marlene Says: *Top it your way! Sprinkle the green bean mixture in the skillet with either 2/3 cup (½ of a 3-ounce can) French fried onions (adds 30 calories per serving), 1/3 cup sliced toasted almonds (adds 20 calories per serving), or 1/3 cup panko breadcrumbs toasted in a pan with 1½ teaspoons onion powder and 1 teaspoon oil (adds 10 calories per serving) before serving. If preferred, scoop the green bean mix into a casserole dish before topping. Bake at 350°F for 15 minutes before serving.*

NUTRITION INFORMATION PER SERVING: (½ cup) Calories 70 | Carbohydrate 12g (Sugars 5g) | Total Fat 1g (Sat Fat 0g) | Protein 2g | Fiber 2g | Cholesterol 0mg | Sodium 140mg | Food Exchanges: 1 Vegetable, ½ Starch | Carbohydrate Choices: 1 | Weight Watcher Plus Point Comparison: 2

Balsamic Green Beans Almandine

IF YOU LOOKING TO MAKE AN EASY SIDE DISH with fresh green beans, this recipe is for you. In ten minutes, you'll have a gorgeous platter of perfectly cooked beans worthy of any occasion. Balsamic vinegar updates this classic dish, while toasted almonds provide the customary crowning touch. (This recipe doubles nicely.)

MAKES **4** SERVINGS

12 ounces green beans, trimmed

2 tablespoons sliced almonds

3 tablespoons balsamic vinegar

1 teaspoon granulated sugar

⅛ teaspoon salt, or to taste

Black pepper to taste

1. Place a large skillet on the stove over medium-high heat. Add the green beans and ⅓ cup water to the skillet, and bring to a boil. Cover, reduce heat to medium-low, and simmer for 3 minutes until beans are almost cooked to your liking.

2. While beans are cooking, place the almonds in a small sauté pan over medium-low heat. Cook for about 3 minutes, shaking the pan, until nuts are lightly browned, watching carefully. Remove from heat.

3. Uncover the beans and cook off any remaining water. Add balsamic vinegar and sugar to the pan, sprinkle with salt and pepper, and sauté for 1 to 2 minutes, or until the glaze has thickened and beans are well coated. Place in a serving dish, sprinkle with the toasted almonds, and serve.

Marlene Says: *To prepare this dish ahead of time, cook the beans as in step 1, either in the skillet or in a pot of simmering water. After 3 minutes, rinse the beans with cold water to stop the cooking, and set aside. Toast the nuts and set aside. When ready to serve, add the beans to pan and proceed with step 3.*

NUTRITION INFORMATION PER SERVING: (½ cup) Calories 50 | Carbohydrate 9g (Sugars 3 g) | Total Fat 1.5g (Sat Fat 0 g) | Protein 2g | Fiber 3g | Cholesterol 5mg | Sodium 150mg | Food Exchanges: 1 Vegetable | Carbohydrate Choices: ½ | Weight Watcher Plus Point Comparison: 1

Skillet-Roasted Smoky Brussels Sprouts

IF YOU'RE STILL A BRUSSELS SPROUTS SKEPTIC, this recipe, with its sweet and smoky flavor, may very well change your mind. Roasting sprouts tones down bitterness and brings out natural sweetness, but it can be a time killer, so instead I use a skillet-fry method to deliver the same result in half the time. After you try these you may just have to admit to your mother that you are finally eating your sprouts.

MAKES 4 SERVINGS

2 slices center-cut bacon

1 teaspoon canola oil

1 pound Brussels sprouts, trimmed and halved

¼ cup minced onion or shallot

1½ tablespoons balsamic vinegar

1 tablespoon brown sugar

⅛ teaspoon salt, or more to taste

Black pepper to taste

1. In a large, nonstick skillet, cook the bacon over medium heat, turning until crisp. Remove bacon, crumble, and set aside.

2. Add the oil to the skillet, increase heat to medium-high, add the Brussels sprouts, and let cook for 5 minutes or until the sprouts start to brown. Add the onion, stir, and cook another minute. Add ⅓ cup water, cover, reduce the heat to medium, and cook for 4 minutes.

3. Remove cover, stir in the balsamic, brown sugar, and salt. Cook for 2 to 3 minutes, stirring to coat the Brussels sprouts. Add the bacon and continue to cook, turning, until sprouts are well browned. Season with additional salt and pepper to taste.

Marlene Says: *Don't let their small size fool you. Brussels sprouts are jam-packed with nutrients and cancer-fighting compounds similar to other cruciferous vegetables like broccoli, cauliflower, and cabbage. The mighty sprouts are high in Vitamin A, potassium, folate, iron, fiber, and Vitamin C.*

NUTRITION INFORMATION PER SERVING: Calories 90 | Carbohydrate 14g (Sugars 6g) | Total Fat 3g (Sat Fat 1g) | Protein 5g | Fiber 4g | Cholesterol 0mg | Sodium 125mg | Food Exchanges: 1 Vegetable, ½ Fat | Carbohydrate Choices: 1 | Weight Watcher Plus Point Comparison: 2

Jalapeño Popper Stuffed Zucchini Boats

I CANNOT LIE, THESE BOATS ARE DOWNRIGHT ADDICTIVE. Picture zucchini stuffed with ooey gooey cheese, peppered with bits of jalapeño pepper, hot out of the oven. During the recipe testing, I actually burned my tongue on the first batch because I couldn't wait to dive in. For a fun finger food appetizer, cut into bite-size pieces—your guests will be "popping" them up in seconds flat.

MAKES 4 SERVINGS

2 medium zucchini (about ¾ pound)

6 tablespoons reduced-fat shredded Cheddar cheese

2 tablespoons light tub-style cream cheese

2 tablespoons light sour cream

1½ teaspoons finely chopped jarred jalapeño peppers

4 tablespoons panko breadcrumbs

1. Preheat the oven to 400°F.

2. Slice the zucchini in half lengthwise. Using a spoon, carefully scoop out the seeds to form zucchini boats. Place on a microwave-safe plate and microwave on high for 1 minute. Blot any moisture from the zucchini with a paper towel, and set aside.

3. In a medium bowl, place Cheddar, cream cheese, sour cream, and jalapeños, and stir well with a fork until smooth. Spread about 2 tablespoons cheese mixture in each of the zucchini boats.

4. Place the stuffed zucchini on a baking sheet, sprinkle each boat evenly with 1 tablespoon of the breadcrumbs, spray well with cooking spray, and bake for 25 minutes, or until the crumb topping is golden brown. Let cool slightly before digging in!

NUTRITION INFORMATION PER SERVING: (1 zucchini boat) Calories 80 | Carbohydrate 6g (Sugars g) | Total Fat 4g (Sat Fat 2g) | Protein 6g | Fiber 1g | Cholesterol 15mg | Sodium 130mg | Food Exchanges: 1 Vegetable, ½ Lean Meat, ½ Fat | Carbohydrate Choices: ½ | Weight Watcher Plus Point Comparison: 2

Better Bean Succotash

TRADITIONAL SUCCOTASH, made with lima beans, corn, and lots of butter, is a Southern favorite. But if you are not a fan of lima beans, you will be pleased to see that, while I have kept the hallmarks of the classic dish, limas are swapped out for hearty, protein-rich edamame (soy beans). The result is a thoroughly modern better-for-you dish with a solid dose of Southern charm. (If you are a succotash purist, feel free to use lima beans.)

MAKES 6 SERVINGS

2 cups frozen corn

1¼ cups shelled edamame beans

1 slice center-cut bacon, cut in half

½ cup chopped onion

1½ teaspoons granulated sugar

¾ teaspoon reduced-sodium seasoned salt

2 medium tomatoes, seeded and chopped (about 1¼ cups)

2 teaspoons butter

2 tablespoons nonfat half-and-half (optional)

1. Place the corn and beans in a medium, microwave-safe bowl. Add 2 tablespoons water, cover, and microwave on high for 4 minutes. Set aside.

2. While the corn is cooking, place the bacon in a large sauté pan over medium heat. Cook until crisp, remove from pan, cool, crumble, and set aside. Add the onion to the pan, and cook for one minute. Sprinkle the sugar over the onions, add 1 tablespoon water, and cook for 2 to 3 more minutes, or until onions soften.

3. Add the seasoned salt and corn mixture to the pan and stir. Stir in the tomatoes, and cook 1 to 2 minutes or until warm. Stir in the butter. Add optional half-and-half, if desired, and cook for 1 to 2 minutes, or until incorporated into the succotash. Top succotash with crumbled bacon and serve.

Marlene Says: *Soybeans are high in omega-3 fatty acids and have twice the protein and fiber of lima beans. Look for shelled edamame (soy) beans in the freezer case.*

NUTRITION INFORMATION PER SERVING: (½ cup) Calories 155 | Carbohydrate 21g (Sugars 5g) | Total Fat 6g (Sat Fat 2g) | Protein 9g | Fiber 5g | Cholesterol 5mg | Sodium 180mg | Food Exchanges: 1 Starch, 1 Lean Meat, 1 Fat | Carbohydrate Choices: 1 | Weight Watcher Plus Point Comparison: 3

Two-Minute Sugar Snap Peas

WHEN I WAS A TEEN, my Italian mother took Chinese cooking classes, and to this day, many of my best Chinese cooking secrets come from her. One of the things she taught me was that Asian pea pods should cook for no longer than two minutes—the same cooking time I use here with slightly heartier sugar snap peas. The addition of a simple, soy-based sauce also has Mom's approval.

MAKES 5 SERVINGS

1 tablespoon reduced-sodium soy sauce

1 teaspoon brown sugar

1 teaspoon sesame oil

½ teaspoon cornstarch

1 pound (or one 15-ounce bag) sugar snap peas

1. Mix together first four ingredients in a small cup. Set aside.

2. Place peas and 2 tablespoons water in a large skillet, and place over medium heat. Bring water to a simmer, cover pan, and cook for 1 minute. Uncover pan, cook off any remaining water, and add soy sauce mixture to pan.

3. Bring to a simmer and cook peas for one more minute while tossing with sauce.

NUTRITION INFORMATION PER SERVING: (²/₃ cup) Calories 45 | Carbohydrate 7g (Sugars 1g) | Total Fat 1g (Sat Fat 0g) | Protein 2g | Fiber 2g | Cholesterol 0mg | Sodium 180mg | Food Exchanges: 1 Vegetable | Carbohydrate Choices: ½ | Weight Watcher Plus Point Comparison: 1

Terrific Tomato Tart

THIS IS THE RECIPE TO SHOWCASE ANY LUSCIOUS, ripe tomatoes you have on hand. With Parmesan cheese and an Italian-seasoned rice crust, the rustic tomato basil tart could be mistaken as a menu offering from an authentic Italian trattoria. Cut it into wedges for a side dish, or with just over 350 calories for the whole tart, enjoy one as your personal entrée, without the guilt or the carbs associated with eating an entire pizza pie.

MAKES 4 SERVINGS

6 tablespoons grated Parmesan cheese, divided

²/₃ cup uncooked instant brown rice

¾ teaspoon garlic powder

¾ teaspoon Italian seasoning, divided

¼ teaspoon salt (optional)

1 large egg white

3 medium Roma tomatoes, cut into ½-inch slices, ends discarded

⅛ teaspoon black pepper, or to taste

2 tablespoons chopped fresh basil

1. Preheat the oven to 400°F. Lightly spray a 9-inch glass pie plate with cooking spray, and sprinkle the bottom evenly with 2 tablespoons Parmesan.

2. Cook the brown rice according to package directions, and place in a medium bowl. When the rice has cooled, mix in garlic powder, ½ teaspoon Italian seasoning, salt, and egg white. Press the rice mixture firmly on the bottom of the prepared pie plate, and set aside.

3. Blot the tomato slices with paper towels to remove excess moisture. Arrange the tomatoes on top of the rice. Sprinkle with pepper and remaining ¼ teaspoon Italian seasoning. Bake for 15 minutes, sprinkle the tomatoes with the remaining 4 tablespoons Parmesan, and bake another 10 minutes.

4. Let cool for 2 minutes, top with basil, cut into wedges, and serve.

NUTRITION INFORMATION PER SERVING: (¼ tart) Calories 90 | Carbohydrate 11g (Sugars 2g) | Total Fat 4g (Sat Fat 2g) | Protein 7g | Fiber 1g | Cholesterol 10mg | Sodium 250mg | Food Exchanges: 1 Starch, ½ Vegetable, ½ Lean Meat | Carbohydrate Choices: 1 | Weight Watcher Plus Point Comparison: 2

Extra Crispy Oven-Baked Steak Fries

THESE DAYS, THE TERM "EXTRA CRISPY" usually means extra fat, but not in these fries. Panko breadcrumbs and Parmesan cheese step up to the plate to create crispy, flavorful steak-cut fries—but with a fraction of the usual fat. The usual cooking time has been trimmed, and the steps are simple, but follow the instructions as written for the best results. Trust me when I say that after many trials—each step counts.

MAKES 5 SERVINGS

2 medium russet potatoes, unpeeled, about 1½ pounds

2 large egg whites

2 tablespoons grated Parmesan cheese

1 teaspoon garlic salt, divided

⅔ cup panko breadcrumbs

⅛ teaspoon black pepper

1. Preheat the oven to 425°F. Cut each potato in half lengthwise, cut each piece in half, and then half again for 8 wedges. Place half the wedges on a large, microwave-safe plate, and microwave on high for 3 minutes.

2. In a shallow bowl, whisk together the egg whites, Parmesan, and ½ teaspoon garlic salt. In another bowl, combine the panko, black pepper, and ½ teaspoon garlic salt.

3. Remove potatoes from microwave and replace with second batch. Brush the cut sides of the each microwaved potato wedge with the egg white mixture, sprinkle with the seasoned panko, and place the wedges skin-side down (pointed-side up) on a baking sheet. Spray lightly with cooking spray, and repeat with the remaining wedges.

4. Cover the baking sheet with foil, and bake for 10 minutes. Remove the foil and bake for another 15 minutes, or until the fries are golden brown. Serve immediately.

Marlene Says: *To make CRISPY OVEN-FRIED CARROTS, substitute 3 medium carrots for the potatoes. Cut each carrot into 6 sticks (cut each carrot in half crosswise, then cut each piece lengthwise, cutting the fat end in half again). Do not microwave the carrots. Simply coat them with the egg white mixture, and then the crumbs. Bake as directed, for 15 minutes covered and 10 minutes uncovered. (Four servings with 85 calories, 16g of carbohydrate, 5g protein, 1g fat, and 1g fiber.)*

NUTRITION INFORMATION PER SERVING: (3 wedges) Calories 130 | Carbohydrate 25g (Sugars 2g) | Total Fat 1g (Sat Fat 0g) | Protein 5g | Fiber 1.5g | Cholesterol 0mg | Sodium 260mg | Food Exchanges: 1½ Starch | Carbohydrate Choices: 1½ | Weight Watcher Plus Point Comparison: 3

Creamy Steakhouse Mashed Potatoes

IMAGINE ALL YOUR FAVORITE STEAKHOUSE SIDE DISHES rolled into one decadent dish, and you have this casserole. When I first thought of combining caramelized onions and creamed spinach into buttery mashed potatoes, I honestly wasn't sure it would work. But does it ever! Topped with Parmesan or bleu cheese, this luscious side dish is a winner. Love bacon? Sprinkle on 3 tablespoons of bacon bits for just 10 calories more per serving. Leftovers reheat beautifully.

MAKES 8 SERVINGS

1½ pounds Yukon Gold potatoes, peeled and cubed

1 teaspoon margarine or butter

1 medium onion, chopped

1 (10-ounce) package frozen chopped spinach, thawed and squeezed dry

½ cup light sour cream

1 (12-ounce) can low-fat evaporated milk, divided

¾ teaspoon salt, or more to taste

½ teaspoon black pepper

¼ cup Parmesan or blue cheese

1. Preheat the oven to 350°F. Spray a 13 x 9-inch baking dish with cooking spray, and set aside.

2. Place the potatoes in a large pot of water, bring to a boil, and cook for 15 to 20 minutes, or until the potatoes are tender.

3. While the potatoes are cooking, heat the margarine in a large, nonstick skillet over medium-low heat. Add the onions and cook, stirring frequently, for 8 to 10 minutes, or until soft and starting to caramelize, adding 1 tablespoon water if needed to keep them soft. Add the spinach and 2 additional tablespoons of water, stir, and cook for another 2 minutes. Set aside.

4. When potatoes are tender, drain, place back in pot, and add the sour cream, half of the evaporated milk, salt, and pepper. Using an electric mixer, blend just until smooth. Add remaining milk and briefly blend again. Stir in the spinach mixture and transfer to the baking dish. Bake for 20 minutes, sprinkle with the Parmesan, and bake another 5 to 10 minutes, or until hot and bubbly. (Potatoes will thicken as they cool.)

DARE TO COMPARE: A side order of loaded mashed potatoes at Applebee's serves up 460 calories, 33 grams of fat, and 1,230 milligrams of sodium.

NUTRITION INFORMATION PER SERVING: (¾ cup) Calories 120 | Carbohydrate 18g (Sugars 6g) | Total Fat 3.5g (Sat Fat 1g) | Protein 7g | Fiber 2g | Cholesterol 15mg | Sodium 350mg | Food Exchanges: 1 Starch, ½ Vegetable, ½ Fat | Carbohydrate Choices: 1 | Weight Watcher Plus Point Comparison: 3

30-Minute Twice-Baked Potatoes

THESE CREAMY, CHEESY TWICE-BAKED POTATOES are made in record time. Microwaving the potatoes saves time, and once stuffed, a hot oven finishes them off in 10 minutes flat. Creamed cottage cheese imparts a lusciously creamy texture, while Cheddar, green onions, and garlic heap on the flavor. Serve these as a side to simple meat entrées or with a salad for the perfect light lunch.

MAKES 4 SERVINGS

2 (10-ounce) baking potatoes

2 green onions, green and white parts, sliced

¾ cup low-fat cottage cheese*

½ cup reduced-fat shredded Cheddar cheese, divided

¼ cup low-fat milk

⅛ teaspoon black pepper

¼ teaspoon garlic powder

1. Preheat the oven to 425°F. Pierce the potatoes with a fork, and place in the microwave. Cook on high for 10 to 12 minutes or until fork-tender.

2. Place the green onions in a small bowl, cover, and microwave for 30 seconds. Set aside.

3. Slice the potatoes in half lengthwise. Scoop out the potato pulp, leaving ¼ inch of potato in the skin, and place pulp in a medium bowl. Blend the cottage cheese in a food processor or with an immersion blender until smooth. Add it to the bowl, along with ¼ cup Cheddar cheese, milk, pepper, garlic powder, and green onions, and beat with an electric mixer until smooth.

4. Pile the filling into the skins, top each potato with 1 tablespoon Cheddar cheese, and bake for 10 minutes.

DARE TO COMPARE: Traditional twice-baked potatoes average 600 calories, over 30 grams of fat, and 1,000 milligrams of sodium.

* Light sour cream can be substituted for cottage cheese. Add 25 calories and 2 grams of fat. Subtract 5 grams of protein.

NUTRITION INFORMATION PER SERVING: (1 stuffed half) Calories 150 | Carbohydrate 22g (Sugars 4g) | Total Fat 2g (Sat Fat 1g) | Protein 11g | Fiber 3g | Cholesterol 5mg | Sodium 250mg | Food Exchanges: 1½ Starch, 1 Lean Meat | Carbohydrate Choices: 1½ | Weight Watcher Plus Point Comparison: 3

10-Minute Mexican-Style Pintos

HERE'S AN AUTHENTIC MEXICAN SIDE DISH to add to your go-to recipe list. Simmer pinto beans with garlic, onions, tomatoes, and cilantro for a punch of flavor, and then add a touch of smoky bacon, and you have "piggy-style" beans. Instead of hours, reduced-sodium canned pinto beans, now easily found in most supermarkets, allow you to get this side dish to the table in mere minutes.

MAKES **4** SERVINGS

1 slice center-cut bacon, chopped

½ cup diced onion

2 garlic cloves, minced

1 (15-ounce) can reduced-sodium pinto beans (not drained)

¾ cup chopped, seeded tomato

2 tablespoons chopped cilantro

Salt, to taste

1. In a small saucepan, cook the bacon over medium heat for 1 to 2 minutes, or until it starts to brown. Add the onion, stir, and cook for 3 to 4 minutes or until translucent (add 1 to 2 teaspoons of water if needed). Stir in the garlic, and cook for 30 seconds.

2. Add beans and tomato, and stir. Using a fork or potato masher, lightly mash some of the beans, if desired. Simmer on low for 3 to 4 minutes, or to desired thickness. Stir in cilantro, and salt to taste, simmer another 30 seconds, and serve.

Marlene Says: *When it comes to value, convenience, and good nutrition, it's hard to beat canned beans. These days, most brands offer reduced-sodium varieties, and that is important in this recipe, which requires them to be undrained.*

NUTRITION INFORMATION PER SERVING: (½ cup) Calories 100 | Carbohydrate 17g (Sugars 2g) | Total Fat 1.5g (Sat Fat 0g) | Protein 6g | Fiber 6g | Cholesterol 0mg | Sodium 135mg | Food Exchanges: 1 Starch, ½ Lean Meat | Carbohydrate Choices: 1 | Weight Watcher Plus Point Comparison: 2

Instant Curried Rice and Pea Pilaf

A TASTE OF INDIA IS JUST MINUTES AWAY in this easy dish that takes advantage of instant brown rice and frozen peas. The tantalizing combination of coconut and curry will win over even the most finicky eaters. Serve it with my Tandoori-Style Grilled Chicken (page 256) and naan bread, and you'll have a feast that will convince your taste buds you've traveled to India.

MAKES **4** SERVINGS

2 teaspoons canola oil

1 large shallot, finely diced (or ⅓ cup diced onion)

⅔ cup instant brown rice

¾ teaspoon curry powder

1 cup reduced-sodium chicken broth

¼ cup nonfat half-and-half

¼ teaspoon coconut extract

⅛ teaspoon salt

¾ cup frozen peas

1. In a medium saucepan, heat the oil over medium-high heat. Add the shallot and sauté for 3 to 4 minutes, or until the onion is translucent.

2. Add brown rice and curry powder, stirring until slightly toasted. Add the broth, nonfat half-and-half, coconut extract, and salt, and bring to a boil. Cover, reduce the heat, and let simmer for 5 minutes. Mix in peas and simmer for an additional 5 to 7 minutes, or until rice is tender.

3. Fluff with a fork and serve.

NUTRITION INFORMATION PER SERVING: (~ ⅔ cup) Calories 120 | Carbohydrate 17g (Sugars 3g) | Total Fat 3g (Sat Fat 0g) | Protein 4g | Fiber 3g | Cholesterol 0mg | Sodium 230mg | Food Exchanges: 1 Starch, ½ Fat | Carbohydrate Choices: 1 | Weight Watcher Plus Point Comparison: 2

Sweet Noodle Kugel

IF YOU ARE UNFAMILIAR WITH "KUGEL," it's a delicious custard-like noodle dish that's quite common in Eastern Europe. In America, it's known mostly for the comfort it serves up on Jewish holidays. My lightened version, still made the old-fashioned way with eggs, butter, cottage cheese, and sour cream, retains the dish's rich heritage with brand-new guilt-free goodness. This sweet-style kugel is a wonderful addition to any brunch.

MAKES 12 SERVINGS

8 ounces extrawide egg noodles

2 tablespoons margarine or butter

4 large egg whites

2 cups low-fat cottage cheese

3 large eggs

⅔ cup no-calorie sweetener*

1 teaspoon cinnamon

¾ teaspoon vanilla extract

1 cup light sour cream

1. Preheat the oven to 350°F. Lightly spray a 13 x 9 x 2-inch glass or ceramic baking dish with nonstick cooking spray.

2. Cook the noodles for one minute less than the minimum cooking time on the package directions. Drain the pasta well, return to the pot, add the margarine, and stir to coat. Set aside. In a large bowl with an electric mixer, beat the egg whites on high speed until soft peaks form. Set aside.

3. Place the cottage cheese, eggs, sweetener, cinnamon, and vanilla in a blender, or a large bowl for an immersion blender, and process until almost smooth. If needed, transfer mixture to a large bowl. Stir in the sour cream, add the noodles, and stir again. Gently fold in the egg whites.

4. Spoon the mixture into the prepared baking dish and smooth the surface. Bake for 35 minutes, or until set.

DARE TO COMPARE: A piece of sweet kugel made the traditional way averages 330 calories, 18 grams of fat, and 29 grams of carbohydrate per serving.

*See page 81 for sweetener options.

NUTRITION INFORMATION PER SERVING: (¾ cup) Calories 160 | Carbohydrate 15g (Sugars g) | Total Fat 5g (Sat Fat 1g) | Protein 11g | Fiber 0g | Cholesterol 75mg | Sodium 220mg | Food Exchanges: 1 Starch, 1 Lean Meat, ½ Fat | Carbohydrate Choices: 1 | Weight Watcher Plus Point Comparison: 4

Quick 'n Easy Any Day Applesauce

THIS SIDE DELIVERS THE FRESH FLAVOR and homemade goodness of applesauce to your table in just 15 minutes. Highly versatile, served warm (my favorite) or cold, applesauce is terrific with meats such as pork chops or ham, as a topping for pancakes and yogurt, or even served alone as a simple dessert. You'll find several of my favorite variations in the Marlene Says section. Extra sauce keeps fresh for 4 days in the fridge.

MAKES 6 SERVINGS

6 golden delicious or other cooking apples (about 2 pounds)

1 tablespoon fresh lemon juice

½ teaspoon cinnamon

1 tablespoon brown sugar

1. Peel, core, and cut apples into 1-inch chunks. (Uniform pieces will even the cooking time.) Place the apples in a deep, microwave-safe casserole dish. Stir in 1 cup water, lemon juice, and cinnamon.

2. Microwave, uncovered, on high for 5 minutes. Stir and mash the apples with a fork. Microwave the apples for another 5 to 7 minutes, or until the apples are tender. Mash the apples, and stir to incorporate the liquid. Stir in the brown sugar, and serve warm or cool. Store in the refrigerator for 3 to 4 days.

Marlene Says: For cinnamon applesauce, stir in another ½ teaspoon cinnamon. For a savory applesauce, stir in ⅛ teaspoon ground cardamom. To make 1½ cups of applesauce that is perfect for topping pancakes and waffles, measure half of the recipe (1½ cups applesauce) into a small bowl, and stir in 2 tablespoons sugar-free maple-flavored syrup, 2 tablespoons water, and ¼ teaspoon cinnamon.

NUTRITION INFORMATION PER SERVING: (½ cup) Calories 75 | Carbohydrate 19g (Sugars 16g) | Total Fat 0g (Sat Fat 0g) | Protein 0g | Fiber 2g | Cholesterol 0mg | Sodium 0mg | Food Exchanges: 1 Fruit | Carbohydrate Choices: 1 | Weight Watcher Plus Point Comparison: 1

Any Day Stuffin' Muffins

MAKE ANY DINNER FEEL SPECIAL with these easy-to-make muffins made of stuffing! A quick sauté of fresh vegetables combined with spices and green onion take packaged stuffing mix to homemade heights. Pack the mix into muffin cups to ensure quick cooking and easy portion control. These muffins rated an enthusiastic two-yums up with my stuffin'-lovin' boys.

MAKES 8 SERVINGS

2 tablespoons margarine or butter

¾ cup diced onions

½ cup diced celery

½ cup diced red pepper

1 teaspoon dried sage, crumbled

1 teaspoon finely chopped fennel seeds, or more to taste

¼ teaspoon black pepper

¼ cup sliced green onion

1 (6-ounce) package lower sodium chicken stuffing mix (like Stove Top)*

2 large egg whites

* I do not recommend using the lower sodium cornbread stuffing mix in the Stove Top brand. Potassium is used to reduce the sodium and it has a bitter metallic taste.

1. Preheat the oven to 425°F. Line 8 muffin cups with foil liners, or lightly spray with nonstick cooking spray.

2. Melt the margarine in a medium sauté pan over medium heat. Add the next 6 ingredients (onions through black pepper), and cook for 6 to 7 minutes, or until vegetables are softened. While the vegetables cook, place 1 ¼ cups water in a microwave-safe measuring cup and heat on high for 2 minutes.

3. Remove the pan from heat, and stir in the green onions and stuffing mix. Add the hot water, and toss lightly with a fork to evenly distribute. Transfer the mixture to a bowl, let cool for 5 minutes, and gently stir in egg whites.

4. Scoop ⅓ cup stuffing into each muffin cup. Spray the muffin tops with cooking spray, and bake for 10 minutes, or until tops are lightly browned.

Marlene Says: *For a SAUSAGE STUFFIN' MUFFIN, remove the meat from 4-ounce link of sausage, add to the sauté pan, break up with a spatula, and cook for 5 minutes before adding the vegetables. Proceed with recipe directions.*

NUTRITION INFORMATION PER SERVING: (1 muffin) Calories 80 | Carbohydrate 13g (Sugars 2g) | Total Fat 2g (Sat Fat 0g) | Protein 2g | Fiber 1g | Cholesterol 0mg | Sodium 150mg | Food Exchanges: ½ Starch, 1 Vegetable | Carbohydrate Choices: 1 | Weight Watcher Plus Point Comparison 2

Quick-Fix Chicken and Turkey Entrées

Parmesan Crusted Chicken

Crispy Ranch Hand Chicken

Speedy Spinach Artichoke Chicken

Any Day Chicken Enchiladas

No Bones Chicken Coq au Vin

Stephen's Pretzel Chicken with Honey Mustard Sauce

20-Minute One Pot Chicken and Bean Stew

Sesame Chicken

Quicker-Than-Takeout Sweet and Sour Chicken

Tandoori-Style Grilled Chicken

Almost Cheesecake Factory Bang-Bang Chicken and Shrimp

Grilled Portobello Turkey Stuffed "Pizzas"

Moist and Flavorful Chicken for Days

Poor Man's Turkey Stroganoff

ITH TODAY'S BUSY LIFESTYLES, chicken is often the answer to quick-fix meals. But even our best go-to chicken dishes can get dull after a while, especially when the recipes are focused more on convenience and health than on tantalizing taste. I'm thrilled to tell you that this chapter will change all that with a dozen fast and fit recipes designed to add a world of exciting flavors to your poultry dinners!

To kick things off, healthy meets heavenly with my cheesy, crispy Parmesan Crusted Chicken. An Italian favorite in its own right, the entrée transforms into a plated masterpiece when served with broccoli on a bed of linguini and drizzled with Light and Luscious All-Purpose Alfredo Sauce (page 189). Its taste and texture will delight your family, while the fat and calorie savings whittle your waistline. Any Day Chicken Enchiladas capture an authentic Mexican feel with rich homemade enchilada sauce elevating the taste. Though it takes just minutes to make, the sauce is richer and more complex tasting (with less sodium) than any you'll find in a can. And the full flavor of Chinese takeout can be delivered to your table in no time flat with Quicker-Than-Takeout Sweet and Sour Chicken. Making this beloved dish at home not only saves time, but it also saves money—and over 700 calories! Pair it with Panda-Style Chicken Chow Mein (page 192), for an at-home Chinese feast.

These dishes and others, like the wonderfully aromatic Tandoori-Style Grilled Chicken, sizzling sweet Sesame Chicken stir-fry, and terrific trattoria-worthy Grilled Portobello Turkey Stuffed "Pizzas" will have you "traveling the world" at dinnertime before you know it. (P.S.—Be sure to check out the pasta, pressure cooker, soups, and salads chapters (pages 172, 196, 122, and 151) for more quick-fix poultry entrées!)

Parmesan Crusted Chicken

THIS IS THE TYPE OF SIMPLE RECIPE you just can't beat having in your "what's for dinner?" repertoire. Skinless boneless chicken breast get the royal crunchy cheesy treatment with a coating of equal parts panko breadcrumbs and Parmesan and a hot skillet. Enjoy it alone with your favorite sides, on top of salad greens, or drizzled with Light and Luscious Alfredo Sauce (page 189). Feel free to double the recipe.

MAKES 2 SERVINGS

3 tablespoons grated Parmesan cheese

3 tablespoons panko breadcrumbs

¼ teaspoon garlic salt

⅛ teaspoon black pepper

1 large egg white

2 boneless, skinless chicken breasts (about ½ pound)

1½ teaspoons olive oil

1. In a shallow bowl, mix together the Parmesan cheese, bread-crumbs, garlic salt, and pepper. In another shallow bowl, beat the egg white until frothy.

2. Wrap the chicken breasts in plastic wrap and place on a cutting board. Gently pound each breast with a mallet until thin (about ¼ inch thick). Dip each chicken breast into the beaten egg to coat, and then roll it in the breadcrumb mixture.

3. Heat the oil in a large nonstick skillet over medium-high heat. Add the chicken and cook for 3 to 4 minutes on each side, turning once or twice while cooking, until both sides are crispy and golden brown, and chicken is cooked through.

Marlene Says: *For a Red Lobster–style Parmesan Crusted Chicken entrée, toss ¾ cup each pasta and cooked broccoli florets with ¼ cup of Light and Luscious Alfredo Sauce (page 189), and top with one Parmesan Crusted Chicken breast. You'll save a trip to the restaurant, a whopping 800 calories, and 55 grams of fat!*

NUTRITION INFORMATION PER SERVING (1 breast) | Calories 195 | Carbohydrate 8g (Sugars 2g) | Total Fat 6g (Sat Fat 2g) | Protein 30g | Fiber 0g | Cholesterol 5mg | Sodium 240 mg | Food Exchanges: 4½ Lean Meat, ½ Starch | Carbohydrate Choices: ½ | Weight Watcher Plus Point Comparison: 5

Crispy Ranch Hand Chicken

BARBECUE CHICKEN AND RANCH DRESSING LOVERS UNITE! This oven-baked chicken is moist, tender, and dare I say, finger-licking good. The buttermilk ranch dressing tenderizes while the barbecue-seasoned breadcrumbs make the chicken crispy, smoky, and delectable. Serve with baked beans and my Apple Poppy Seed Slaw (page 162) for a hearty, home-on-the-range meal at home.

MAKES 4 SERVINGS

⅓ cup low-fat buttermilk

2 tablespoons light mayonnaise

½ teaspoon garlic powder

½ teaspoon dried parsley

½ teaspoon onion powder

¼ teaspoon black pepper

Pinch of salt

¾ cup panko breadcrumbs

¼ cup dry breadcrumbs

2 teaspoons canola oil

2 teaspoons barbecue seasoning, divided

4 boneless, skinless chicken breasts (about 1 pound)

1. Preheat the oven to 425°F.

2. To make the dressing, in a small bowl, stir together the first 7 ingredients (buttermilk through salt). In a medium shallow bowl, mix together crumbs, oil, and 1½ teaspoons barbecue seasoning.

3. Wrap the chicken breasts in plastic wrap and gently pound to ¼-inch thickness. Spread 1 teaspoon of dressing on one side of a chicken breast, and dip the chicken breast, dressing-side down, in the seasoned breadcrumbs. Repeat with other side, and place on baking sheet. Sprinkle lightly with barbecue seasoning. Repeat with remaining chicken breasts.

4. Spray the chicken breasts with cooking spray, and bake for 12 to 14 minutes, or until coating is golden brown and chicken is cooked. Serve each chicken breast with 1 tablespoon of ranch dressing.

Marlene Says: *Barbecue seasonings (or rubs) are easily found in the spice aisle. I like McCormick brand Grill Mates barbecue seasoning. It's also great sprinkled on pork and roasted potatoes.*

NUTRITION INFORMATION PER SERVING: (1 chicken breast) Calories 240 | Carbohydrate 13g (Sugars 2g) | Total Fat 8g (Sat Fat 2g) | Protein 27g | Fiber 0g | Cholesterol 75mg | Sodium 480mg | Food Exchanges: 3½ Lean Meat, 1 Starch | Carbohydrate Choices: 1 | Weight Watcher Plus Point Comparison: 6

Speedy Spinach Artichoke Dip Chicken

YOU CAN HAVE CRAVE-ABLE, OH-SO-CREAMY DIP—and even eat it for dinner! Inspired by the ever popular spinach artichoke dip, this quick-fix skillet dish features juicy chicken topped with creamy, melt-y hot dip, and takes as little as 15 minutes from prep to plate. Feel free to whip up extra dip to serve with raw veggies for a yummy next-day snack.

MAKES 4 SERVINGS

1 cup thinly shredded fresh spinach

½ cup drained quartered artichoke hearts

¼ cup plus 4 teaspoons grated Parmesan cheese, divided

3 tablespoons light mayonnaise

½ teaspoon minced garlic

½ teaspoon onion powder

¼ teaspoon black pepper

2 tablespoons shredded part-skim mozzarella

4 boneless, skinless chicken breasts (about 1 pound)

1. Place the spinach and artichoke hearts in a medium, microwave-safe bowl, cover, and cook on high for 1 minute. Remove from microwave and stir in ¼ cup Parmesan, mayonnaise, garlic, onion powder, and black pepper. Stir in mozzarella and set aside.

2. Wrap the chicken breasts in plastic wrap and gently pound to ⅛- to ¼-inch thickness. Spray a large, nonstick skillet with cooking spray, and place over medium-high heat. Add the chicken and cook for 2 to 3 minutes on each side, until well browned and almost cooked through.

3. Spoon ¼ cup of the "dip" onto each breast, and spread to cover. Add scant ¼ cup of water to the skillet, cover, and cook 1 minute, or until the chicken is cooked through, "dip" is hot, and cheese melted. Sprinkle 1 teaspoon of Parmesan over each breast and serve.

DARE TO COMPARE: The Spinach Artichoke Dip appetizer at Applebee's—just like this recipe—has 28 grams of protein. But instead of 200 calories and 8 grams of fat, it has 1,350 calories and 92 grams of fat. This dippy dish also delivers an 85% savings in sodium and 95% less carbs.

NUTRITION INFORMATION PER SERVING: (1 breast) Calories 200 | Carbohydrate 4g (Sugars 0g) | Total Fat 8g (Sat Fat 2g) | Protein 28g | Fiber 1g | Cholesterol 80mg | Sodium 320mg | Food Exchanges: 4½ Lean Meat, ½ Fat | Carbohydrate Choices: 0 | Weight Watcher Plus Point Comparison: 5

Any Day Chicken Enchiladas

MY HOMEMADE CHICKEN ENCHILADAS are easy enough to make anytime you get the enchilada craving, but still want to keep calories in check. I use basic pantry staples to whip up a rich-tasting, tortilla-worthy sauce (superior to any canned version), and my Moist and Flavorful Chicken for Days recipe on page 260 for the chicken. I find the perfect Tex-Mex side to be the Three-Minute Tomato and Avocado Salad on page 155.

MAKES 4 TO 8 SERVINGS

4 tablespoons chili powder

4 teaspoons flour

1 teaspoon ground cumin

1 teaspoon granulated sugar

½ teaspoon garlic powder

½ teaspoon dried oregano

⅛ teaspoon salt

4 tablespoons tomato paste

1 (14.5-ounce) can reduced-sodium chicken broth

2 cups shredded cooked chicken breast

¾ cup shredded reduced-fat Mexican Blend cheese

8 (6-inch) corn tortillas

¼ cup chopped green onion

1. Preheat the oven to 375°F. To make the enchilada sauce, in a medium saucepan over medium-low heat, combine the first 7 ingredients (chili powder through salt), and warm for 2 minutes. Stir in the tomato paste and ½ cup water, whisking until smooth. Whisk in the chicken broth, increase heat to medium, and bring to a boil. Cover, reduce heat, and simmer on low for 5 minutes.

2. To soften the tortillas, sprinkle 4 tortillas with water, wrap in a clean dish or paper towel, and microwave on high power for 45 seconds. (Repeat with remaining tortillas as you need them.)

3. Spread ¼ cup enchilada sauce on the bottom of a 13 x 9 x 2-inch baking pan. Spread each tortilla with 1 tablespoon sauce and top with ¼ cup chicken, 1 tablespoon cheese, and 1 teaspoon green onion. Roll the tortilla to cover filling, and place in baking pan seam-side down. Repeat with remaining tortillas.

4. Stir 2 tablespoons water into the remaining enchilada sauce and pour over the enchiladas, and top with remaining cheese and green onions. Cover with foil and bake for 15 to 20 minutes.

NUTRITION INFORMATION PER SERVING: (1 enchilada) Calories 150 | Carbohydrate 16g (Sugars 1g) | Total Fat 4g (Sat Fat 1g) | Protein 15g | Fiber 2g | Cholesterol 35mg | Sodium 310mg | Food Exchanges: 1½ Lean Meat, 1 Starch, ½ Fat | Carbohydrate Choices: 1 | Weight Watcher Plus Point Comparison: 4

No Bones Chicken Coq au Vin

FIFTY YEARS AGO, through her cookbook and television series, Julia Child single-handedly made the classic French one-pot chicken dish, Coq au Vin, into an American favorite. My rendition delivers all the essential ingredients—chicken, bacon, onions, mushrooms, and wine—but instead of hours, this mouthwatering stew cooks up in only 30 minutes. Serve it for the authentic taste of rustic French cuisine and as a valid excuse to say, "Bon Appétit!"

MAKES 4 SERVINGS

⅔ cup frozen pearl onions, thawed

4 boneless, skinless chicken breasts (about 1 ¼ pound)

2 tablespoons all-purpose flour

2 slices center-cut lean bacon

1 8-ounce package sliced mushrooms,

¾ cup dry red wine

½ cup reduced-sodium chicken broth

2 tablespoons tomato paste

¾ teaspoon dried thyme

¼ teaspoon black pepper

⅛ teaspoon salt, or to taste

Fresh parsley for garnish (optional)

1. Place the pearl onions and 2 tablespoons water in a small, microwave-safe bowl, cover, and cook on high for 3 minutes. Uncover, drain, and set aside. Wrap the chicken breasts in plastic wrap and gently pound to ¼- to ½-inch thickness. Sprinkle flour over both sides and set aside.

2. In a large, nonstick skillet, cook the bacon over medium-high heat until crisp. Crumble, and set aside. Add the chicken, and cook for 2 to 3 minutes per side, or until well browned and barely cooked through. Transfer the chicken to a plate.

3. Reduce the heat to medium, add the pearl onions, and cook for 2 minutes, while stirring. Add the mushrooms, and cook for 3 minutes, or until softened. Add bacon and remaining ingredients, stirring to incorporate the tomato paste. Bring to a boil, and simmer for 3 to 5 minutes, allowing sauce to slightly thicken.

4. Add chicken back to the pan, turn to coat both with sauce, and simmer an additional 3 to 5 minutes, or until the sauce is thickened to taste. Garnish with parsley, if desired, and serve.

NUTRITION INFORMATION PER SERVING: (1 chicken breast plus sauce) Calories 230 | Carbohydrate 13g (Sugars 3g) | Total Fat 4.5g (Sat Fat 1g) | Protein 28g | Fiber 1g | Cholesterol 75mg | Sodium 220mg | Food Exchanges: 4 Lean Meat, 1 Vegetable, ½ Starch | Carbohydrate Choices: 1 | Weight Watcher Plus Point Comparison: 5

Stephen's Pretzel Chicken with Honey Mustard Sauce

THE DAY I WAS TESTING THIS RECIPE, I asked my son Stephen to "sample it" as he was running out the door. It took only one bite to stop him in his tracks. Crunchy pretzels and tangy mustard are a perfect match as they seal the juices of the white meat chicken, but I think the creamy honey mustard dipping sauce sealed the deal for Stephen, who ate a full serving on his way out—and another when he returned. It's now his dish.

MAKES 4 SERVINGS

4 boneless, skinless chicken breasts (about 1 pound)

²/₃ cup crushed pretzels (about 1 ounce)

½ teaspoon mustard powder

1 teaspoon onion powder

½ teaspoon black pepper

2 tablespoons plus 4 teaspoons Dijon mustard, divided

2 tablespoons white wine vinegar

1 tablespoon light mayonnaise

2 teaspoons honey

2 teaspoons olive oil

1. Preheat the oven to 425°F. Spray a large baking pan with cooking spray. Wrap the chicken breasts in plastic wrap and gently pound to ¼-inch thickness. Set aside.

2. In a wide flat bowl, place the pretzel crumbs, mustard powder, onion powder, and ½ teaspoon pepper, and stir to combine.

3. Smear ½ teaspoon of Dijon on each side of breast, and roll chicken in the crumb mixture until evenly coated (use finer crumbs to cover bare spots). Place chicken on prepared baking sheet, lightly spray with cooking spray, and bake for 15 to 18 minutes, or until cooked through.

4. While chicken is baking, in a small bowl, whisk together the remaining Dijon, vinegar, mayonnaise, honey, olive oil, a pinch of black pepper, and 1 tablespoon of water. Serve each chicken breast with 1 tablespoon of the sauce.

NUTRITION INFORMATION PER SERVING: (1 chicken breast with sauce) Calories 240 | Carbohydrate 16g (Sugars 3g) | Total Fat 8g (Sat Fat 0.5g) | Protein 26g | Fiber less than 1g | Cholesterol 75mg | Sodium 650mg | Food Exchanges: 3½ Lean Meat, 1 Starch, ½ Fat | Carbohydrate Choices: 1 | Weight Watcher Plus Point Comparison: 6

20-Minute One Pot Chicken and Bean Stew

HERE'S ANOTHER CLASSICALLY INSPIRED one-pot chicken dinner that's quick and tasty. This dish is reminiscent of a cassoulet, a French peasant-style stew typically composed of garlicky white beans and various meats, including chicken and cured pork or sausages. A crisp green salad and a slice of crusty bread are my preferred accompaniments.

MAKES **4** SERVINGS

2 teaspoons olive oil

1 small onion, diced

1 medium carrot, peeled and diced

1 tablespoon minced garlic

3 slices (or 2 ounces) Canadian bacon

½ teaspoon liquid smoke

½ cup dry white wine (or water)

1 (14-ounce) can reduced-sodium chicken broth

1 (15-ounce) can cannellini beans, rinsed and drained

2 cups shredded cooked boneless, skinless chicken breast

1 (14-ounce) can fire-roasted diced tomatoes

¾ teaspoon dried thyme

Fresh black pepper (optional)

1. Heat the oil in a large soup pot over medium heat. Add the onion and carrot, and cook for 3 to 4 minutes, or until the onion starts to soften. Add minced garlic and cook for 1 minute. Chop the Canadian bacon into ½-inch pieces and add it to the pan, along with the liquid smoke.

2. Add the remaining ingredients to the pot, crushing the thyme between your fingers. Simmer for 10 minutes, or until the carrots are tender. Season with black pepper, if desired.

Marlene Says: *The convenience of canned products pushes up the sodium. Using no-salt-added, fire-roasted, or diced tomatoes reduce the sodium by 200 milligrams of sodium per serving. Omitting the Canadian bacon will save another 200 milligrams.*

NUTRITION INFORMATION PER SERVING: (1½ cups) Calories 285 | Carbohydrate 25g (Sugars 6g) | Total Fat 5g (Sat Fat 0g) | Protein 27g | Fiber 7g | Cholesterol 60mg | Sodium 790mg | Food Exchanges: 4 Lean Meat, 1 Starch, 2 Vegetable | Carbohydrate Choices: 1½ | Weight Watcher Plus Point Comparison: 6

Sesame Chicken

SESAME CHICKEN IS YET ANOTHER CHINESE DISH LOVED for its sweet and salty sauce, often delivered with a bit of heat. An ample amount of quickly cooked fresh vegetables star in this version, which instead of excessive sugar and sodium, offers over a day's worth of Vitamins A and C. Toasting the sesame seeds is easy. Simply place seeds in a small sauté pan and heat for a minute or two, or until they start to brown.

MAKES 4 SERVINGS

1 tablespoon cornstarch

3 tablespoons granulated no-calorie sweetener*

2 tablespoons brown sugar

3 tablespoons reduced-sodium soy sauce

1 tablespoon white vinegar

Pinch of red pepper flakes

1 garlic clove, minced (1 teaspoon)

8 ounces boneless, skinless chicken breast, cut in 1-inch pieces

2 tablespoons cornstarch

1 tablespoon canola oil

2 cups broccoli florets

1 large red pepper, chopped

1 (8-ounce) can sliced water chestnuts

2 teaspoons sesame oil

4 teaspoons toasted sesame seeds

1. In a small saucepan, whisk the first 7 ingredients (cornstarch through garlic) together with ⅔ cup water. Place the pan over medium-high heat, bring to a low simmer, and cook for 2 minutes, or until the sauce thickens and clears. Remove from heat and set aside.

2. Dredge the chicken pieces with the cornstarch and shake off excess. Heat the canola oil in a large, nonstick wok or skillet over medium-high heat. Add the chicken and cook for 4 to 5 minutes, or until well browned on all sides and the chicken is barely cooked through. Transfer the chicken to a bowl.

3. Add the broccoli, pepper, and 2 tablespoons water to the wok. Cover and steam for 2 minutes. Remove lid, cook off any remaining water, and add the water chestnuts, chicken, and sauce, and drizzle with the sesame oil. Simmer for 2 minutes, stirring until chicken and vegetables are well coated with sauce. Garnish with sesame seeds.

*See page 81 for sweetener options.

NUTRITION INFORMATION PER SERVING: (1¼ cups) Calories 190 | Carbohydrate 22g (Sugars 8g) | Total Fat 5g (Sat Fat 0.5g) | Protein 15g | Fiber 6g | Cholesterol 35mg | Sodium 450mg | Food Exchanges: 2 Lean Meat, 2 Vegetable, 1 Starch, ½ Fat | Carbohydrate Choices: 1½ | Weight Watcher Plus Point Comparison: 5

Quicker-Than-Takeout Sweet and Sour Chicken

I LOVE CHINESE FOOD. Sweet, sour, salty, and sometimes spicy, it's a cuisine that isn't shy when it comes to flavor. Unfortunately, most Asian restaurant dishes are equally as bold about the enormous amounts of sugar, fat, and calories they deliver. Here moist white chicken and crisp vegetables bask in a sweet and sour sauce that is sure to cure your craving for takeout.

MAKES 4 SERVINGS

⅓ cup rice vinegar

⅓ cup no-calorie granulated sweetener*

3 tablespoons ketchup

1 tablespoon reduced-sodium soy sauce

1 teaspoon fresh or jarred minced ginger

2 tablespoons plus 2 teaspoons cornstarch, divided

1 medium carrot

1 pound boneless, skinless chicken breast, chopped

3 teaspoons canola oil, divided

1 medium green bell pepper, cut into 1-inch chunks

½ cup sliced water chestnuts

½ cup pineapple chunks, fresh or canned (drained)

1. In a small bowl, whisk together first 5 ingredients (vinegar through ginger), 2 teaspoons cornstarch, and ¼ cup water. Set aside.

2. Peel carrot and cut into ½-inch pieces. Place the carrots and 2 tablespoons water in a small, microwave-safe bowl, cover, and microwave for 3 minutes. Uncover, drain, and set aside.

3. Toss the chicken pieces with remaining 2 tablespoons cornstarch to coat. Heat 2 teaspoons of the oil in a large, nonstick skillet over medium-high heat. Add half the chicken and cook 4 to 5 minutes, or until well browned on all sides and chicken is cooked through. Transfer to a bowl and repeat with the remaining chicken pieces. Set chicken aside.

4. Heat the remaining teaspoon oil in the skillet, add bell pepper, and cook for 2 minutes. Add the carrots and water chestnuts, and cook for 1 minute. Stir in the pineapple and vinegar mixture, reduce heat to low, and cook for 2 to 3 minutes, stirring constantly, until the sauce thickens and clears. Add the chicken to the pan, toss to coat, and serve.

DARE TO COMPARE: According to the Center for Science in the Public Interest, the average order of sweet and sour chicken has over 1,000 calories—and has more breading than meat!

*See page 81 for sweetener options.

NUTRITION INFORMATION PER SERVING: (1 cup) Calories 260 | Carbohydrate 20g (Sugars 6g) | Total Fat 9g (Sat Fat 0g) | Protein 25g | Fiber 2g | Cholesterol 70mg | Sodium 340mg | Food Exchanges: 3½ Lean Meat, 1 Starch, ½ Vegetable | Carbohydrate Choices: 1½ | Weight Watcher Plus Point Comparison: 7

Tandoori-Style Grilled Chicken

WHETHER OR NOT YOU ARE A FAN OF INDIAN FOOD, this Tandoori chicken is so tantalizing, it may very well become the star of your chicken repertoire. A scoop of yogurt, a squeeze of lemon, and a few shakes from the spice rack is all it takes to create a fragrant and exotic marinade. I used chicken thighs for their deep, rich flavor. Boneless thighs cook faster, but bone-in comes with extra flavor. The choice is yours.

½ cup plain low-fat Greek yogurt

1 tablespoon minced garlic

1 tablespoon minced ginger

2 teaspoons ground coriander

2 teaspoons ground cumin

1 teaspoon paprika

¾ teaspoon salt

½ teaspoon cayenne powder

Juice of ½ lemon

8 skinless chicken thighs, about 2 pounds

1. In a large bowl, whisk together first 9 ingredients (yogurt through lemon juice). Add the chicken, and stir to coat. Cover and marinate in the refrigerator for at least 2 hours, and up to overnight.

2. Remove the chicken from refrigerator. Shake the thighs lightly to remove excess yogurt mixture (or lightly pat off using a paper towel). Let sit while heating your grill.

3. Grill chicken for 15 to 20 minutes for boneless thighs and 20 to 25 minutes for bone-in thighs, turning halfway and cooking to 165°F.

Marlene Says: *As a rule of thumb, only 50% of the weight of bone-in, skin-on chicken is meat. When comparing cost, the boneless, skinless variety is a good deal if it doesn't cost more than twice that with both skin and bone.*

NUTRITION INFORMATION PER SERVING: (1 thigh) Calories 150 | Carbohydrate 2g (Sugars 1g) | Total Fat 5g (Sat Fat 1g) | Protein 23g | Fiber 0g | Cholesterol 100mg | Sodium 100mg | Food Exchanges: 3 Lean Meat, 1 Fat | Carbohydrate Choices: 0 | Weight Watcher Plus Point Comparison: 4

Almost Cheesecake Factory Bang-Bang Chicken and Shrimp

MY SON JAMES LOVES CURRY DISHES, so when he told me how good the bang-bang chicken dish at the Cheesecake Factory was, I had to make it. In order to streamline both calories and labor, I took the elements James loved best and created my own bangin' Cheesecake-style dish. For "Cheesecake" flair, top each serving with 1 tablespoon of toasted coconut and 1 teaspoon of chopped peanuts (adds 50 calories). (P.S.—The ingredient list is long, but the dish is not difficult or time-consuming.)

MAKES 4 SERVINGS

¾ cup nonfat half-and-half

2 tablespoons brown sugar

1 tablespoon cornstarch

½ teaspoon coconut extract

¼ teaspoon salt

1 teaspoon canola oil

½ pound boneless, skinless chicken breasts, cubed

½ pound large shrimp, cleaned and peeled

½ teaspoon black pepper

1 teaspoon minced garlic

1 teaspoon minced ginger

1 cup chopped onion

2 teaspoons curry powder

1 cup frozen peas, thawed

1 medium zucchini, julienned

1 medium carrot, julienned

1 cup reduced-sodium chicken broth

1. In a small bowl, whisk together the first 5 ingredients (half-and-half through salt). Set aside.

2. Heat the oil in a large, nonstick skillet over medium-high heat. Add the chicken and cook for 3 minutes, stirring occasionally, until lightly browned. Add shrimp and black pepper, stir, and cook for 2 minutes, or until shrimp are barely pink. Transfer to a plate and set aside.

3. Add the garlic and ginger to the skillet, and cook for 30 seconds. Add the onion and cook for 3 to 4 minutes, or until nearly translucent. Sprinkle curry powder over the onions. Stir in the peas, carrot, and zucchini, and cook for 2 minutes.

4. Add the chicken broth and half-and-half mixture, stir again, and simmer for 1 to 2 minutes, or until the sauce thickens. Return the chicken and shrimp to the skillet, and simmer until meat is hot and sauce thickens. Serve topped with optional peanuts and coconut.

DARE TO COMPARE: An order of Bang-Bang Chicken and Shrimp has 1,343 calories, 44 grams of fat, and almost 2,000 milligrams of sodium.

NUTRITION INFORMATION PER SERVING: (1½ cups) Calories 280 | Carbohydrate 28g (Sugars 15g) | Total Fat 5g (Sat Fat 1g) | Protein 30g | Fiber 5g | Cholesterol 85mg | Sodium 420mg | Food Exchanges: 3½ Lean Meat, 1½ Vegetable, ½ Starch | Carbohydrate Choices: 1½ | Weight Watcher Plus Point Comparison: 6

Grilled Portobello Turkey Stuffed "Pizzas"

I LOVE IT WHEN READERS SHARE their favorite recipes. Marilyn Polka sent me a real winner with this one. The next time you fire up the grill, consider a change from the usual burgers and dogs, and try these easy stuffed mushrooms. In ten minutes, with just a handful of ingredients, you'll have personal "pizzas" that are meaty, cheesy, and saucy—without the side of carbs and sodium. As an alternative, you can bake the caps in a preheated 400°F oven for 20 minutes.

MAKES 4 SERVINGS

4 medium portobello mushrooms, 4 to 5 inches in diameter

½ teaspoon canola oil

8 ounces lean ground turkey

¾ cup marinara sauce, jarred or from page 190

½ teaspoon dried oregano

½ cup shredded part-skim mozzarella

4 slices green bell pepper, cut into ¼-inch rings

1. Preheat a grill to 350°F. Set out 4 (12 x 12-inch) pieces of aluminum foil on the counter. Remove the mushroom stems by gently snapping them off. With a tablespoon, gently scrape the gills from the underside of the mushrooms. Spray the tops of the mushroom caps with cooking spray, and place each cap, sprayed-side down, on a piece of foil.

2. Heat the oil in a large, nonstick skillet with cooking spray and set over medium-high heat. Crumble in the turkey and cook, stirring often, until starting to brown, about 5 to 7 minutes. Stir in the marinara sauce and oregano and cook for 3 to 5 minutes. Remove from heat.

3. Spread ¼ of the meat mixture on each mushroom cap, top each cap with 2 tablespoons mozzarella and a bell pepper ring. Loosely wrap the foil around the mushroom caps, and grill for 10 minutes, or until the mushroom is cooked.

Marlene Says: *Did you know mushrooms are magical when it comes to good health? Low in calories, and high in selenium and vitamin D, mushrooms have been shown to have both anti-tumor and anti-inflammatory properties.*

NUTRITION INFORMATION PER SERVING: (1 pizza) Calories 180 | Carbohydrate 7g (Sugars 2g) | Total Fat 8g (Sat Fat 3g) | Protein 20g | Fiber 2g | Cholesterol 60mg | Sodium 320mg | Food Exchanges: 2½ Lean Meat, 1 Vegetable, ½ Fat | Carbohydrate Choices: ½ | Weight Watcher Plus Point Comparison: 5

Moist and Flavorful Chicken For Days

THIS RECIPE IS A REAL TIMESAVER; cook once and have enough chicken for several meals. Cooking chicken breasts with the bone-in and skin-on keeps the meat moist and flavorful. Removing the skin after cooking removes the guilt! One large split breast yields enough to serve two for dinner, still leaving you with 2 breasts, or 4 cups of cubed or shredded meat.

| | MAKES 6 SERVINGS |

4 large bone-in, skin-on chicken breasts (about 3 pounds)

2 teaspoons olive oil

½ teaspoon seasoned salt

1. Preheat the oven to 400°F. Cover a rimmed baking sheet with foil and set aside.

2. Place the chicken breasts on the baking sheet. Gently loosen the chicken skin (do not detach) and drizzle each chicken breast with ½ teaspoon olive oil, using your fingers to spread the oil. Sprinkle about ⅛ teaspoon seasoned salt over the oiled chicken, and replace the skin on the breast meat.

3. Bake the chicken for 35 to 40 minutes, or until chicken is done and reads 165°F on the thickest part of the breast. Remove chicken from oven, remove skin and eat now, or let cool. Remove the skin, and cube, shred, or chop the chicken for later use.

Marlene Says: *For a delicious, easy herbalicious entrée, combine the olive oil with 1 teaspoon chopped fresh rosemary and ¼ teaspoon of lemon zest. Spread the mixture on the underside of the chicken breasts, sprinkle with salt, and bake as directed.*

NUTRITION INFORMATION PER SERVING: (4 ounces chicken, about 1 cup shredded) Calories 125 | Carbohydrate 0g (Sugars 0g) | Total Fat 3g (Sat Fat 1g) | Protein 28g | Fiber 0g | Cholesterol 10mg | Sodium 100mg | Food Exchanges: 3½ Lean Meat | Carbohydrate Choices: 0 | Weight Watcher Plus Point Comparison: 3

Poor Man's Turkey Stroganoff

THIS RECIPE TAKES MY SKILLET BEEF STROGANOFF from Eat What You Love *and gives it a tasty turkey twist while keeping the convenience of one-pan cooking. You still get the classic stroganoff flavors of sour cream, mushrooms, and onions, and despite being made on a budget, you'll feel rich when dining on this. Served with wide egg noodles in true stroganoff style will only set you back an additional 105 calories.*

MAKES 4 SERVINGS

1 cup reduced-fat sour cream

1 tablespoon coarse-grain mustard

1 teaspoon canola oil

1 pound lean ground turkey

1 medium onion, chopped

1 teaspoon minced garlic

1 pound mushrooms, sliced

½ teaspoon dried thyme

2 tablespoons all-purpose flour

1 cup reduced-sodium beef broth

Black pepper to taste

½ teaspoon salt (optional)

2 tablespoons chopped fresh parsley

3 cups cooked wide noodles (optional)

1. In a small bowl, stir together sour cream and mustard. Set aside.

2. Heat the oil in a very large, nonstick skillet over medium-high heat, and crumble in the turkey. Cook for 3 to 4 minutes, or just until browned. Remove from skillet and set aside.

3. Add the onion to the hot pan and cook for 3 minutes. Add the garlic and sauté for 30 seconds. Add the mushrooms, and crush the thyme in with your fingers. Stir and cook for 3 to 4 more minutes, or until the onion and mushrooms are soft. Sprinkle the flour over the onion mixture, and stir.

4. Add the broth and cook, stirring, until the mixture bubbles and thickens. Reduce heat to medium-low, stir in the turkey, black pepper, and salt, and cook for 1 minute. Stir in the sour cream mixture. Cook briefly until slightly thickened and hot; do not boil. Sprinkle with parsley and serve over cooked noodles, if preferred.

NUTRITION INFORMATION PER SERVING: (1½ cups) Calories 330 | Carbohydrate 17g (Sugars 8g) | Total Fat 14g (Sat Fat 6g) | Protein 30g | Fiber 3g | Cholesterol 100mg | Sodium 380mg | Food Exchanges: 4 Lean Meat, 1½ Vegetable, ½ Carbohydrate, 1 Fat | Carbohydrate Choices: 1 | Weight Watcher Plus Point Comparison: 8

Lean Beef, Pork, and Seafood

15-Minute Meat Loaf Dinner

Skillet Shepherd's Pie

James's Orange Beef

No-Fail Roast Beef

Filet Mignon with Creamy Crab Topping

Better than Shake 'n Bake Pork Chops

Pork Tenderloin with Blackberry Barbecue Sauce

Skillet Pork Chops with Buttermilk Gravy

Porchetta-Style Pork Loin

Company's Coming Maple Glazed Ham

15-Minute Garlicky Baked Shrimp

Fast-Fix Buffalo Salmon

Tuscan Tilapia

Chuck's Rub Barbecued Salmon

Fish 'n Chips

Grilled Fish with Mango Salsa

LIKE MANY FAMILIES TODAY, mine has become more conscientious about eating red meat, but that's not to say we don't still don't love eating beef (and pork, too!). Fortunately, choosing leaner cuts, like those marked "round" or "lean," and employing healthier cooking techniques—along with showing some love to poultry, fish, and meatless meals—has allowed me to keep flavorful beef and succulent pork healthfully on my family's plates.

With easy recipes for everything from casual weeknights to entertaining, this chapter shows you how to bring out the best in beef, pork, and seafood. In a hurry? How about a 15-Minute Meat Loaf Dinner in which the tasty combination of meat loaf and potatoes cooks up perfectly *together* in just 10 minutes! (You'll find that trick on page 265.) When you need to impress, pull out all the stops with Filet Mignon with Creamy Crab Topping. This easy-to-make, eye-popping dish offers the rich decadence of the steakhouse classic Steak Oscar for a fraction of the steakhouse price (on your wallet as well as your waistline!). Served with Creamy Steakhouse Mashed Potatoes (page 233) and steamed asparagus, it's utter perfection. When it comes to "the other white meat," pork doesn't get any better than my Skillet Pork Chops with Buttermilk Gravy. These chops are topped with spicy buttermilk gravy and have a sassy heat that will have you eagerly anticipating the next bite. Better Bean Succotash (page 228) is an ideal Southern-style plate partner.

As the perfect counterpoint, the chapter concludes with six nutritious seafood offerings. From a crispy 15-Minute Garlicky Baked Shrimp that will have you licking the plate, to a tasty, heart-healthy Fast-Fix Buffalo Salmon, and a gorgeous, company-worthy Grilled Fish with Mango Salsa, I guarantee these recipes will have your family and friends excited about eating fish and seafood the recommended twice a week.

BACON

As the saying goes, "Everything tastes better with bacon." Apparently a lot of folks agree as the estimated annual consumption of bacon in the United States is a hefty 18 pounds per person. The reality is that the irresistible taste of smoky, salty bacon simply sizzles, whether it's served up with eggs for breakfast, or as an ice cream topping for dessert! But it's no secret that traditional pork bacon is high in fat and sodium. In this book you will find a number of better-for-you ways to enjoy the great taste of the king of pork, including how to use smaller quantities in more creative ways and still keep that great bacon taste. To achieve this goal, here are five favorite guilt-free swaps that can help bring home the bacon:

Five Fabulous "Bacon" Tips:

1. **CENTER CUT BACON:** With less total fat, saturated fat, and sodium than traditional pork bacon, center cut bacon is an authentic bacon best bet. Cut closer to the bone, it's naturally up to 30% leaner and has just 20 to 25 calories per cooked slice. The sodium level varies by brand, but lower sodium varieties have as little as 50 milligrams of sodium per slice.

2. **TURKEY BACON:** This non-pork alternative has a similar fat content as center cut bacon. Compare labels as nutritional content, especially sodium (which is often higher in turkey varieties) varies by brand.

3. **LIQUID SMOKE:** Liquid smoke is the liquefied cooled smoke of smoldering wood chips. It's all natural, free of carcinogens, and great for adding a smoky kick—without calories, sodium, or fat—to any recipe. It's a favorite ingredient of mine. Caution: use sparingly. A small amount adds a nice smoky flavor, but too much ruins the dish.

4. **JARRED REAL BACON BITS:** It doesn't get more convenient than pre-cooked lean bits of real bacon that can be sprinkled on everything from eggs to potatoes at a moment's notice. A tablespoon has just 25 calories and 1.5 grams of fat. They are not low in sodium, but you only need a small shake to add a ton of flavor.

5. **CANADIAN-STYLE BACON:** While it says bacon, it's actually fully-cooked, thinly sliced, smoked pork loin, and more like ham. Canadian Bacon is very lean, but still high in sodium. Hold the salt and add chopped Canadian Bacon to egg dishes for a meaty taste with minimal extra sodium. It also ranks as a high protein, low fat choice for those less sensitive to sodium.

15-Minute Meatloaf Dinner

IN KICKING OFF THIS CHAPTER, I wanted to give you something easy and fun to make, and this meatloaf dinner delivers on all accounts. Stuff raw potatoes with a barbecue-glazed meatloaf mix, and amazingly, after only 10 minutes in the microwave, both are cooked to perfection. Serve these stuffed potatoes with a salad, and you have a complete meal that's worth repeating. See Marlene Says to cook two servings.

MAKES 2 TO 4 SERVINGS

6 ounces lean ground beef

6 ounces lean ground pork

½ cup finely chopped onion

⅓ cup quick-cooking oats

½ cup shredded carrot

1 large egg

1 large egg white

2 tablespoons tomato paste

½ teaspoon dried thyme, crushed

¼ teaspoon black pepper

½ teaspoon garlic salt, divided

2 medium baking potatoes, about 12 ounces each

4 tablespoons barbecue sauce

1. In a medium bowl, with a spoon or by hand, combine the first 10 ingredients (ground beef through black pepper) with ¼ teaspoon of the garlic salt, until just uniformly mixed. Set aside.

2. Slice each potato in half lengthwise. Slice a small piece from the bottom of each half so the halves sit flat. Then with a teaspoon, or melon baller, scoop out about 3 tablespoons of the raw potato flesh (to make a boat-like cavity). Sprinkle the potatoes lightly with remaining ¼ teaspoon of garlic salt.

3. Evenly spoon the meat into potatoes, pressing it lightly into the space and creating a smooth mound. Brush or spread 1 tablespoon of barbecue sauce on top to cover all of the meat. Place the potatoes on a large, microwave-safe plate, and cook on high for 10 minutes, or until a thermometer registers 155°F.

Marlene Says: *Streamline the preparation of this recipe by making the meatloaf mix ahead of time. Then, either make the complete recipe, or use half to make two stuffed potatoes and save or freeze the rest for another meal. The meatloaf mix will hold 2 to 3 days in the fridge and a month or more in the freezer.*

NUTRITION INFORMATION PER SERVING: (1 stuffed potato half) Calories 315 | Carbohydrate 35g (Sugars 9g) | Total Fat 6 g (Sat Fat 2g) | Protein 30g | Fiber 5g | Cholesterol 75mg | Sodium 370mg | Food Exchanges: 3 Lean Meat, 2½ Starch, ½ Fat | Carbohydrate Choices: 2½ | Weight Watcher Plus Point Comparison: 7

Skillet Shepherd's Pie

A FAVORITE FROM ACROSS THE POND, the term Shepherd's Pie truly defines what we think of as a satisfying, stick-to-your-ribs supper. I've streamlined this British classic by skipping the baking and getting the job done in the skillet. My sneaky cauliflower-potato mix adds extra nutrients but decreases carbs in the must-have layer of mashed potatoes, and while this may be lighter than the original, it sure doesn't taste like it.

MAKES 5 SERVINGS

3 cups cubed Yukon Gold potatoes

3 cups cauliflower florets

¼ cup light sour cream

¾ teaspoon garlic powder, divided

¼ teaspoon salt, or to taste

¼ plus ⅛ teaspoon black pepper, divided

¼ cup finely chopped green onion

1 small onion, chopped

1 pound lean ground beef

3 tablespoons tomato paste

1 tablespoon Worcestershire sauce

½ teaspoon dried thyme

2½ cups frozen peas and carrots

1½ cups reduced-sodium beef broth

1 tablespoon cornstarch

1. Place the potatoes in a medium pot of water, bring to a boil, and cook for 5 minutes. Add the cauliflower, reduce heat, and cook for 10 to 15 minutes, or until the potatoes and cauliflower are tender. Drain into in a colander, and press down on the mixture with a pot lid to remove excess water. Return them to the pot, add sour cream, ¼ teaspoon garlic powder, ¼ teaspoon salt, and ⅛ teaspoon black pepper, and using a hand or electric mixer, process until smooth (do not overmix). Stir in green onion, cover, and keep warm.

2. While potatoes are cooking, spray a large, nonstick skillet with cooking spray, and place over medium-high heat. Add onion, crumble in beef, and cook for 5 minutes, or until meat is browned. Add the next 5 ingredients (tomato paste through broth) plus remaining black pepper and garlic powder, and stir to combine. Reduce heat to medium, and simmer for 5 minutes.

3. Preheat the broiler. In a small bowl, whisk cornstarch with 2 tablespoons water, add to the skillet, and simmer 1 minute, stirring, until the sauce thickens slightly. Spread the mashed potatoes over the meat and place the skillet under the broiler for 5 minutes, or until the potatoes are lightly browned.

NUTRITION INFORMATION PER SERVING: (1½ cups) Calories 295 | Carbohydrate 32g (Sugars 5g) | Total Fat 8g (Sat Fat 4g) | Protein 31g | Fiber 6g | Cholesterol 60mg | Sodium 325mg | Food Exchanges: 2½ Lean Meat, 1½ Starch, 1½ Vegetable | Carbohydrate Choices: 2 | Weight Watcher Plus Point Comparison: 8

James's Orange Beef

NAMING A RECIPE AFTER EACH OF MY BOYS in every one of my cookbooks is a tradition for me. They both eagerly taste test, and sometimes even assist me, when testing new recipes. Occasionally, when one finds a dish he really loves, he eagerly claims it as his own. In the case of this re-worked dish, I didn't have to ask James twice if this should be his. Add a pinch of red pepper flakes if you like your Asian food spicy.

MAKES 4 SERVINGS

¼ cup orange juice

¼ cup low-sugar orange marmalade

1 tablespoon brown sugar

2 tablespoons reduced-sodium soy sauce

1 tablespoon rice vinegar

1½ teaspoons cornstarch

¼ teaspoon ground ginger

¼ teaspoon black pepper

1 pound lean boneless sirloin, partially frozen

1 tablespoon cornstarch

2 teaspoons canola or peanut oil

1 medium onion, cut in half, and halves sliced lengthwise in ¼-inch strips

1 large bell pepper, cut into ¼-inch strips

1 teaspoon sesame oil

¼ cup chopped green onions, green and white parts

1. In a small saucepan, whisk together the first 8 ingredients. Place the pan over medium heat, and bring to a low simmer. Cook until sauce clears. Remove from heat and set aside.

2. Thinly slice the steak across the grain, and place in a medium bowl. Add the cornstarch and toss to coat the meat. Heat the oil in a large, nonstick skillet or wok over medium-high heat until hot. Add the beef, and stir-fry for 3 to 4 minutes, or until no longer pink. Remove from skillet.

3. Add the onion and bell pepper to the skillet, and stir-fry for 3 to 4 minutes. Add the sauce mixture, sesame oil, and beef to the skillet, stirring well to coat. Top with green onions and serve.

DARE TO COMPARE: The Orange Peel Beef at P. F. Chang's contains a rather un-a-peeling 850 calories and 2,500 milligrams of sodium.

NUTRITION INFORMATION PER SERVING: (1 cup) Calories 255 | Carbohydrate 18g (Sugars 13g) | Total Fat 8g (Sat Fat 2g) | Protein 25g | Fiber 3g | Cholesterol 70mg | Sodium 330mg | Food Exchanges: 3½ Lean Meat, 1 Starch, ½ Vegetable | Carbohydrate Choices: 1 | Weight Watcher Plus Point Comparison: 6

No-Fail Roast Beef

MY FAMILY AND I FELL IN LOVE with this roast beef. It uses a very lean cut of beef, but the cooking technique keeps it moist and flavorful, without a lot of sodium (compared to deli roast beef, it's a 50% sodium savings). The leftover roast is fantastic for roast beef sandwiches, such as my Beef "Fil-A" Sandwich on page 142.

MAKES 10 TO 12 SERVINGS

2½- to 3-pound eye of the round roast

2 teaspoons garlic salt with parsley

1 teaspoon pepper, or more to taste

2 teaspoons canola oil

1. Lay a large piece of plastic wrap on a flat surface. Place the roast on the plastic, pat it dry, and rub the surface with the garlic salt and pepper. Roll the roast in the plastic wrap, and refrigerate for at least 4 hours (or overnight).

2. Remove the roast from the refrigerator 30 minutes before cooking. Preheat the oven to 250°F.

3. In a large skillet over medium-high heat, heat the oil until very hot. Add the roast and sear on all sides until well browned, about 8 to 10 minutes. Transfer the roast to a shallow baking dish.

4. Cook for approximately 1 hour and 30 minutes, or until temperature reads 130°F with an instant read thermometer (start checking the temperature after 1 hour and 15 minutes). Turn off the heat and leave it in the oven for 15 to 20 minutes longer, or until the temperature reaches 140°F (for medium). Let the meat rest 10 minutes and slice very thin.

Marlene Says: *Always rely on a meat thermometer, not the written cooking time, to determine when your meat is done. The size, thickness, and initial temperature of the meat, along with the actual temperature of your oven, all influence timing. An instant read thermometer is a cook's best friend.*

NUTRITION INFORMATION PER SERVING: (4 ounces cooked) Calories 150 | Carbohydrate 0g (Sugars 0g) | Total Fat 3.5g (Sat Fat 1.5g) | Protein 26g | Fiber 0g | Cholesterol 40mg | Sodium 190mg | Food Exchanges: 4 Lean Meat | Carbohydrate Choices: 0 | Weight Watcher Plus Point Comparison: 4

Filet Mignon with Creamy Crab Topping

THIS SUMPTUOUS STEAKHOUSE-STYLE ENTRÉE does not disappoint. Meltingly tender filet gets the royal treatment "Oscar-style" when topped with crab and draped with rich-tasting béarnaise sauce. The béarnaise sauce here is pure magic, super-easy-to-make, and tastes like the real deal—with just one-third of the calories! Prepare it just before serving for the best results. I suggest serving this steak with steamed fresh asparagus and my Creamy Steakhouse Mashed Potatoes (page 235). See page 332 for more menu ideas.

MAKES 4 SERVINGS

4 ounces lump crab meat

4 (5-ounce) filets mignon, 1 inch thick

Salt and pepper to taste

¼ cup egg substitute

¼ cup light mayonnaise

¼ cup light sour cream

½ teaspoon dried tarragon

1½ teaspoons white wine vinegar

⅛ teaspoon Old Bay Seasoning

1. Preheat the broiler or grill. Place the crab meat on a plate, and set aside. Pat the filets dry and season with salt and pepper to taste.

2. Grill or broil filets for 5 to 6 minutes per side for medium rare. Add 1 to 2 minutes per side to cook to medium (or 145°F for medium rare and 155°F for medium). Remove filets from grill, top each with 2 tablespoons crab meat, cover with foil, and set aside for 5 minutes to rest.

3. While steaks are cooking, prepare the sauce. Place the remaining ingredients (egg substitute through Old Bay) in a very small saucepan over low heat. Keep the heat low, and while whisking constantly, heat the sauce for 1 minute, or until mixture is smooth and coats a spoon.

4. To serve, transfer crab-topped steaks to dinner plates, and top each with 2 tablespoons sauce.

DARE TO COMPARE: A typical steakhouse "Steak Oscar" has 800 calories, 50 grams of fat, and over a day's worth of cholesterol—before you add the side dishes. Plop those on the plate, and you're looking at 1,200 calories, or more.

NUTRITION INFORMATION PER SERVING: (1 topped steak) Calories 310 | Carbohydrate 3g (Sugars 0g) | Total Fat 16g (Sat Fat 6g) | Protein 38g | Fiber 0g | Cholesterol 125mg | Sodium 290mg | Food Exchanges: 4 Lean Meat, 2 Fat | Carbohydrate Choices: 0 | Weight Watcher Plus Point Comparison: 8

Better than Shake 'n Bake Pork Chops

IF YOU HAVE A SPICE DRAWER, you're just a shake away from making the best pork chops on the block. Even though good ol' packaged Shake 'n Bake really does produce a supermoist and flavorful pork chop, I was up for the challenge to make a fast-fix crumb coating of my own that's better for your health, your taste buds—and your wallet. After several rounds of testing (with half the usual sodium), these chops live up to my "better" claim.

MAKES 4 SERVINGS

½ cup panko breadcrumbs

¼ unseasoned dry breadcrumbs

1 tablespoon canola oil

¾ teaspoon paprika

¾ teaspoon celery salt

¼ teaspoon baking powder

¼ teaspoon garlic powder

¼ teaspoon onion powder

¼ teaspoon oregano

⅛ teaspoon salt

4 lean pork chops (about 1¼ pounds)

1. Preheat oven to 425°F. Line sheet pan with foil.

2. In a medium bowl, mix all of the ingredients together, except the pork chops.

3. Moisten pork chops slightly with water, and coat with breadcrumb mixture. Place pork chops on a baking sheet, lightly coat with cooking spray, and bake for 15 minutes, or until done (about 145°F).

NUTRITION INFORMATION PER SERVING: (1 chop) Calories 240 | Carbohydrate 9g (Sugars 1g) | Total Fat 8g (Sat Fat 2g) | Protein 32g | Fiber 0g | Cholesterol 125mg | Sodium 390mg | Food Exchanges: 4 Lean Meat | Carbohydrate Choices: ½ | Weight Watcher Plus Point Comparison: 6

Pork Tenderloin with Blackberry Barbecue Sauce

GET YOUR BARBECUE FIX ALL YEAR LONG with succulent smoky pork tenderloin. Inspired by a recipe from Sunset magazine, berries, jam, ginger, and barbecue flavors blend beautifully into a lip-smacking barbecue sauce. Frozen blackberries are always in season (and actually work best here) and liquid smoke gives that barbecue essence without having to fire up the grill in the dead of winter. This sauce is as equally sweet and sassy when served over chicken.

MAKES 4 SERVINGS

2 teaspoons canola oil

½ teaspoon liquid smoke

¼ teaspoon salt

¼ teaspoon black pepper

1¼ pounds pork tenderloin, trimmed

Sauce

⅔ cup frozen blackberries, thawed

3 tablespoons sugar-free blackberry jam

¼ cup hickory barbecue sauce (like KC Masterpiece)

½ teaspoon minced ginger

1. Preheat the oven to 400°F. In a small bowl, whisk together the oil, liquid smoke, salt, and pepper. Using your hands, rub the pork with the oil mixture, and massage well into the surface.

2. Spray a large, nonstick skillet lightly with cooking spray, and place over medium-high heat. Add the tenderloin and brown well on all sides. Transfer the pork to a baking sheet and roast for 20 minutes, or until a meat thermometer reads 145°F. Remove from the oven, cover, and let rest 5 to 10 minutes.

3. While the pork roasts, place the blackberries in a small saucepan, and press them with a fork to release the juice. Add the jam, barbecue sauce, and ginger, and cook over low heat for 2 to 3 minutes, or until sauce bubbles.

4. Slice the meat and top with barbecue sauce.

NUTRITION INFORMATION PER SERVING: (4 ounces meat and sauce) Calories 220 | Carbohydrate 12g (Sugars 6g) | Total Fat 7g (Sat Fat 2g) | Protein 28g | Fiber 1g | Cholesterol 80mg | Sodium 360mg | Food Exchanges: 4 Lean Meat, ½ Fruit, ½ Starch | Carbohydrate Choices: 1 | Weight Watcher Plus Point Comparison: 6

Skillet Pork Chops with Buttermilk Gravy

HERE'S A PORK CHOP RECIPE THAT'S GOT SOUTHERN COMFORT written all over it. I cook the chops in a regular nonstick skillet, but feel free to pull out your cast iron for this one. The highlight here is the easy buttermilk gravy. Tangy, with a bit of heat, it's knock-your-socks-off good. My Sour Cream and Onion Smashed Potatoes from Eat More of What You Love *and Better Bean Succotash (page 228) are some favorite sides.*

MAKES 4 SERVINGS

1½ teaspoons onion powder

1½ teaspoons garlic powder

¼ teaspoon salt

⅛ teaspoon cayenne pepper

4 bone-in center-cut pork chops

¼ cup all-purpose flour

½ teaspoon dried thyme

2 teaspoons canola oil

1 cup reduced-sodium chicken broth

½ cup low-fat buttermilk

Black pepper to taste

1. In a wide, flat bowl or plate, combine the onion and garlic powders, salt, and cayenne. Sprinkle scant ½ teaspoon of the spice mix onto one side of each chop. Add the flour and crush the dried thyme into the remaining spice mix, then lightly dredge the pork chops in the flour mixture, tapping off the excess flour.

2. In a small bowl or measuring cup, whisk together the broth with 2 tablespoons of remaining flour mix, and set aside.

3. Heat the oil in a medium, nonstick skillet over medium-high heat. Add the pork chops and brown them, cooking for about 2 minutes on each side. Remove them from the pan and set aside. Whisk the broth mixture again, pour it into the skillet, simmer until thickened, and whisk in the buttermilk.

4. Return the pork chops to pan, and simmer them in the gravy for 3 to 5 minutes, or until pork registers 145°F, and the gravy is thickened to your liking.

Marlene Says: *I love boneless, center-cut pork chops for their leanness and quicker cooking time, but opt for bone-in in this skillet dish to ensure a tender chop. Thin cut boneless chops can also be used.*

NUTRITION INFORMATION PER SERVING: (1 chop plus gravy) Calories 250 | Carbohydrate 6g (Sugars 2g) | Total Fat 10g (Sat Fat 3g) | Protein 31g | Fiber 0g | Cholesterol 80mg | Sodium 350mg | Food Exchanges: 4 Lean Meat, ½ Starch | Carbohydrate Choices: ½ | Weight Watcher Plus Point Comparison: 6

Porchetta-Style Pork Loin

WHEN I'M ASKED WHAT I COOK FOR DINNER GUESTS, this pork recipe immediately comes to mind. Porchetta is the traditional Italian way of roasting pork. Garlic, fennel, black pepper, and rosemary seasonings provide both an intoxicating aroma and an intense burst of flavor in every bite. And it couldn't be simpler—apply the spice rub and refrigerate until it's time to pop it in the oven. Talk about easy entertaining!

MAKES 6 TO 8 SERVINGS

2 ½- to 3-pound pork loin roast, trimmed

4 garlic cloves, sliced

1 tablespoon fennel seed, crushed

2 teaspoons coarsely ground black pepper

2 teaspoons garlic salt with parsley

2 teaspoons fresh rosemary, minced

1 tablespoon olive oil

1. To stud the roast with garlic, using a sharp paring knife, cut ½- to 1-inch slits into the pork loin, and insert the garlic slices.

2. Place the pork loin on a large piece of plastic wrap (about 10 inches longer than the length of the roast). Evenly sprinkle the roast with the fennel, pepper, garlic salt, and rosemary. Drizzle the olive oil over the roast. With your hands, pat the seasoning onto the roast, covering the entire surface.

3. Wrap the roast tightly with the plastic wrap and refrigerate for 2 hours or overnight.

4. Preheat the oven to 425°F, remove the roast from the refrigerator, and unwrap. Place on a foil-lined roasting pan, and bake for 30 to 35 minutes, or until a thermometer registers 140°F. Let the roast rest for 10 minutes before slicing.

NUTRITION INFORMATION PER SERVING: (4 ounces) Calories 260 | Carbohydrate 1g (Sugars 0g) | Total Fat 12g (Sat Fat 3g) | Protein 36g | Fiber 0g | Cholesterol 50mg | Sodium 350mg | Food Exchanges: 4 Lean Meat, 1 Fat | Carbohydrate Choices: 0 | Weight Watcher Plus Point Comparison: 6

Company's Coming Maple Glazed Ham

IT WOULDN'T BE EASTER WITHOUT A HAM. The good news is that, if you are looking to put a ham on your table at holiday time, or any time of year, most hams are very lean. The bad news is that festive hams not only come with the usual salt, but also loads of sugar. To curb the sugar, but not the special-occasion taste, I've created a tantilizing low-sugar glaze. To significantly reduce the sodium, cook the ham using the alternative technique that follows the recipe.

1 (5- to 7-pound) cooked ham

Whole cloves (optional)

Glaze:

½ cup sugar-free maple-flavored syrup

½ cup reduced-sugar orange marmalade

3 tablespoons brown sugar

2 teaspoons whole grain or Dijon mustard

1 teaspoon soy sauce

1 teaspoon cornstarch

1. Remove the ham from the refrigerator and let sit at room temperature for 30 minutes.

2. Preheat the oven to 325°F. Place ham cut-side down in a roasting pan, cover with foil, and cook for 1 to 1¼ hours, or until 140°F.

3. While ham is cooking, whisk together all glaze ingredients in a small pot. Place pot over medium heat and bring to a low simmer. Cook for 2 minutes, or until mixture is smooth and has thickened.

4. Remove ham from oven, remove foil, and cover with ¾ of the glaze. Turn oven temperature up to 425°F, and return ham to oven. Cook for 20 minutes, baste with remaining glaze, and cook for 10 more minutes, or until glaze bubbles. Remove from oven and let set 15 to 20 minutes before serving.

Marlene Says: To reduce the sodium in a whole ham, place it in a large pot with cold water, bring to a boil, and simmer for 15 minutes per pound, or until ham is cooked. Place ham cut-side down in roasting pan, brush on the glaze, and cook at 400°F for 15 to 20 minutes, or until the glaze is hot (reduces sodium by approximately 30%).

NUTRITION INFORMATION PER SERVING: (4 ounces lean ham and 1 tablespoon glaze) Calories 170 | Fat 6g (Sat Fat 2g) | Carbohydrate 8g (sugar 5g) Fiber 0g | Protein 22g | Sodium 900mg | Food Exchanges: 4 Lean Meat, ½ Carbohydrate | Weight Watcher Plus Point Comparison: 4

15-Minute Garlicky Baked Shrimp

THIS OVEN-BAKED, SCAMPI-STYLE DISH topped with yummy buttery breadcrumbs does double duty as both an appetizer and an entrée. As an entrée, I suggest pasta or a baked potato side and a green salad (pop potatoes into the microwave, as this dish cooks quickly!). For an appetizer, I suggest leaving the tails on and providing small plates.

MAKES 4 SERVINGS

1¼ pounds large to extra large shrimp, peeled and deveined

Zest of one lemon

3–4 garlic cloves, minced

½ teaspoon paprika

¼ teaspoon salt (optional)

⅔ cup panko breadcrumbs

2 tablespoons butter, melted

2 tablespoons grated Parmesan cheese

⅛ teaspoon black pepper

Fresh parsley for garnish (optional)

1. Preheat the oven to 400°F.

2. Place the shrimp in a large bowl. Add the zest, garlic, paprika, and salt, if desired, and toss well. Arrange the shrimp in a baking dish, laying them flat and close together.

3. In a small bowl, mix the panko crumbs with butter, Parmesan, and black pepper. Sprinkle the panko mixture over the shrimp, pat it onto the shrimp lightly, and bake for 12 to 15 minutes, or until shrimp is cooked and crumbs are brown. Sprinkle with parsley, if desired.

DARE TO COMPARE: An order of shrimp scampi with pasta at the Cheesecake Factory clocks in at 1,200 calories. For a decadent meal for a fraction of the "price," serve this pasta drizzled with my Light and Luscious All-Purpose Alfredo Sauce on page 189.

NUTRITION INFORMATION PER SERVING: (4 ounces shrimp) Calories 190 | Carbohydrate 8g (Sugars 1g) | Total Fat 7g (Sat Fat 3g) | Protein 23g | Fiber 0g | Cholesterol 170mg | Sodium 220mg | Food Exchanges: 3 Lean Meat, ½ Starch | Carbohydrate Choices: 1 | Weight Watcher Plus Point Comparison: 5

Fast-Fix Buffalo Salmon

IT DOESN'T GET ANY EASIER when it comes to getting a healthy dinner on the table in a hurry. This recipe came about quite unplanned. Left with an extra piece of salmon, and too tired to cook, I coated the salmon with "wing" sauce and threw it in the microwave, with little expectations. What emerged was one of the best salmon dishes I have ever tasted—in less than four minutes! If you like both salmon and Buffalo wings, you'll love this. (P.S.—This is fabulous on sandwiches and in salads!)

MAKES 2 SERVINGS

1 tablespoon reduced-fat sour cream

4 teaspoons Frank's Red Hot sauce (I used Red Hot Wings style), divided

2 (5-ounce) fresh or thawed salmon fillets

2 teaspoons chopped green onion

1. In a small bowl, combine sour cream with 2 teaspoons of water; set aside.

2. Spread 1 teaspoon of the hot sauce over the top of each salmon fillet. Turn the salmon over, sauce-side down, and place both fillets on a large, microwave-safe plate. Seal the plate with plastic wrap, ensuring the plate is totally covered for proper cooking.

3. Microwave on high for 2 minutes. Remove the fish from microwave, and discard the plastic wrap. If there is skin on the fish, remove it with a fork, and gently scrape off any dark meat. Using a spatula, flip the fillets, and spread another teaspoon of hot sauce over the top of each fillet. Cover the plate with another piece of plastic wrap, and microwave on high for 1 minute for ¾-inch-thick fillets (90 seconds for 1-inch-thick fillets).

4. Remove the fish from microwave, drizzle each fillet with the sour cream mixture, and sprinkle with green onions. Serve immediately.

Marlene Says: *To bake this in a conventional oven, lay the fillets in a baking dish, cover with sauce, and bake at 400°F uncovered for 20 minutes.*

NUTRITION INFORMATION PER SERVING: (1 fillet) Calories 270 | Carbohydrate 1g (Sugars 1g) | Total Fat 16g (Sat Fat 3g) | Protein 29g | Fiber 0g | Cholesterol 85mg | Sodium 240mg | Food Exchanges: 4 Medium Fat Meat | Carbohydrate Choices: 0 | Weight Watcher Plus Point Comparison: 7

Tuscan Tilapia

WHEN IT COMES TO SERVING FISH at our house, tilapia is my hands-down favorite because of its clean, light flavor and versatility. We eat it so much that I keep frozen tilapia, sold in two-pound bags of individually wrapped, perfectly proportioned pieces, in my freezer at all times. With this recipe, you get crispy, Italian-seasoned tilapia that's been known to convert more than one fish hater into a fish lover.

| MAKES 4 SERVINGS

4 (5-ounce) tilapia fillets

2 tablespoons tomato paste

1 tablespoon light mayonnaise

¼ cup dry breadcrumbs

¼ cup panko breadcrumbs

1 teaspoon Italian seasoning

1 teaspoon garlic salt (with parsley)

⅛ teaspoon black pepper

2 tablespoons grated Parmesan cheese

1. Preheat the oven to 400°F. Spray a baking sheet with cooking spray. Pat the fish fillets dry with a paper towel. Combine the tomato paste and mayonnaise, and spread one side of each filet with 2 teaspoons of the tomato mixture.

2. In a small bowl, combine the breadcrumbs, panko, Italian seasoning, garlic salt, and pepper. Sprinkle the mixture evenly over the coated side of each fillet, pressing the crumbs lightly to help them stick. Sprinkle each fillet with 1½ teaspoons Parmesan cheese.

3. Transfer the fillets, coating side up, to the prepared baking sheet, and bake for 12 to 14 minutes, or until the fish is golden brown and flakes easily when tested with a fork.

Marlene Says: *Individually wrapped frozen fish filets defrost quickly when set in warm water. Cooking should take place shortly thereafter for food safety.*

NUTRITION INFORMATION PER SERVING: (1 fillet) Calories 180 | Carbohydrate 10g (Sugars 1g) | Total Fat 4g (Sat Fat 2g) | Protein 26g | Fiber 0g | Cholesterol 30mg | Sodium 430mg | Food Exchanges: 4 Lean Meat, 1 Starch | Carbohydrate Choices: 1 | Weight Watcher Plus Point Comparison: 4

Chuck's Rub Barbecued Salmon

IN OUR FAMILY, THE RUB THAT ADORNS this salmon is affectionately known as "Chuck rub," after my husband. After mixing and matching ingredients in various rub recipes, and from a multitude of grill "experts," Chuck finally came up with one that always left everyone clamoring for more. While the fish portion of this recipe is sized for four, you will have enough rub to make this dish two more times. Or do as I do, and use it on chicken and/or shrimp.

| MAKES 4 SERVINGS

Rub

2 tablespoons brown sugar

1½ tablespoons chili powder

2 teaspoons salt, coarse grind preferred

1½ teaspoons ground cumin

¾ teaspoon paprika

¾ teaspoon black pepper

¼ teaspoon dry mustard

⅛ teaspoon cinnamon

Salmon

4 (5-ounce) salmon fillets, rinsed and patted dry

1. For the rub, in a small bowl, combine all the ingredients, and stir to mix well. Note that you will have ample rub left over for future use.

2. Heat the grill to medium-high. Coat one side of each salmon fillet with 1 teaspoon rub (coat the side without skin if fillets are not skinless).

3. Place the salmon on the hot grill, rub-side down, and cook each side for 5 minutes (for 1-inch fillets), or until fish flakes apart easily. Serve salmon with the rub-side up.

DARE TO COMPARE: Farm-raised salmon is richer and milder in flavor than wild-caught salmon. A 4-ounce portion can have as much as 4 grams of fat and almost 40 calories. I averaged the two for my analysis.

NUTRITION INFORMATION PER SERVING: (1 fillet) 225 Calories | Carbohydrate 2g (Sugars 2g) | Total Fat 12g (Sat Fat 1g) | Protein 28g | Fiber 0g | Cholesterol 10mg | Sodium 225 mg | Food Exchanges: 4 Medium Fat Meat | Carbohydrate Choices: 0 | Weight Watcher Plus Point Comparison: 6

Fish 'n Chips

CRUNCHY BAKED POTATO CHIPS lend crunch to the coating, while the fish finds itself rolled "n" in this healthy take on fried fish. After trying several types of chips, baked "Kettle-style" were found to retain their crunch best upon baking. Pair this with the Extra Crispy Oven-Baked Steak Fries (page 232) for a true fish and chips meal.

MAKES 4 SERVINGS

1 ounce (or 1 cup) reduced fat potato chips

¼ cup panko breadcrumbs

¼ teaspoon thyme

⅛ teaspoon black pepper

2 tablespoons light mayonnaise

1 teaspoon malt or apple cider vinegar

4 (4- to 5-ounce) pieces cod (or other white fish), patted dry

1. Preheat oven to 425°F. Place the potato chips in a plastic bag, seal, and crush into roughly fine pieces. Place the crumbs in a small bowl, crush the thyme in with your fingers, add the breadcrumbs and pepper, and mix well. Set aside.

2. In another small bowl whisk together mayonnaise and vinegar. Coat the top of each piece of fish with 1½ teaspoons of the mayonnaise mixture. Sprinkle with 2 rounded tablespoons of crumb mixture, and pat well. Transfer fish fillets to an ungreased baking sheet and spray the tops lightly with baking spray.

3. Bake fish for 12 to 14 minutes or until topping is golden brown and fish flakes easily with a fork.

NUTRITION INFORMATION PER SERVING (1 piece): Calories 170 | Carbohydrate 9g (Sugars 1g) | Total Fat 4.5 (Sat Fat 1.5 g) | Protein 29g | Fiber 0g | Cholesterol 70mg | Sodium 190mg | Food Exchanges: 4 Lean Meat, ½ Starch | Carbohydrate Choices: ½ | Weight Watcher Plus Point Comparison: 4

Grilled Fish with Mango Salsa

RESTAURANT FLAVOR AND FLAIR CAN BE HAD in mere minutes with the vibrant sweet salsa that adorns this dish. The perfect compliment to any type of grilled fish (or chicken), the tropical topper is also delicious served on tacos or chips. Serve this dish with a green salad and a whole grain roll or serving of grains for a super-slim meal saturated with good health and great taste.

MAKES 4 SERVINGS

1 mango, peeled, pitted, and chopped (or 1 cup chopped frozen mango, thawed)

⅓ cup chopped red bell peppers

¼ cup diced red onion, rinsed and drained

2 tablespoons chopped fresh cilantro

Juice of ½ lime

1 teaspoon granulated sugar

Pinch salt

4 5-ounce white fish fillets (cod, red snapper, halibut or tilapia)

2 teaspoons olive oil

Paprika for sprinkling

1. In a medium bowl, combine the first 7 ingredients (mango through salt). Cover, and place in the refrigerator (This can be done up to 2 days ahead of time.)

2. Sprinkle the oil over the fish and rub to coat. Sprinkle a light coating of paprika onto each of the fillets. Preheat the grill on medium-high or place a nonstick grill pan over medium-high heat. When hot, place the fish on the grill paprika-side down and cook for 3 minutes, or until underside is lightly browned. Turn fish and cook 3 to 4 more minutes, or unitl fish flakes apart easily when teased with a fork.

3. Place fish on plates or a serving tray and top with ⅓ cup salsa on each serving. Garnish with additional cilantro if desired.

Marlene Says: *While fatty fish like salmon and trout get kudos for their heart healthy omega-3 fatty acid content, lower-fat fish are also powerhouses of good nutrition. Cod (and other mild white fish), are high in B-vitamins, including B6 and B12 necessary for energy and proper metabolism.*

NUTRITION INFORMATION PER SERVING: (1 fillet with salsa) Calories 170 | Carbohydrate 9 g (Sugars 6g) | Total Fat 3g (Sat Fat 0 g) | Protein 30g | Fiber 1g | Cholesterol 5mg | Sodium 100 mg | Food Exchanges: 4 Lean Meat, ½ Fruit | Carbohydrate Choices: ½ | Weight Watcher Plus Point Comparison: 4

Pies, Cakes, Cupcakes, and Frostings

No-Bake Banana Caramel Cream Cheese Pie

Deep-Dish Double Berry Rhubarb Pie

10-Minute Peanut Butter Pretzel Pie

90-Calorie Vanilla Cupcakes

Luscious Coconut Cupcakes

Cherry-Filled Black Forest Cupcakes

Carrot Zucchini Cake

Old-Fashioned Orange Buttermilk Cake

Coconut Layer Cake with
Creamy Coconut Cream Cheese Frosting

Heavenly Strawberry Cake Roll

My Unbelievable Chocolate Cake (Classic or Gluten-Free)

Molten Chocolate Lava Cakes

Whipped Cream Cheese Frosting

Chocolate Fudge Glaze

IF YOU LOVE TO BAKE BUT DON'T LOVE THE TIME or effort it often takes, you are going to love this chapter. Healthy-yet-easy is the order of the day, with over a dozen fuss-free recipes for pies and cakes, all under 240 calories per serving (for sweetener options, see page 81).

Temperamental crusts and complicated fillings are a thing of the past in three of my easiest pies to date. Your family and friends are sure to go bananas over my No-Bake Banana Caramel Cream Cheese Pie. A premade graham cracker crust helps deliver this blue ribbon–worthy pie in just 15 minutes. Even more impressive than how little time it takes to make is the 600 calories and 50 grams of fat you save, per slice, when compared to a similar slice of cheesecake.

Then there are the cakes that are truly a piece of cake to make—even if you've never baked before. Take the Boston Cream Pie Cupcakes, which take just a bowl and a whisk to make. They begin with my incredibly moist 90-Calorie Vanilla Cupcakes. Once cooled, they're filled with vanilla pudding (revved up with more vanilla), and capped off with quick-fix dark Chocolate Fudge Glaze. Delectable from top to bottom, they are each just 150 calories! The same one-bowl vanilla cake batter forms the base of my Coconut Layer Cake with Creamy Coconut Cream Cheese Frosting and Luscious Coconut Cupcakes. Without the usual sticks of butter and cups of sugar, the calories plummet. Cupcakes that once topped 610 calories are now just 135 each! Chocolate, of course, is a dessert must, and you can satisfy your craving with my rich-tasting, but decadently slim, 210-calorie ooey gooey Molten Chocolate Lava Cakes. With a 75% reduction in the usual calories, they're an absolute dream for chocolate lovers everywhere.

No-Bake Banana Caramel Cream Cheese Pie

A DESSERT WITH A NAME LIKE THIS NEEDS LITTLE INTRODUCTION, but I can't resist. Imagine slices of sweet banana atop a graham cracker crust, layered with luscious cheesecake filling and drizzled with creamy caramel—all put together in 10 minutes. The hardest part of this recipe, besides believing that a slice has a whopping 75% less calories than a regular piece of banana or caramel cheesecake, is waiting the hour for the pie to chill.

MAKES 8 SERVINGS

1 large banana, sliced

1 prepared reduced-fat graham cracker crust

¼ cup light tub-style cream cheese

¼ cup nonfat cream cheese, room temperature

⅓ cup light sour cream

¼ cup granulated no-calorie sweetener (or 6 packets)*

1 teaspoon vanilla extract

2 cups light whipped topping, thawed

1 tablespoon sugar-free caramel ice cream topping

1. Place the banana slices on the bottom of the graham cracker crust, and set aside.

2. In a medium bowl, with an electric mixer on medium speed, beat the cream cheeses, sour cream, sweetener, and vanilla until smooth. Gently fold in the whipped topping.

3. Spread the cream cheese mixture over the bananas, smoothing the top. Drizzle on the caramel syrup and refrigerate for at least 1 hour before serving.

> **DARE TO COMPARE:** A piece of Fresh Banana Cheesecake at the Cheesecake Factory has 925 calories, and almost 2 days' worth of saturated fat. The caramel-style slice tops even that with 1080 calories, 44 grams of saturated fat, and more than a meal's worth of carbs.

*See page 81 for sweetener options.

NUTRITION INFORMATION PER SERVING: (⅛ pie) Calories 210 | Carbohydrate 26g (Sugars 15g) | Total Fat 9g (Sat Fat 4.5g) | Protein 4g | Fiber less than 1g | Cholesterol 10mg | Sodium 210mg | Food Exchanges: 1½ Carbohydrate, 2 Fat | Carbohydrate Choices: 1½ | Weight Watcher Plus Point Comparison: 6

Deep-Dish Double Berry Rhubarb Pie

WHEN MOST PEOPLE HEAR "DEEP-DISH PIE," they picture a pie that's a mile high. In culinary lingo, however, a deep-dish pie is also a pie made with a single crust containing a deep layer of filling—and that is what you find here. Tart, fresh rhubarb is paired with strawberries and raspberries, then topped with a tender crust. The result is a pie big on fruit flavor, without the usual fat, making it one deeply delicious guilt-free treat.

MAKES 8 SERVINGS

3 cups chopped rhubarb, (about 1 pound)

3 cups fresh strawberries, quartered

1½ cups fresh or frozen raspberries

1 cup granulated no-calorie sweetener*

¼ cup cornstarch

2 tablespoons brown sugar

1 teaspoon orange zest

½ package refrigerated pie crust, or 1 single-crust pie pastry

1. Preheat the oven to 375°F. Set aside a large 10-inch-diameter x 2-inch-deep pie plate.

2. In a large bowl, combine the rhubarb, strawberries, and raspberries. In a small bowl, combine the remaining ingredients, sprinkle over the fruit, and toss lightly to mix. Pour the fruit into the pie plate.

3. Place the pie dough on a lightly floured surface, and lightly roll out into an 11-inch-diameter round. Place the pie crust on top the fruit, crimp the edges, and cut 4 vents in the pie crust. Bake for 40 minutes, or until fruit juices are bubbling. Remove from oven and let cool 2 hours or overnight, to allow filling to thicken.

*See page 81 for sweetener options.

NUTRITION INFORMATION PER SERVING: (1 slice) Calories 165 | Carbohydrate 24g (Sugars 9g) | Total Fat 7g (Sat Fat 2g) | Protein 2g | Fiber 5g | Cholesterol 0mg | Sodium 105mg | Food Exchanges: 1 Carbohydrate, ½ Fruit, 1 Fat | Carbohydrate Choices: 1½ | Weight Watcher Plus Point Comparison: 5

10-Minute Peanut Butter Pretzel Pie

I CAN'T IMAGINE WRITING A DESSERT CHAPTER without including a chocolate peanut butter recipe, especially one as delectable as this five-ingredient, ultra smooth, frozen delight. And, like the best no-bake peanut butter pies, it takes just minutes to assemble. The crowning touch is a pretzel garnish, which provides the perfect sweet and salty taste experience.

MAKES 8 SERVINGS

3 cups light, no-sugar-added vanilla ice cream, slightly softened

⅓ cup creamy peanut butter

1 chocolate or Oreo pre-made pie crust

1 tablespoon sugar-free chocolate ice cream topping

⅓ cup roughly crushed pretzels

1 cup light whipped topping (optional garnish)

1. In a medium bowl, combine the ice cream and peanut butter until well mixed. Spoon the mixture into the crust and smooth the top. Drizzle the filling with ice cream topping, and sprinkle the pretzels over the pie.

2. Freeze for at least 2 hours before serving. Let pie sit at room temperature for 5 minutes before cutting and garnishing with whipped topping, if desired.

DARE TO COMPARE: A traditional slice of frozen peanut butter pie made with cream cheese and whipped topping has 650 calories—including a full day's worth of saturated fat and sugar.

NUTRITION INFORMATION PER SERVING: (1 slice) Calories 235 | Carbohydrate 28g (Sugars 14g) | Total Fat 13g (Sat Fat 4g) | Protein 6g | Fiber 4g | Cholesterol 0mg | Sodium 230mg | Food Exchanges: 2 Carbohydrate, 2 Fat | Carbohydrate Choices: 2 | Weight Watcher Plus Point Comparison: 7

90-Calorie Vanilla Cupcakes

SO SKINNY AND SO GOOD, these vanilla cupcakes truly take the cake. Like their namesake 90-Calorie Chocolate Cupcakes from Eat More of What You Love, these are the slimmest, moistest cupcakes I know of. The fact they only take one bowl and spoon to make is an added bonus. Dust them with powdered sugar for a 100-calorie treat, top them with Whipped Cream Cheese Frosting (page 304) for parties, or get fancy and turn them into Boston Cream Pie Cupcakes! (See Marlene Says, below.)

MAKES 12 CUPCAKES

¾ cup low-fat milk

½ cup granulated no-calorie sweetener*

½ cup light mayonnaise

2 tablespoons granulated sugar

1½ teaspoons vanilla extract

¼ teaspoon almond extract

1 large egg

1½ cups cake flour

1 teaspoon baking powder

¼ teaspoon baking soda

1. Preheat the oven to 325°F. Place cupcake liners in 12-cup muffin tin and spray with nonstick cooking spray (alternately, foil liners can be used and do not require spraying).

2. In a large bowl, whisk together the first 7 ingredients (milk through egg) until smooth. Gradually sift in the flour, baking powder, and baking soda, and stir until smooth.

3. Scoop ¼ cup of batter into each muffin cup. Bake for 13 to 15 minutes, or until the center springs back when touched or a toothpick comes out clean.

Marlene Says: *To make* BOSTON CREAM PIE CUPCAKES, *use an apple corer to remove a plug from the center of each cupcake. Fill each cupcake with 2 teaspoons low-calorie prepared vanilla pudding (two sugar-free vanilla pudding cups provide the right amount), and top with 2 teaspoons Chocolate Fudge Glaze (page 305). Each cupcake has 135 calories, 24 grams of carb, and 4 grams of fat (1½ carb choices and 3 plus points.)*

*See page 81 for sweetener options.

NUTRITION INFORMATION PER SERVING: (1 cupcake) Calories 90 | Carbohydrate 14g (Sugars 3g) | Total Fat 3g (Sat Fat 0.5g) | Protein 2g | Fiber 0g | Cholesterol 20mg | Sodium 160mg | Food Exchanges: 1 Carbohydrate | Carbohydrate Choices: 1 | Weight Watcher Plus Point Comparison: 2

Luscious Coconut Cupcakes

EARLY IN MY COOKBOOK CAREER, I was told that a (now) very well-known food celebrity sealed the deal for her first cookbook with a plate full of her luscious coconut cupcakes. As you would expect, I immediately searched for the esteemed recipe. My inclination to try it, however, was quickly tempered when I noted the recipe called for four sticks of butter and five cups of sugar! With a mere fraction of the fat and sugar, these luscious coconut-y "cakes" are every bit as cookbook-worthy. Enjoy!

MAKES 12 CUPCAKES

6 tablespoons shredded sweetened coconut, divided

1 recipe 90-Calorie Vanilla Cupcakes batter (opposite page)

1 recipe Coconut Whipped Cream Cheese Frosting (page 304)

1. Preheat the oven to 325°F. Place cupcake liners in 12-cup muffin tin and spray with nonstick cooking spray (alternately, foil liners can be used and do not require spraying). Place 4 tablespoons coconut in a small baking pan and bake for 5 minute, shaking once or twice, or until coconut is lightly browned. Set aside for garnishing.

2. Prepare the cupcake batter according to directions, adding the remaining 2 tablespoons of coconut before sifting in the flour.

3. Scoop ¼ cup of batter into each muffin cup. Bake for 13 to 15 minutes, or until the center springs back when touched or a toothpick comes out clean.

4. To assemble cupcakes, frost with coconut whipped cream cheese frosting and sprinkle each cupcake with 1 teaspoon toasted coconut.

DARE TO COMPARE: Not so luscious, a traditional coconut cupcake with cream cheese frosting can have as many as 610 calories and two days' worth of added sugar.

NUTRITION INFORMATION PER SERVING: (1 cupcake) Calories 135 | Carbohydrate 18g (Sugars 6g) | Total Fat 6g (Sat Fat 3g) | Protein 3g | Fiber 0g | Cholesterol 20mg | Sodium 220mg | Food Exchanges: 1 Carbohydrate, 1 Fat | Carbohydrate Choices: 1 | Weight Watcher Plus Point Comparison: 4

Cherry-Filled Black Forest Cupcakes

FOR THIS RECIPE, I took my favorite chocolate cupcakes, stuffed them with luscious cherries, topped them with dreamy whipped cream frosting, and sprinkled them with chocolate shavings. Just like the famous Black Forest cake, but with only 160 calories, these beauties are perfect for holidays, birthdays, showers . . . or simply anytime you want a celebration-worthy sweet treat.

MAKES 12 CUPCAKES

6 tablespoons cocoa powder

¾ cup granulated no-calorie sweetener*

2 tablespoons brown sugar

⅓ cup low-fat milk

1½ teaspoons vanilla extract

1 large egg

½ cup light mayonnaise

1 cup all-purpose flour

1 teaspoon baking powder

1 teaspoon baking soda

½ (20-ounce) can no-sugar-added (or lite) cherry pie filling

½ teaspoon almond extract

2 tablespoons granulated no-calorie sweetener*

1 recipe Whipped Cream Cheese Frosting (page 304)

12 teaspoons finely grated or shaved dark chocolate

1. Preheat the oven to 325°F. Line 12 muffin cups with liners and spray with nonstick cooking spray (alternately, foil liners can be used and do not require spraying).

2. Place cocoa powder in a large bowl. Add ½ cup warm water and whisk until smooth. Whisk in the next 6 ingredients (sweetener through mayonnaise), until mixture is smooth. Gradually sift in flour, baking powder, and baking soda, and stir until well mixed.

3. Scoop ¼ cup of batter into each muffin cup. Bake for 13 minutes or until the center springs back when touched or a toothpick comes out clean. While cupcakes are baking, in a medium bowl, combine the pie filling, almond extract, and 2 tablespoons sweetener. Set aside.

4. To assemble cupcakes, when cupcakes are cool, using an apple corer (or small knife), remove a plug from the center of the cupcake. Spoon 3 cherries with some of the gel into the center of the cupcake. Top with 2 tablespoons frosting, and dust with chocolate shavings.

*See page 81 for sweetener options.

NUTRITION INFORMATION PER SERVING: (1 cupcake) Calories 160 | Carbohydrate 22g (Sugars 7g) | Total Fat 6 g (Sat Fat 2g) | Protein 4g | Fiber 1g | Cholesterol 25mg | Sodium 280mg | Food Exchanges: 1½ Carbohydrate, 1 Fat | Carbohydrate Choices: 1½ | Weight Watcher Plus Point Comparison: 4

Carrot Zucchini Cake

MOST CARROT CAKES ARE WHAT I CALL HEALTHY IMPOSTERS—they sound like a healthy option, but the truth is, they're not. Instead, this carrot cake is not only moist and delicious—it's good for you too! Perfect for toting, a dusting of powdered sugar is all it needs. Use half white whole wheat flour to turn it into a wholesome pick-me-up afternoon snack or breakfast treat. Or go all-out yummy and spread it with my Coconut Whipped Cream Cheese Frosting (page 304).

MAKES 20 SERVINGS

2 cups all-purpose flour

2 teaspoons baking soda

1 teaspoon baking powder

2 teaspoons cinnamon

1½ teaspoons ground allspice

½ teaspoon ground ginger

¼ cup unsweetened applesauce

¼ cup canola oil

2 large eggs

1 teaspoon vanilla extract

1¼ cups granulated no-calorie sweetener*

¾ cup low-fat buttermilk

1 cup finely grated carrot

1 cup grated blotted dry zucchini

1. Preheat the oven to 350°F. Coat a 13 x 9-inch cake pan with non-stick cooking spray.

2. In a medium bowl, whisk together the first 6 ingredients (flour through ginger).

3. In a large bowl, whisk together the next four ingredients (applesauce through vanilla). Whisk in the sweetener and buttermilk. Stir in the carrot and zucchini, and mix well. Add the flour mixture, and stir to mix well.

4. Transfer the batter into the prepared pan. Bake for 25 to 30 minutes, or until a toothpick inserted in the center of the cake comes out clean. Let cake cool in the pan on a wire rack. Prepare frosting according to recipe. Frost cake and serve or refrigerate.

*See page 81 for sweetener options

NUTRITION INFORMATION PER SERVING: (1 piece) Calories 150 | Carbohydrate 18g (Sugars 3g) | Total Fat 6g (Sat Fat 1.5g) | Protein 4g | Fiber less than 1g | Cholesterol 30mg | Sodium 270mg | Food Exchanges: 1 Starch, 1 Fat | Carbohydrate Choices: 1 | Weight Watcher Plus Point Comparison: 4

Old-Fashioned Orange Buttermilk Cake

PERFECT IN ITS SIMPLICITY, this cake is both homey and elegant. With a slightly higher ratio of eggs to flour than usual, it's light and airy, making it the perfect base for fresh berries, custard toppings or light whipped cream. Buttermilk adds tenderness, and the orange adds a burst of fresh flavor. Serve it instead of shortcake for a delicious beautiful berry topped dessert.

MAKES 8 SERVINGS

¾ cup granulated no-calorie sweetener*

¼ cup margarine or butter, softened

¼ cup granulated sugar

2 large eggs

2 large egg whites

1¼ cups cake flour, divided

1½ teaspoons baking powder

½ teaspoon baking soda

½ cup low-fat buttermilk

½ cup light orange juice

1 teaspoon orange zest

1. Preheat the oven to 350°F. Spray a 9-inch round baking pan with nonstick baking spray.

2. In a large bowl, with an electric mixer on medium speed, beat the sweetener, margarine, and sugar together for 2 minutes. Add the eggs and egg whites, and beat for 2 more minutes until the mixture is smooth.

3. In a medium bowl, sift together the flour, baking powder, and baking soda. By hand, stir one-half of the flour mixture into the creamed mixture. Stir in the buttermilk, the remaining flour, and the orange juice with zest, stirring each time until ingredients are just incorporated.

4. Pour the batter into the prepared pan and smooth the top. Bake for 20 to 23 minutes or until the center of the cake springs back when touched or a toothpick inserted into the center comes out clean. Cool cake on wire rack.

Marlene Says: *A light dusting of powdered sugar is all this cake needs. The easiest way to dust is put a couple of teaspoons into a small fine meshed strainer. Always dust just before serving.*

*See page 81 for sweetener options.

NUTRITION INFORMATION PER SERVING: (1 piece) Calories 165 | Carbohydrate 24g (Sugars 8g) | Total Fat 6g (Sat Fat 2g) | Protein 4g | Fiber 0g | Cholesterol 45mg | Sodium 260mg | Food Exchanges: 1½ Carbohydrate, 1 Fat | Carbohydrate Choices: 1½ | Weight Watcher Plus Point Comparison: 5

Coconut Layer Cake with Creamy Coconut Cream Cheese Frosting

THIS CAKE MADE ME DO THE HAPPY DANCE! After numerous tries, I stumbled upon the perfect batter for the cake (yes, my 90-Calorie Vanilla Cupcakes, page 292), and was transported right to coconut heaven. With a triple dose of coconut flavor, this tender cake is all a coconut cake should be. To make a tall, party-style double layer cake, see the Marlene Says.

MAKES 8 SERVINGS

4 tablespoons shredded sweetened coconut, divided

¾ cup low-fat milk

½ cup granulated no-calorie sweetener*

½ cup light mayonnaise

3 tablespoons granulated sugar

1 teaspoon vanilla extract

1½ teaspoon coconut extract

1 large egg

1½ cups cake flour

1 teaspoon baking powder

½ teaspoon baking soda

1 recipe Coconut Whipped Cream Cheese Frosting (page 304)

1. Preheat the oven to 325°F. Spray an 8-inch round baking pan with nonstick baking spray. Place 2 tablespoons coconut in a small baking pan. Add to the oven, bake for 5 minutes, or until lightly browned, and set aside for garnishing.

2. In a large bowl, whisk together next 7 ingredients (milk through egg) until smooth. Sift in the flour, baking powder, and baking soda. Add the remaining 2 tablespoons of the coconut, and whisk until smooth.

3. Pour the batter into the prepared pan and smooth the top. Bake for 20 to 22 minutes, or until the center of the cake springs back when touched or a toothpick inserted into the center comes out clean. Cool cake on wire rack for 10 minutes, remove from pan, and let cool completely.

4. Using a sharp serrated knife, carefully slice the cake in half. Place the bottom half of cake on a cake plate, and top with half of the frosting, smoothing with a cake spatula. Place the top half on the frosted bottom half, and spread with remaining frosting. Sprinkle with toasted coconut.

Marlene Says: *To make this big and tall, double the batter recipe and bake the layers according to the directions in step 3. When layers are cool, fill and top with a double recipe of frosting. Makes 16 servings.*

*See page 81 for sweetener options.

NUTRITION INFORMATION PER SERVING: (⅛ cake) Calories 205 | Carbohydrate 27g (Sugars 7g) | Total Fat 9g (Sat Fat 4.5g) | Protein 5g | Fiber 1g | Cholesterol 35mg | Sodium 320mg | Food Exchanges: 2 Carbohydrate, 2 Fat | Carbohydrate Choices: 2 | Weight Watcher Plus Point Comparison: 5

Heavenly Strawberry Cake Roll

WHILE MAKING A CAKE ROLL can be challenging, there's no need to be intimidated here. Angel food cake mix simplifies the process and produces a heavenly cake that's sinfully delicious. Even if your final result looks a bit messy, you'd be hard-pressed to find a strawberry dessert that tastes as divine as this with only 120 calories and 1 gram of fat per serving.

MAKES 10 SERVINGS

½ box angel food cake mix (1 cup plus 2 tablespoons dry mix)

1 large egg white

4 teaspoons powdered sugar, divided

1½ cups light whipped topping, thawed

2 tablespoons reduced-sugar strawberry jam

1 cup thinly sliced fresh strawberries

1. Preheat the oven to 325°F. Coat a 10 x 12-inch jelly roll pan with nonstick cooking spray. Line bottom of pan with wax paper, lightly spray with cooking spray, and set aside.

2. In a large bowl, with an electric mixer, make angel food cake according to package directions, using ½ cup plus 2 tablespoons water and the egg white. Pour batter into the prepared pan. Using a spatula, completely level batter. Bake for 15 minutes, or until cake is springy to the touch and edges appear dry. (Do not over-bake, or the cake will crack when it is rolled.)

3. Lay a smooth kitchen towel onto a counter. Sift 2 teaspoons powdered sugar evenly onto the towel. As soon as the cake comes out of the oven, turn it onto a towel, remove wax paper, and roll it up (towel and all), starting with the short side. Let cool.

4. For the filling, in a medium bowl, combine 2 tablespoons of whipped topping with preserves, and stir to blend. Fold in remaining topping. Unroll the cake, and cover it with the filling, leaving a ½-inch border around the edges. Top the filling with sliced strawberries. Re-roll the cake, cover with plastic wrap, and refrigerate until ready to serve.

5. To serve, remove plastic wrap, dust the cake with the remaining powdered sugar, and slice cake in 1-inch slices.

NUTRITION INFORMATION PER SERVING: (1 slice) Calories 150 | Carbohydrate 23g (Sugars 18g) | Total Fat 6g (Sat Fat 3.5g) | Protein 3g | Fiber 0g | Cholesterol 20mg | Sodium 180mg | Food Exchanges: 1½ Carbohydrate, 1 Fat | Carbohydrate Choices: 1½ | Weight Watcher Plus Point Comparison: 4

My Unbelievable Chocolate Cake
(Classic or Gluten-Free)

IF YOU OWN ANY OF MY BOOKS, there is a good chance you have already made my unbelievable chocolate cake. It has become a signature recipe, and for good reason—in mere minutes, using only one bowl and a whisk, you have a perfectly delicious, guilt-free chocolate cake. I am excited to share that, for the first time, I can offer a simple way to make this cake gluten-free—without any loss of its unbelievable ease, taste, or texture. As I say, "Everyone deserves chocolate cake!" Please see Marlene Says for more information.

MAKES 9 SERVINGS

¼ cup canola oil

1 large egg

1 teaspoon vanilla extract

¼ cup packed dark brown sugar

1 cup no-calorie granulated sweetener*

1 cup buttermilk

1¼ cups cake flour

1 teaspoon baking powder

1 teaspoon baking soda

¼ cup Dutch-process cocoa powder

¼ cup hot water

1. Preheat the oven to 350°F. Coat an 8 x 8-inch baking pan with nonstick baking spray.

2. In a large bowl, whisk together the oil and egg until the mixture is frothy and thick. Add the vanilla, brown sugar, and sweetener. Beat with a whisk for 2 more minutes until the mixture is thick and smooth and the sugars have been thoroughly incorporated into the mixture. Whisk in the buttermilk.

3. Sift in the flour, baking powder, baking soda, and cocoa powder, and whisk for 1 to 2 minutes, or until the batter is smooth. Add the water and whisk until smooth. (Batter will be thin.) Pour the batter into the prepared pan, and tap the pan on the counter to level the surface and to help remove any air bubbles.

4. Bake for 18 to 20 minutes, or until the center springs back when touched or a toothpick inserted into the center comes out clean. Do not overbake. Cool the cake on a wire rack.

Marlene Says: *After much searching and testing I've found a gluten-free flour blend worthy of this cake (and the other recipes in this book). My choice, Cup4Cup gluten-free flour, can be found online, in many markets, and all Williams-Sonoma stores. Use it 1:1 for any wheat flour.*

*See page 81 for sweetener options.

NUTRITION INFORMATION PER SERVING: (1 slice) Calories 160 | Carbohydrate 22g (Sugars 8g) | Total Fat 7g (Sat Fat 1g) | Protein 3g | Fiber 1g | Cholesterol 25mg | Sodium 180mg | Food Exchanges: 1½ Carbohydrate, 1 Fat | Carbohydrate Choices: 1½ | Weight Watcher Plus Point Comparison: 5

Molten Chocolate Lava Cakes

THESE DARK CHOCOLATE LAVA CAKES, with their ooey gooey chocolaty centers, are the real deal. Yep, they taste just like the ones served at a restaurant, but at a fraction of the calories and fat. I find Hershey's Special Dark chocolate bars a convenient and delicious chocolate option. With other chocolates, use 2 ounces of chocolate for the batter, and 1 ounce, divided, for pressing in the centers. (In a pinch, melt ⅓ cup semisweet chocolate chips for the batter and press ½ tablespoon into each cake.)

MAKES 4 SERVINGS

3 ounces dark chocolate (2 (1.45-ounce) Hershey's Special Dark bars or 6 squares from a 6.8-ounce bar)

1 tablespoon butter

2 tablespoons low-fat milk

1 teaspoon vanilla extract

3 large eggs, room temperature, separated, divided

2 tablespoons cocoa powder, preferably Dutch-processed

2 tablespoons all-purpose flour

1 tablespoon granulated sugar

1 tablespoon powdered sugar (optional for dusting)

1. Preheat the oven to 400°F. Set the oven rack to lower third of oven. Lightly spray four 6-ounce ramekins with cooking spray. Set aside.

2. Reserve either 8 squares of chocolate from the small bars, or 2 from the large one. Place remaining chocolate in a medium, microwave-safe bowl with the butter and microwave on high for 60 seconds, or until chocolate is mostly melted. Remove and stir until smooth. Whisk in milk, vanilla and egg yolks until smooth. Sift in cocoa powder and flour, and whisk to combine.

3. In a medium bowl, with an electric mixer on high speed, beat the egg whites until foamy. Gradually add 1 tablespoon sugar and beat to soft peaks. Fold ⅓ of the egg whites into the chocolate mixture to lighten, and then gently fold in remaining whites.

4. Divide the batter among the ramekins. If using the small chocolate bars, press 2 squares into the center of each cake. For the larger bar, cut one square in half and press into each cake. Bake for 8 to 9 minutes, or until tops are just firm to the touch and the cakes still jiggle slightly in center. Let cool for 2 minutes and serve immediately with a dusting of powdered sugar, if desired.

DARE TO COMPARE: At Roy's restaurant, classic Melting Hot Chocolate Soufflé cake (served plain) clocks in with 930 calories, including two days' worth of added sugar, a day's worth of fat, and an entire meal's worth of carbohydrates.

NUTRITION INFORMATION PER SERVING: (1 lava cake) Calories 210 | Carbohydrate 21g (Sugars 15g) | Total Fat 12g (Sat Fat 7g) | Protein 7g | Fiber 2g | Cholesterol 150mg | Sodium 85mg | Food Exchanges: 1½ Carbohydrate, 1 Lean Meat, 1½ Fat | Carbohydrate Choices: 1½ | Weight Watcher Plus Point Comparison: 6

Whipped Cream Cheese Frosting

I'VE TWEAKED THIS CREAM CHEESE FROSTING several times over the years, and I have to say that this is my fluffiest, creamiest version yet. Delicious as is, it's also very versatile. Flavor it with coconut (instructions follow), almond, peppermint, or other extracts, chocolate, a couple of tablespoons of jam, or grated citrus zest to create the perfect topping for any type of cake. Start with a small amount of any add-in you choose, and increase in small amounts to taste. Keep in mind the flavor will intensify as the frosting sits.

MAKES 1½ CUPS

⅓ cup tub-style reduced-fat cream cheese

¼ cup nonfat cream cheese, room temperature

¼ cup granulated no-calorie sweetener (or 6 packets)*

1¼ cups light whipped topping

1. In a small bowl, with an electric mixer on medium, beat the cream cheeses until smooth. Add the sweetener and beat for 1 minute longer.

2. On slow speed, beat in half of the whipped topping until fluffy and just combined. Using a rubber spatula, carefully fold in the remaining whipped topping.

Marlene Says: *To make Coconut Whipped Cream Cheese Frosting, add ½ teaspoon of coconut extract in step 1.*

*See page 81 for sweetener options.

NUTRITION INFORMATION PER SERVING: (2 tablespoons) Calories 35 | Carbohydrate 2.5g (Sugars 2g) | Total Fat 2g (Sat Fat 7g) | Protein 1g | Fiber 0g | Cholesterol 0mg | Sodium 70mg | Food Exchanges: ½ Fat | Carbohydrate Choices: 0 | Weight Watcher Plus Point Comparison: 1

Chocolate Fudge Glaze

IT'S SAID THAT ONE SHOULDN'T MESS WITH SUCCESS, so I won't. But if you remember the sticky, shiny, chocolaty glaze I used on my Ooey Gooey Peanut Butter Stuffed Chocolate Cupcakes in Eat More of What You Love, *I share it again here as the perfect glaze for my Boston Cream Pie Cupcakes (page 292) and Easy Icebox Éclair Squares (page 319). Don't forget that, warm from the microwave, it is excellent as an ice cream topping or a dip for strawberries.*

MAKES ½ CUP

3 tablespoons semisweet chocolate chips

3 tablespoons nonfat half-and-half

½ cup granulated no-calorie sweetener*

½ teaspoon vanilla extract

½ cup powdered sugar, sifted

⅓ cup cocoa powder, preferably Dutch-processed

1. Place the chocolate chips in a medium bowl.

2. In a microwave-safe bowl, combine the nonfat half-and-half and the sweetener. Place in the microwave and heat for 1 minute. Pour over the chocolate chips, add the vanilla, and stir until the chocolate chips are melted and the mixture is smooth.

3. With an electric mixer on low speed, beat in the powdered sugar until smooth. Sift in the cocoa powder, and beat again until smooth.

*See page 81 for sweetener options.

NUTRITION INFORMATION PER SERVING: (2 teaspoons) Calories 35 | Carbohydrate 7g (Sugars 3g) | Total Fat 1g (Sat Fat 0g) | Protein 0g | Fiber 0g | Cholesterol 0mg | Sodium 70mg | Food Exchanges: ½ Carbohydrate | Carbohydrate Choices: ½ | Weight Watcher Plus Point Comparison: 1

Cookies, Creamy Favorites, and More

Double Chocolate Softies

Peanut Butter Oatmeal Chocolate Chip Cookies

Coconut Almond Cookies

Lemon Meringue Pie Meringues

James's Spicy Ginger Cookie Coins

Cherry Berry Crunch

Five-Ingredient Strawberry Blossom Pudding Cups

Jammin' Cheesecake Squares

Easy Icebox Éclair Squares

Tiramisu

Marvelous Strawberry Mousse

Supercreamy Pumpkin Pie Cups

Red Velvet Cheesecake Cupcakes

Blackberry Bread Pudding

Homemade Frozen Fruit Pops

WHEN IT COMES TO THINGS I LOVE TO EAT, dessert is near the top of my list! I could (and often do) eat dessert every day, but those I especially love are seasonal sweets—sweets made with seasonal ingredients or eaten at holidays throughout the year. For instance, I can't imagine not eating cookies at Christmas, fruity gems in spring, pumpkin goodies in autumn, or cool creamy treats in the hot summer. If you are reading this, my guess is that you may feel the same way too.

This section is chock-full of delectable desserts for any day, and every season. And, best of all, these low in sugar, fat, and calorie goodies can be enjoyed by *everyone*—guilt-free! Spring means fresh strawberries and the perfect time to whip up my Five-Ingredient Strawberry Blossom Pudding Cups. Though they take only minutes to make, these creamy pink cups give the impression that you worked on them for hours! Or grab a blender and get skinny with Marvelous Strawberry Mousse. At 100 slim calories, this delightful dessert with its intense burst of fresh strawberry flavor, won't burst you out of your bathing suit. Come summer you can cool off with cool, creamy Easy Icebox Éclair Squares or get patriotic with sweet Cherry Berry Crunch. Both are perfect for summer celebrations and get you out of the kitchen quick.

When the leaves start falling it's time for my Supercreamy Pumpkin Pie Cups. (I guarantee that no one will miss the traditional fat-laden crust.) You'll also find plenty to indulge in come holiday season. From my son James's Spicy Ginger Cookie Coins to gluten-free Peanut Butter Oatmeal Chocolate Chip Cookies to yep, the oh-so creamy Red Velvet Cheesecake Cups, I am positive that these desserts will make the season brighter for every one and every body!

FOR THE LOVE OF
NUTS

If you've ever said no to nuts over worries of weight gain, I've got great news for you! Studies show those who eat up to 250 calories of nuts a day weigh no more than those who don't. Moreover, nuts are incredibly nutritious! They are high in heart healthy monounsaturated and omega-3s fatty acids, rich in protein, vitamin E, minerals, and antioxidants, packed with fiber, belly filling and gluten-free. If that isn't enough, eating nuts regularly can reduce your risk for heart disease and type 2 diabetes. It's good to get nutty!

Health benefits aside, creamy, salty, and delectably crunchy nuts are just plain delicious. And despite their small size, it doesn't take many to improve any dish. From cereals and salads to cookies and cakes, nuts add amazing texture, flavor, and crunch. Nuts can also pump up the protein in smoothies, as peanut butter does in my PB & J Smoothie, be used instead of flour, as almonds are in my Gluten-free Oatmeal Spice Bars (page 90), or even be made into milk (see page 38).

A serving size of nuts is one ounce and the number of nuts in an ounce varies by the type of nut. To keep calories in check, whether cooking or snacking, here are the nutritional stats for some of my favorite (healthiest) nuts:

NUT	Approx # of nuts	Calories (kcal)	Protein (g)	Total Fat (g)	Saturated fat (g)	Carbs (g)	Fiber (g)
Almonds	24	160	6	14	1	6	4
Cashews	18	160	4	13	3	9	1
Pecans	19 (halves)	200	3	20	2	4	3
Pistachios	49	160	4	18	1.5	8	3
Walnuts	14 (halves)	190	4	18	1.5	4	2
Peanuts	28 (~1 ½ tbsp. nut butter)	160	5	14	2	5	2.5

Double Chocolate Softies

THERE IS NO BETTER WAY TO SAY "I LOVE YOU," than with a double dose of chocolate. Fill the cookie jar with these cakey chocolate drops, and you'll get nothing but smiles all around. You can also save some for later, simply seal cooled cookies in a plastic bag and freeze. Whenever you need a lift, pop one in the microwave for 15 to 20 seconds and enjoy.

MAKES 20 SERVINGS

1 cup plus 2 tablespoons all-purpose flour

¼ cup cocoa powder (preferably Dutch-processed)

½ teaspoon baking soda

½ cup granulated no-calorie sweetener*

⅓ cup margarine or butter, softened

¼ cup brown sugar

¼ cup (or 3.5-ounce container) prune puree

1 large egg

1 teaspoon vanilla extract

1 tablespoon low-fat milk

⅓ cup mini chocolate chips

1. Preheat the oven to 375°F. Spray a cookie sheet with non-stick cooking spray.

2. In a small bowl, combine the flour, cocoa, and baking soda. Set aside.

3. In a medium bowl, with an electric mixer, beat the next 4 ingredients (sweetener through puree) until smooth and creamy. Add the egg and vanilla and beat well. Gently stir in the flour mixture, add the milk, and stir to incorporate. Stir in the chocolate chips.

4. Drop level tablespoons of dough onto the cookie sheet. Press cookies flat (a wet finger works best), and bake the cookies for 6 to 8 minutes (These are best when slightly soft. Do not over-bake.) Remove from pan and cool on rack.

*See page 81 for sweetener options.

NUTRITION INFORMATION PER SERVING: (1 cookie) Calories 65 | Carbohydrate 10g (Sugars 4g) | Total Fat 3g (Sat Fat 1g) | Protein 1g | Fiber 1g | Cholesterol 10mg | Sodium 55mg | Food Exchanges: ½ Carbohydrate, ½ Fat | Carbohydrate Choices: ½ | Weight Watcher Plus Point Comparison: 2

Peanut Butter Oatmeal Chocolate Chip Cookies

LOADED WITH CREAMY PEANUT BUTTER, chewy oatmeal, and *sweet chocolate chips, these flourless, gluten-free whole grain cookies hit the favor trifecta when it comes to everyone's favorite cookies. The only downside is that they may disappear as fast as you can bake them up. Don't be surprised if you start hiding your own secret stash.*

MAKES 16 SERVINGS

½ cup smooth peanut butter

⅓ cup granulated no-calorie sweetener*

½ teaspoon baking soda

3 tablespoons brown sugar

1 large egg

1 teaspoon vanilla

1¼ cups quick oats

⅓ cup mini chocolate chips

1. Preheat the oven to 350°F. Spray a cookie sheet with non-stick cooking spray.

2. In a medium bowl, with an electric mixer, beat the peanut butter, sweetener, baking soda, and brown sugar until well creamed. Add the egg and vanilla, and beat until smooth. Stir in the oats and the chocolate chips.

3. Roll the dough, by level tablespoons, into 1-inch balls. Place onto a greased baking sheet, and flatten the cookies by pressing down on the dough with a spatula or the bottom of a glass.

4. Bake for 8 to 10 minutes, or until cookies are golden brown on the bottom but still slightly soft in the center. Remove from the oven and let cool on the baking sheet for 5 minutes. Remove to wire racks to finish cooling.

Marlene Says: *When making these for someone on a strict gluten-free diet, check the label on the oats. While oats are naturally gluten free, not all brands guarantee they are processed in gluten-free facilities.*

*See page 81 for sweetener options.

NUTRITION INFORMATION PER SERVING: (1 cookie) Calories 95 | Carbohydrate 8g (Sugars 3g) | Total Fat 6g (Sat Fat 1.5g) | Protein 3g | Fiber 1g | Cholesterol 10mg | Sodium 40mg | Food Exchanges: ½ Carbohydrate | Carbohydrate Choices: ½ | Weight Watcher Plus Point Comparison: 3

Coconut Almond Cookies

WHILE I AM NOT ABOUT TO GIVE UP MY BELOVED PEANUT BUTTER anytime soon, it now shares a shelf with rich, nutty almond butter. I find almond butter is super satisfying—and a little goes a long way (a single tablespoon smeared on a banana is a terrific snack). The higher ratios of healthy fats and moderate amount of carbohydrates in these confection-like flourless cookies, make them a smart choice for those watching their blood sugar.

MAKES 12 SERVINGS

½ cup almond butter

6 tablespoons granulated no-calorie sweetener*

3 tablespoons brown sugar

2 tablespoons egg substitute (or ½ large egg, beaten)

½ teaspoon coconut extract

¼ teaspoon baking soda

¼ cup quick-cooking oats

1. Preheat the oven to 350°F.

2. Combine the first 6 ingredients (almond butter through baking soda) in a medium bowl, and stir until well mixed. Add the oats and stir until dough is formed. Dough will be soft and sticky.

3. Place by tablespoons on an ungreased baking sheet, and pat the dough with your finger until almost flat.

4. Bake for 7 to 8 minutes, or until cookies are golden brown. Remove from the oven and let cool on the baking sheet for 5 minutes. Remove to wire racks to finish cooling.

Marlene Says: *Calorie, fat, and sugar content is very similar for both almond and peanut butters, but almond butter has the edge when it comes to micronutrients. A single 2-tablespoon serving delivers 40% of your daily requirement of Vitamin E and 8% of of calcium and iron.*

*See page 81 for sweetener options.

NUTRITION INFORMATION PER SERVING: (1 cookie) Calories 95 | Carbohydrate 8g (Sugars 5g) | Total Fat 6g (Sat Fat 0.5g) | Protein 3g | Fiber 1g | Cholesterol 0mg | Sodium 35mg | Food Exchanges: ½ Carbohydrate, ½ Lean Meat, 1 Fat | Carbohydrate Choices: ½ | Weight Watcher Plus Point Comparison: 3

Lemon Meringue Pie Meringues

CALLING ALL LEMON PIE LOVERS! These simple, light-as-a-feather meringue cookies boast a delicate crunch and a sweet lemony taste that will remind you of the classic pie. Make them for special occasions, like bridal and baby showers, or serve them with bowls of berries and frozen yogurt for a taste of all things summer.

MAKES 20 SERVINGS

3 large egg whites

¼ teaspoon cream of tartar

⅔ cup granulated sugar

1½ teaspoons fresh lemon juice

1½ teaspoons lemon zest

⅛ teaspoon vanilla

1. Preheat the oven to 225°F. Line 2 cookie sheets with silicone liners or parchment. Set aside.

2. Place the egg whites, cream of tartar, and sugar in a metal mixing bowl, and place over a pan of simmering water. Heat for 2 to 3 minutes, or until sugar dissolves and egg whites are slightly warm.

3. Remove the bowl from the heat and beat the egg whites with an electric mixer on high for 4 to 5 minutes or until very stiff peaks form. With a spatula, gently fold in the lemon juice, zest, and vanilla, being careful not to deflate meringue mixture.

4. Using a tablespoon, immediately spoon the meringue mixture onto the cookie sheets. Bake for 1 hour, or until cookies lift cleanly off the cookie sheet. Turn off the oven, and leave the cookies in the oven for 15 minutes. Remove and cool on a rack. Store cookies in an airtight container.

> **DARE TO COMPARE:** You need to eat a dozen of these meringues to equal the carbohydrates in one piece of Marie Callender's Lemon Meringue Pie. To match just the calories, you need to eat the entire batch!

NUTRITION INFORMATION PER SERVING: (1 meringue) Calories 30 | Carbohydrate 7g (Sugars 7g) | Total Fat 0g (Sat Fat 0g) | Protein 1g | Fiber 0g | Cholesterol 0mg | Sodium 10mg | Food Exchanges: ½ Carbohydrate | Carbohydrate Choices: ½ | Weight Watcher Plus Point Comparison: 1

James's Spicy Ginger Cookie Coins

MOVE OVER CHOCOLATE CHIP AND OATMEAL, this shiny, sparkly cookie has some serious sass. Spiced with ginger and cloves and darkly flavored with molasses, these are a holiday favorite. But as my son James recently reminded me, there's no need to wait for the holidays to enjoy them!

MAKES 24 COOKIES

½ cup margarine or butter, softened

¾ cup granulated no-calorie sweetener*

1 large egg

⅓ cup molasses

2 cups all-purpose flour

1 teaspoon baking soda

1 teaspoon cinnamon

1 teaspoon ginger

½ teaspoon ground cloves

1 large egg white

2 teaspoons granulated sugar

1. Preheat the oven to 350°F. In a large bowl, with an electric mixer, beat the margarine, sweetener, egg, and molasses until light and creamy. Set aside.

2. In another bowl, whisk together next 5 ingredients (flour through cloves). Add to the creamed mixture, and mix well.

3. Roll the dough by level tablespoons into balls, and place 1 inch apart on an ungreased baking sheet. Flatten cookies with the bottom of a drinking glass. Whisk the egg white in a small bowl. Brush each cookie lightly with egg white, and sprinkle lightly with sugar. Bake for 10 to 12 minutes. Remove to a wire rack to cool.

*See page 81 for sweetener options.

NUTRITION INFORMATION PER SERVING: (1 cookie) Calories 70 | Carbohydrate 10g (Sugars 3g) | Total Fat 3g (Sat Fat 1g) | Protein 1g | Fiber 0g | Cholesterol 5mg | Sodium 75mg | Food Exchanges: 1 Carbohydrate, ½ Fat | Carbohydrate Choices: 1 | Weight Watcher Plus Point Comparison: 2

Cherry Berry Crunch

DESSERTS BAKED AND/OR SERVED IN SMALL JARS are both fun and festive. And after seeing the smiles on the faces of those I served this to, I definitely recommend it. Bake, cool, and twist on a lid, and they are the perfect travel-ready dessert for picnics and potlucks. Served with a dollop of creamy whipped topping, they are stellar for Fourth of July celebrations. No jars? Feel free to use ramekins, or even a single baking dish. Cherries and blueberries are lovely together.

MAKES 6 SERVINGS

1 (20-ounce) can light cherry pie filling

1 cup fresh blueberries

¼ teaspoon almond extract

2 tablespoons plus ⅓ cup no-calorie sweetener, divided*

¼ cup all-purpose flour

3 tablespoons quick oats

½ teaspoon cinnamon

1 tablespoon margarine or butter

1. Preheat the oven to 375°F. In a medium bowl, stir together the pie filling, blueberries, extract, and 2 tablespoons sweetener. Divide the mixture evenly into six 4-ounce jars or six 6-ounce ramekins, placing about ½ cup of filling in each.

2. In a small bowl, combine remaining sweetener, flour, oats, and cinnamon. Cut in margarine, and sprinkle 2 tablespoons topping onto each. Bake for 20 to 25 minutes or until bubbling. Let cool 15 minutes before serving.

Marlene Says: *Alternately, place the fruit mixture in a 1½-quart baking dish, sprinkle evenly with topping and bake as directed.*

*See page 81 for sweetener options.

NUTRITION INFORMATION PER SERVING: (1 jar or generous ½ cup) Calories 140 | Carbohydrate 25g (Sugars 15g) | Total Fat 4g (Sat Fat 1g) | Protein 2g | Fiber 2g | Cholesterol 0mg | Sodium 40mg | Food Exchanges: 1 Fruit, ½ Starch, ½ Fat | Carbohydrate Choices: 1½ | Weight Watcher Plus Point Comparison: 4

Five-Ingredient Strawberry Blossom Pudding Cups

WHEN YOU NEED A WOW-WORTHY DESSERT for last minute guests, I've got you covered. Here, creamy white chocolate pudding and fresh strawberries get a sophisticated makeover in mere minutes using my secret kitchen tool: an egg slicer! This gadget saves knife time (and fingertips) while making picture-perfect strawberry petals for a stunning dessert presentation. Use 4-ounce jars for a garden party look.

MAKES **4** SERVINGS

1½ cups low-fat milk

1 package sugar-free white chocolate pudding

1 cup light whipped topping

8 to 10 medium fresh strawberries, washed, stems removed

4 frozen or fresh blackberries

1. Pour milk in a medium bowl. Whisk the milk while slowly adding the pudding mix. Whisk mixture until smooth. Gently fold in the whipped topping. Divide mixture between four 6-ounce ramekins or 4-ounce jars.

2. Slice strawberries using an egg slicer (or by hand lengthwise). Place a blackberry in the center of each cup of pudding. Starting at the center, insert the strawberry slices, stem end down, around the blackberry. Insert a second layer, between the empty spaces, to create flower effect. Refrigerate for at least 15 minutes, and up to 1 day before serving.

Marlene Says: *Dark chocolate and vanilla puddings also pair well here.*

NUTRITION INFORMATION PER SERVING: (1 pudding cup) Calories 110 | Carbohydrate 18g (Sugars 9g) | Total Fat 2.5g (Sat Fat 2g) | Protein 3g | Fiber 1g | Cholesterol 0mg | Sodium 350mg | Food Exchanges: 1 Carbohydrate, ½ Fat | Carbohydrate Choices: 1 | Weight Watcher Plus Point Comparison: 3

Jammin' Cheesecake Squares

THESE CREAMY CHEESECAKE SQUARES are as pretty to look at as they are delicious to eat. A quick swirl of jam adds the final flourish to a sweet cream cheese filling atop a vanilla wafer crust. I leave the jam flavor up to you. I find strawberry and raspberry both lovely, but blackberry is the family favorite.

MAKES 9 SERVINGS

¾ cup crushed vanilla wafers

2 tablespoons margarine or butter, melted

8 ounces light tub-style cream cheese

4 ounces nonfat cream cheese, room temperature

⅔ cup granulated no-calorie sweetener*

2 teaspoons cornstarch

1 large egg

1 large egg white

1 tablespoon fresh lemon juice

¾ teaspoon vanilla extract

¼ teaspoon almond extract

½ cup light sour cream

¼ cup sugar-free jam

1. Preheat the oven to 325°F. Coat an 8 x 8-inch square pan with cooking spray. To make the crust, mix the wafer crumbs and margarine together in a medium bowl. Press the crust mixture in an even layer onto the bottom of the prepared pan. Place the crust in the freezer while preparing the filling.

2. In a medium bowl, beat the cream cheeses, sweetener, and cornstarch together with an electric mixer. Beat in the egg, egg white, lemon juice, and extracts until mixture is just smooth. Do not overmix. Gently fold in the sour cream. Pour the filling onto the crust and spread evenly.

3. Place the jam in a small, microwave-safe bowl and microwave on high for 20 to 25 seconds and stir. If the jam is too thin, stir slightly to cool. Carefully place small spoonfuls of the jam on top of the cheesecake batter. Swirl a thin knife back and forth through the puree and top of the batter to create a marbleized effect.

4. Bake for 18 to 20 minutes, or until the edges are firm and the center is set but still slightly soft. Cool at room temperature for 20 minutes, then refrigerate for at least 2 hours before cutting into squares.

*See page 81 for sweetener options.

NUTRITION INFORMATION PER SERVING: (1 bar) Calories 180 | Carbohydrate 17g (Sugars 9g) | Total Fat 11g (Sat Fat 4g) | Protein 7g | Fiber 0g | Cholesterol 35mg | Sodium 210mg | Food Exchanges: 1 Carbohydrate, 1 Lean Meat, 1 Fat | Carbohydrate Choices: 1 | Weight Watcher Plus Point Comparison: 5

Easy Icebox Éclair Squares

ICEBOX CAKES DATE BACK TO THE 1920s AND '30s when the novel idea of using wafer cookies to create an overnight "cake," became a popular sensation. The fact that cookies (and graham crackers) soften in the fridge when layered with pudding or cream to create a cake-like layer still amazes me. With no cooking required, icebox desserts are at the top of the class when it comes to convenience. This cool, éclair-like dessert is perfect for hot days.

MAKES 9 SERVINGS

1 (4-serving size) package sugar-free instant vanilla pudding mix

1½ cups low-fat milk

½ teaspoon vanilla extract

2 cups light whipped topping

9 full sheet graham crackers, divided

Chocolate Fudge Glaze, (page 305)

1. In a medium bowl, whisk the pudding mix into the milk until mixture is smooth and no lumps remain. Fold in the vanilla and whipped topping.

2. Break the sheets of graham crackers in half. Arrange 9 (of the 18) halves to line the bottom of an 8-inch square pan. (Note that there will be a small space between each cracker and the sides of the pan.)

3. Top the crackers with the pudding, spreading evenly to cover. Arrange the remaining 9 graham cracker halves over the pudding.

4. Prepare the chocolate fudge glaze, and while it is still warm, spread it evenly over the graham crackers. Refrigerate 8 hours or overnight before serving. Cut 3 times each way to serve.

NUTRITION INFORMATION PER SERVING: (¹⁄₉ of recipe) Calories 155 | Carbohydrate 25g (Sugars 14g) | Total Fat 4g (Sat Fat 3g) | Protein 3g | Fiber 1g | Cholesterol 0mg | Sodium 200mg | Food Exchanges: 1½ Carbohydrate, ½ Fat | Carbohydrate Choices: 1½ | Weight Watcher Plus Point Comparison: 3

Tiramisu

AUTHENTIC VERSIONS OF THIS BELOVED DESSERT are made with a rich, smooth Italian cream cheese called mascarpone. Unfortunately, mascarpone combined with the cream, egg yolks, and sugar in a traditional tiramisu sends fat and calories skyrocketing. Originally developed for a lighter baking class at a professional cooking school, my luscious tiramisu has all the classic taste with just a fraction of the original fat and calories. Or as they say in Italy, it's "bellissimo."

| MAKES 6 SERVINGS

4 ounces mascarpone cheese*

4 ounces nonfat cream cheese, room temperature

¼ cup low-fat ricotta cheese

2 tablespoons light sour cream

½ cup plus 3 tablespoons no-calorie granulated sweetener, divided**

¾ cup light whipped topping

1 tablespoon instant coffee

1 tablespoon brandy (optional)

1 (3-ounce) package soft ladyfingers

1 teaspoon cocoa powder, preferably Dutch-processed

½ ounce semisweet chocolate, shaved (optional)

1. In a medium mixing bowl, beat the cheeses, sour cream, and ½ cup sweetener with an electric mixer until creamy and smooth. Fold in the light whipped topping and set aside.

2. Place ¾ cup water in a small, microwave-safe bowl or saucepan. Add the instant coffee, remaining 3 tablespoons of sweetener, and brandy, if desired, and heat for on high for 1 minute.

4. To assemble, place half of the ladyfingers on the bottom of a 1-quart baking dish. Brush ladyfingers with half of the coffee mixture. Top with half of the cheese mixture, spread until smooth, and repeat.

5. Sift the cocoa powder over the top of the tiramisu. Top with the shaved chocolate, if desired, and refrigerate for at least 4 hours before serving.

DARE TO COMPARE: An order of Tiramisu at Carrabba's Italian restaurant has 1060 calories, including over a days' worth of fat and 2½ days worth of saturated fat!

*Can replace with 4 ounces light tub-style cream cheese and 2 tablespoons light sour cream.

**See page 81 for sweetener options.

NUTRITION INFORMATION PER SERVING: (⅙ of recipe) Calories 160 | Carbohydrate 9g (Sugars 3g) | Total Fat 11g (Sat Fat 4g) | Protein 5g | Fiber 1g | Cholesterol 0mg | Sodium 135mg | Food Exchanges: ½ Carbohydrate, 1 Lean Meat, 2 Fat | Carbohydrate Choices: ½ | Weight Watcher Plus Point Comparison: 5

Marvelous Strawberry Mousse

SUPER-LOW IN CALORIES, this pretty pink mousse delivers big strawberry flavor. Please don't be deterred by the cottage cheese. Creamed until smooth, it blends seamlessly with the sour cream and whipped topping to create a nutritious mousse that delivers 6 grams of protein, a healthy dose of Vitamin C, and 10% of your daily calcium requirement. This is a sweet treat you can feel really good about eating!

MAKES 8 SERVINGS

1 package unflavored gelatin

2 cups fresh sliced strawberries

1 cup low-fat cottage cheese

½ cup low-fat sour cream

2 tablespoons granulated sugar

6 tablespoons granulated no-calorie sweetener*

¼ teaspoon almond extract

¾ cup light whipped topping

1. In a small, microwave-safe bowl, sprinkle the gelatin over ¼ cup of water. Let set for 3 minutes. Microwave for 30 seconds on high to dissolve gelatin, and set aside.

2. Place the strawberries in a blender and blend until pureed. Add the cottage cheese and blend until completely smooth.

3. Add the sour cream, sugar, sweetener, almond extract, and gelatin mixture, and pulse to blend. Pour into a medium bowl, and gently fold in whipped topping. Pour into individual cups or stemmed glasses, if desired. Refrigerate for at least 2 hours before serving.

Marlene Says: *To create Strawberry Mousse Blossom Cups, divide mousse into small jars or ramekins and top with strawberries per the instructions on page 317.*

*See page 81 for sweetener options.

NUTRITION INFORMATION PER SERVING: (½ cup) Calories 100 | Carbohydrate 8g (Sugars 10g) | Total Fat 5g (Sat Fat 3.5g) | Protein 6g | Fiber 1g | Cholesterol 20mg | Sodium 110mg | Food Exchanges: ½ Carbohydrate, 1 Lean Meat, ½ Fat | Carbohydrate Choices: ½ | Weight Watcher Plus Point Comparison: 2

Supercreamy Pumpkin Pie Cups

NO ONE WILL MISS THE CRUST when they eat these creamy pumpkin custard cups. Inspired by a recipe from a famous Food Network chef, cream cheese adds an extra luscious quality to traditional pumpkin pie filling, while the gentle heat of a water bath ensures a silky smooth result every time. Top each serving with whipped topping and a pecan half if you please for a simple, yet showstopper, dessert.

½ cup light tub-style cream cheese

1 (15-ounce) can 100% pure pumpkin puree

2 teaspoons cornstarch

2 large eggs

¾ cup granulated no-calorie sweetener*

2 tablespoons brown sugar

1 ½ teaspoons cinnamon

½ teaspoon ground ginger

¼ teaspoon ground nutmeg

1 teaspoon vanilla extract

1 (12-ounce) can low-fat evaporated milk

1. Preheat the oven to 350°F. Place eight 6-ounce ramekins or custard cups in a deep baking pan.

2. In a medium bowl, using an electric mixer, beat the cream cheese on medium speed until smooth. Beat in the pumpkin, cornstarch and eggs. Add sweetener, brown sugar, spices, and vanilla, and beat briefly. Add evaporated milk and beat until smooth.

3. Pour ½ cup of mixture into in each ramekin. Place the baking pan in the oven and pour hot water into it until it reaches halfway up the sides of ramekins.

4. Bake for 35 to 40 minutes, or until a knife inserted in center of a ramekin comes out clean. Carefully remove ramekins from water bath, cool at room temperature, then refrigerate 8 hours or overnight.

5. Just before serving, combine whipped topping and bourbon, if desired, or vanilla in a small bowl. Top each ramekin with 2 tablespoons topping and 1 pecan half.

DARE TO COMPARE: A piece of the pumpkin pie that inspired this custard clocks in at 500 calories, seven times the fat, and three times the carbs.

*See page 81 for sweetener options.

NUTRITION INFORMATION PER SERVING: (1 custard cup) Calories 135 | Carbohydrate 15g (Sugars 10g) | Total Fat 4g (Sat Fat 2.5g) | Protein 7g | Fiber 2g | Cholesterol 60mg | Sodium 150mg | Food Exchanges: 1 Starch, 1 Lean Meat, ½ Fat | Carbohydrate Choices: 1 | Weight Watcher Plus Point Comparison: 3

Red Velvet Cheesecake Cupcakes

CHEESECAKE, CUPCAKES, AND RED VELVET—what's not to love?! Gorgeously red and sinful only in taste, these wondrous "cakes" in a cup, clock in at 150 slim calories each. New twists on old favorites don't always match the original, but I think you'll agree this is a stellar red velvet dessert.

MAKES 12 SERVINGS

⅔ cup crushed chocolate graham crackers

3 tablespoons plus 1 cup granulated no-calorie sweetener,* divided

2 tablespoons plus ¼ cup cocoa powder, divided

2 tablespoons margarine or butter, melted

1 cup low-fat cottage cheese

8 ounces light tub-style cream cheese

1½ tablespoons red food coloring

2 tablespoons cornstarch

2 tablespoons granulated sugar

1 teaspoon vanilla extract

¼ teaspoon almond extract

2 large eggs

½ cup light sour cream

1½ cups light whipped topping

1. Preheat the oven to 300°F. Place cupcake liners in 12-cup muffin tin (and spray with nonstick cooking spray if not using foil liners).

2. In a small bowl, stir together graham cracker crumbs, 3 tablespoons sweetener, 2 tablespoons cocoa powder, and margarine. Press 1 rounded tablespoon into the bottom of each muffin cup. Place muffin tin in the freezer while preparing the filling.

3. Using a food processor, or immersion blender, blend the cottage cheese until smooth. Transfer to a bowl and add cream cheese, remaining sweetener, ¼ cup cocoa powder, and next 5 ingredients (food coloring through extracts). Beat mixture with an electric mixer on low until smooth. Add the eggs and beat until just blended. Stir in the sour cream.

4. Spoon 3 tablespoons of the filling into each muffin cup and spread until level. Bake for 15 to 18 minutes, or until cheesecakes are set but centers jiggle slightly. Cool to room temperature. Chill in the refrigerator until firm, at least 2 hours. When cool, frost or top with 2 tablespoons whipped topping.

DARE TO COMPARE: A single piece of the Ultimate Red Velvet Cake Cheesecake topped with whipped cream at the Cheesecake Factory has a staggering 1,540 calories and 3 days' worth of saturated fat.

*See page 81 for sweetener options.

NUTRITION INFORMATION PER SERVING: (1 cupcake) Calories 150 | Carbohydrate 13g (Sugars 6g) | Total Fat 7g (Sat Fat 4.5g) | Protein 7g | Fiber less than 1g | Cholesterol 30mg | Sodium 230mg | Food Exchanges: 1 Carbohydrate, 1 Lean Meat, ½ Fat | Carbohydrate Choices: 1 | Weight Watcher Plus Point Comparison: 4

Blackberry Bread Pudding

THERE'S SOMETHING GRAND ABOUT BLACKBERRIES, which is why I love to feature them in recipes as special as this one. Fresh or frozen, these fabulous fruit gems turn basic bread pudding into a berry-licious delight. When using frozen berries, thaw them just slightly before using. One of my favorite ways to "bake" this is actually in a slow cooker. See the "Marlene Says" for directions. (P.S.—This is wonderful for brunch!)

MAKES 8 SERVINGS

6 cups cubed slightly dried French bread

1½ cups fresh or frozen blackberries

2 cups low-fat milk

¾ cup nonfat half-and-half

2 large eggs

2 large egg whites

⅔ cup granulated no-calorie sweetener*

1 tablespoon vanilla extract

1 teaspoon cinnamon

¼ teaspoon nutmeg

1 tablespoon granulated sugar

Powdered sugar (optional for dusting)

1. Preheat the oven to 350°F. Coat an 11 x 17-inch baking pan with cooking spray.

2. Spread ½ of the bread cubes in the baking dish. Sprinkle the blackberries evenly across the bread, and top with remaining the bread cubes.

3. In a medium bowl, whisk together the next 8 ingredients (milk through nutmeg). Pour over bread cubes. Sprinkle the sugar evenly over the top of the pudding.

4. Cover the baking pan with foil and bake for 30 minutes. Remove the foil and bake another 20 to 30 minutes or until the bread pudding is nicely browned on top. Serve warm or at room temperature. Dust with powdered sugar, if desired.

Marlene Says: *To use a slow cooker, follow steps 1 through 3, layering bread and berries in a 5- to 6-quart slow cooker. Cover and cook for 3 hours on low.*

*See page 81 for sweetener options.

NUTRITION INFORMATION PER SERVING: (¾ cup) Calories 140 | Carbohydrate 22g (Sugars 8g) | Total Fat 2g (Sat Fat 1g) | Protein 8g | Fiber 2g | Cholesterol 50mg | Sodium 180mg | Food Exchanges: 1½ Carbohydrate, 1 Lean Meat | Carbohydrate Choices: 1½ | Weight Watcher Plus Point Comparison: 3

Homemade Frozen Fruit Pops

NO NEED TO HEAD TO THE STORE for frozen sweet confections with this handy recipe. Simply blend juice, fruit, and a touch of corn syrup together, and freeze. Colorful fresh blueberries enhance the taste and appeal of my strawberry pops; feel free to tuck a few pieces of fresh pineapple or bananas into my tropical mango popsicle as well, if you please. Simple ingredients, real fruit, and no preservatives make these nutritional all-stars.

MAKES 4 FRUIT POPS

MANGO ORANGE

1 cup frozen mango

1 cup light orange juice

2 teaspoons light corn syrup or agave nectar

1. Combine all of the ingredients in a blender and blend until almost smooth, or to your liking.

2. Pour about ⅓ cup of mixture into a popsicle mold, or into a 6-ounce paper cup. If using a cup, cover with foil and place a popsicle stick through the foil into the center of the popsicle. Freeze until firm.

NUTRITION INFORMATION PER SERVING: (1 fruit pop) Calories 55 | Carbohydrate 15g (Sugars12g) | Total Fat 0g (Sat Fat 0g) | Protein 0g | Fiber 1g | Cholesterol 0mg | Sodium 10mg | Food Exchanges: 1 Fruit | Carbohydrate Choices: 1 | Weight Watcher Plus Point Comparison: 1

STRAWBERRY BLUEBERRY

¾ cup frozen strawberries (about 5 medium)

1 cup reduced-calorie cranberry juice

2 teaspoons light corn syrup or agave nectar

½ cup fresh blueberries

1. Combine strawberries, juice, and corn syrup in a blender, and blend until smooth.

2. Pour ⅓ cup of strawberry mixture into a popsicle mold, or into a 6-ounce paper cup. Insert 5 to 6 blueberries (spread to your liking) into the strawberry mixture. Cover with foil, and place a popsicle stick through the foil into the center of the popsicle. Freeze until firm.

NUTRITION INFORMATION PER SERVING: (1 fruit pop) Calories 45 | Carbohydrate 11g (Sugars7g) | Total Fat 0g (Sat Fat 0g) | Protein 0g | Fiber 1g | Cholesterol 0mg | Sodium 10mg | Food Exchanges: 1 Fruit | Carbohydrate Choices: 1 | Weight Watcher Plus Point Comparison: 1

Menus for
EVERY DAY,
EVERY OCCASION,
and
EVERY ONE!

Sunday Brunch Southern-Style

Easy Family-Style Italian Supper

Better Burger Barbecue

Everyday Asian Takeout

Spectacular Steakhouse-Style Celebration

Garden Fresh Summer Supper

Any Day Mexican Fiesta

Slim and Speedy Seafood Special

IF YOU'VE EVER WONDERED, "what should I serve with this?" or "how best would I do that?" or you simply love to entertain, this section is for you. Coming from a large family where Sunday dinners and holiday celebrations are relished, instilled in me a love for entertaining. In words unspoken it was clear that every feast was infused with love. Today, I am blessed with both the nutrition and culinary backgrounds that not only allow me to create equally wonderful beloved meals—but to create ones that everyone can enjoy!

The following are eight complete menus using the recipes in this book to help you create memorable meals for your own family and friends. From a Southern brunch to enjoy on a lazy Sunday to a spectacular steakhouse celebratory meal, to a Fresh Summer Supper packed with the bounty of the season and the quickest, tastiest, slimming week night supper, every menu has been perfectly balanced—for good health, visual appeal, and of course, great taste.

There are also plenty of planning tips for ease of preparation, some easy decorating tips, and a few eye-opening comparisons that show how significant the savings are when several of my better-for-you recipes are combined to create a better-for-you meal (most of the menus boast a calorie savings of 1,000 calories or more!). Best of all, I've tested all the recipes and crunched all the numbers so you can relax assured that the menus will delight all your guests—including those with diabetes or on weight loss diets.

Finally, don't hesitate to add your own personal touch. Feel free to make substitutions or mix and match within the menus with your favorite recipes—including the more than 500 recipes in *Eat What You Love* and *Eat More of What You Love!* Entertaining with good health and great taste has never been more fun.

Sunday Brunch Southern–Style

There's nothing better than a leisurely Sunday brunch with family or friends, especially when the menu is easy, healthy, and delicious! For a stress-free morning prepare the cupcakes and the frosting the day before. Store the cooled cupcakes in an airtight container and the frosting in the refrigerator. Prep the fruit and make up the Bloody Mary mix (virgin-style, if you prefer) and place in the fridge as well. Come Sunday morning prepare the savory biscuits, set out your beverages and fruit, and frost and display the cupcakes. Just before serving prepare the eggs and gravy. (P.S.—Leftover biscuits pair wonderfully with pork chops or roasted chicken.)

BBQ Bloody Marys *(page 55)*

Fresh Fruit

Savory Southern-Style Biscuits, Eggs, and Gravy *(page 68)*

Luscious Coconut Cupcakes *(page 293)*

Freshly Brewed Coffee

Easy Family-Style Italian Supper

Get out your checkered table cloth! I guarantee you'll have your family racing to the table with this cheesy Italian menu. Parmesan cheese does double duty appearing in both the dressing and the ziti and ditto the ricotta, which is as delicious in the ziti as it is in the Tiramisu. Make the Tiramisu the day before and this menu can be on the table in forty-five minutes, start to finish. The trick is getting the ziti prepped and in the oven, then making the salad. Have guests chip in with setting the table. Looking for even more cheesy goodness? Instead of rolls serve the Everyday Garlic Toast from *Eat More of What You Love* (you'll find them on page 235). Buon appetito!

Italian "House" Salad with Cheesy Italian Dressing *(page 154)*

Better-for-You Three Cheese Baked Ziti *(page 178)*

Whole Wheat Rolls or Breadsticks

Tiramisu *(page 320)* or

Lemon Meringue Pie Meringues *(page 313)*

Better Burger Barbecue

While chicken breasts, steak, and fish are all great grilling favorites, nothing says barbecue better than a juicy burger! Here's my timeline for getting this bodacious meal on the table with a minimum of fuss: At least two hours before the meal, prepare the delectable peanut butter pie and place it in the freezer. One hour before, make the sweet and tangy slaw and refrigerate. Thirty minutes before, prepare the steak fries. When the foil comes off the fries (they have about ten minutes left to cook), it's time to grill the burgers!

Raspberry Lemonade *(page 40)*

Bodacious "50-50" Bacon 'n Beef Burgers *(page 149)*

Apple Poppy Seed Slaw *(page 162)*

Extra Crispy Oven-Baked Steak Fries *(page 232)*

10-Minute Peanut Butter Pretzel Pie *(page 290)*

DARE TO COMPARE: The combined "savings" you reap from this bodacious menu—per serving—is 125 grams of fat, 6 carb servings, and over 1,500 calories!

Everyday Asian Takeout

Whether you love to take out Asian-style chicken or beef, noodles or stir-fried veggies, or all of the above, you will find them all here. Crunchy egg rolls are always a hit, but for an even easier option check out the lettuce wraps on page 120. Both entrées are fast and fit, so the choice is up to you. If you or those you love are strictly watching carbs, then opting for snap peas over the chow mein yields enough carb savings to enjoy both an egg roll and a cookie! The savings of the full menu when compared to takeout is over 1,000 calories! P.S.—To create an "Asian"-themed table, all it takes is to mix a single piece of Asian patterned china (like a tea cup, side plate or bowl) per place setting with white or solid-colored china. Don't forget the chopsticks!

Easy Baked Egg Rolls *(page 119)*

Quicker-Than-Takeout Sweet and Sour Chicken *(page 254)* or

James Orange Beef *(page 268)*

Panda-Style Chicken Chow Mein *(side dish, page 187)* or

Two-Minute Sugar Snap Peas *(page 229)*

Coconut Almond Cookies *(page 312)*

Green Tea

Spectacular Steakhouse-Style Celebration

This showstopping menu is grand enough for any occasion! Do it up right by setting the table with a white table cloth, nice china, flowers, and/or candles. Prep everything for the wedge salads early in the day. Place the wedges on individual plates and dress them up to an hour before the meal, storing them in the fridge. Perfect for easy entertaining, the potatoes can be made much earlier in the day as they finish off in the oven. Simply rewarm them just before serving. If you prefer to have the dessert completed before the meal, then choose the cheesecake cupcakes. Otherwise, for the Lava Cake recipe, separate the eggs and prepare the chocolate mixture through step 2, before the meal and finish the recipe when coffee is served. It'll take you just a few minutes. (P.S.—To make the menu gluten-free, simply swap gluten-free chocolate cookies for the graham crackers using the cheesecake cupcake option).

Spectacular Steakhouse Wedge Salad with
Blue Cheese Dressing *(page 156)*

Filet Mignon with Creamy Crab Topping *(page 270)*

Steamed Asparagus

Creamy Steakhouse Mashed Potatoes *(page 233)*

Molten Chocolate Lava Cakes *(page 303)* or
Red Velvet Cheesecake Cupcakes *(page 324)*

Garden Fresh
Summer Supper

This menu is all about taking advantage of seasonal veggies; luscious vine-ripened tomatoes, tender zucchini, fragrant basil, and luscious berries are the stars of the meal! If you prefer an all-vegetarian menu, you'll find instructions for making Caprese Pasta Pomodoro in the headnote on page 191. Want to add some fresh summer corn to the menu? Be my guest! High in healthy antioxidants, this tried-and-true menu also packs 10 grams of heart-healthy fiber.

Iced Green Tea Refresher *(page 39)*

Jalapeño Popper Stuffed Zucchini Boats *(page 226)*

Pasta with Chicken and Fresh Pomodoro Sauce *(page 174)* or
Caprese Pasta Pomodoro *(page 174)*

Whole Wheat Rolls or Breadsticks

Five-Ingredient Strawberry Blossom Puddng Cups *(page 317)* or
Cherry Berry Crunch *(page 315)*

Any Day Mexican Fiesta

While my family loves eating Mexican food, what I appreciate most are easy full-flavored meals that can be put together with little time or fuss. This menu satisfies us both! For example, it takes just ten minutes to ready the delicious homemade sauce for the enchiladas, ten minutes to make the beans, and only three minutes to make the salad garnish. Start by making the enchiladas, and while they are in the oven you can easily finish the rest. And don't forget the presentation. Years ago I bought a colorful Mexican-style table runner and can't tell you how much it has been used. Simply throw one on the table and it looks like you are having a fiesta. A bowl full of limes and/or tortilla chips makes a great centerpiece, and jars of hot sauce are both decorative and functional. Bowls of sour cream, cheese, additional cilantro, and salsa can also be placed on the table as extra garnishes. Prefer something spicy? Try the Chipotle Beef Barbacoa on page 206.

Three-Minute Tomato and Avocado Salad *(page 155)*

Any Day Chicken Enchiladas *(page 248)*

10-Minute Mexican-Style Pintos *(page 236)*

Fresh Pineapple or No-Bake Banana Caramel
Cream Cheese Pie *(page 288)*

Skinny Margaritas *(page 56)*

Slim and Speedy Seafood Special

So slim, so speedy, so good! The greatest part of this fast-fix menu is that with sweet, savory, creamy, and even nutty elements, watching what you eat doesn't taste like you're missing or depriving yourself of anything at all. And, the entire thing clocks in under 400 calories, with less than 10 grams of fat (and only 9 plus points!). If you prefer shellfish, substitute in the 15-Minute Garlicky Baked Shrimp (page 278). If you want dessert, berries are an excellent choice.

Crunchy Cucumbers with Fresh Dilled Ranch Dressing *(page 159)* or

Bagged Salad Mix with Reduced-Fat Dressing

Tuscan Tilapia *(page 281)*

Balsamic Green Beans Almandine *(page 224)*

Baked Potato with Light Sour Cream
(One half 10-ounce potato with 1½ tablespoons light sour cream)

Marlene Says: *With less than 400 calories and under 10 grams of fat, this carb-concious menu will slim you down fast!*

acknowledgments

FOUR YEARS AGO I WOULD HAVE NEVER IMAGINED MYSELF WRITING acknowledgements for my third *Eat What You Love* cookbook! Of course none of this would have even been possible without the support of my fabulous "kochbook" fans. Without fail, when I am at my most tired, a comment, review or email appears from a lovely reader who shares how my recipes or books have improved their life, or the life of someone they love. These messages lift my spirits, inspire me, and provide me with the fuel to continue doing what I do. Thank you. While I have said this before, the time and collective effort it takes to create a cookbook such as this never ceases to amaze me (or my supportive husband and sons!). Hours of research precede countless days of shopping and recipe testing, which leads to long nights on the computer. Beyond my personal assistants, a collective team of dedicated professionals ensure my work is translated into a tasty and beautiful book. For this, my many thanks go to:

- Chef Judy LaCara, Megan Westersund and Rachel Forman-Lau, my tireless kitchen assistants who smiled and never wavered through hectic days and endless cooking trials. Judy, thank you for your ideas, typing expertise, and attention to detail, Megan, for your flexibility and willingness to help, and Rachel, your culinary expertise and shopping prowess. You made a fantastic team!

- Charisse Petruno, Megan Waldrop, and chef's Michaele Musel and Kara Ricciardi for your time, energy and delectable contributions.

- Interns Kelly Sloan and James Koch for your online savvy and kitchen contributions.

- Caroline Gottesman Kaufman for your excellent research and copy contributions, Deanna Segrave-Daly for your delicious prowess with finding just the right words, and to friend and longtime colleague PJ Dempsey for your ongoing editorial as well as personal support.

- My wonderful styling and photography team; stylist Bonne DiTomo, and prop stylist Mariellen Melker, with special thanks to my uber stylist Carol Haffey and photographer Steve Legato. Your incredible skills are topped only by your unending generosity.

- Chris Navratil and editor Jennifer Kasius at Running Press for their unwavering support, Frances Soo Ping Chow and Susan Van Horn for designing another beautiful book, and Jeanne Emanuel for ongoing assistance, encouragement, and sales contributions.

- The wonderful folks at QVC; Christina Pennypacker, Andrea Alfonso, Courtney Rapp, and Candace Stitt as well as to all the stellar hosts, with a special shout to Mr. David Venable. Thank you David for your warmth, kindness and support. You make me do the happy dance!

- Last, but not least, my family and friends whose enthusiasm and blessings mean world to me. Nancie, thank-you for always being there for me, and Chuck, Stephen and James—I love you—everyday.

index

notes

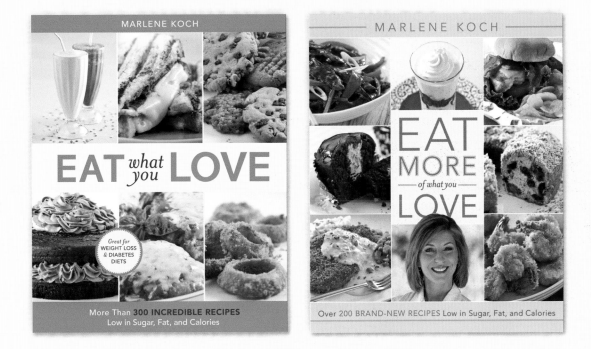

Also Available from Marlene's

EAT what you LOVE

COOKBOOKS SERIES!

MORE FROM MARLENE....

Visit Marlene online at **www.marlenekoch.com** *today for:*

• A week's worth of sample weight loss/carb-controlled menus featuring delectable *Eat More of What You Love—Everyday!* recipes

• Marlene's Free Monthly Newsletter with Sensational New Recipes and Healthy Eating Tips

• Featured Seasonal Recipes

And personalized nutrition tools to help you feel your best!

• Personal Calorie Calculator

• Carbohydrate Budget Calculator

• Body Mass (BMI) Calculator

Connect with Marlene:

Facebook: **https://www.facebook.com/kochmarlene**
(Like, share and comment on Recipes, free give-aways and more....)

Twitter: **@marlenekoch**

Question? Comment? Connect or click on:

"Ask Marlene" at **www.marlenekoch.com** where Good Health is always delivered with Great Taste!